The Mustard Seed:

A Story of Life & Faith

By

Todd White

First published by Dog Ear Publishing
4010 W. 86th Street, Ste H
Indianapolis, IN 46268
www.dogearpublishing.net

ISBN: 978-159858-914-6

This book is printed on acid-free paper.
This book is a work of Fiction. Places, events, and situations in this book are purely
Fictional and any resemblance to actual persons, living or dead, is coincidental.

Printed in the United States of America

For Grandpa.

Your love is the clay
by which I sculpt my life.

Acknowledgments

I'd like to thank my parents, my bride-to-be Jolie, and a vast collection of friends, family, and even strangers who have taught me valuable lessons throughout my life.

<u>*Preface*</u>

This is a work of fiction. However, the plot and characters in this book are based on my authentic spiritual and intellectual journey. That journey occurred in my early-to-mid twenties as I adjusted to the peaks and valleys of the "Real World." Before I entered that world – back when I was in high school and college - I always hungered for a book that could address "life issues" in an honest, straightforward, and dare I say *inspiring* way. Since I couldn't find such a book, I decided to write one of my own.

I offer this book as my humble attempt to address such "life issues" (love and faith, friendship and work, truth and morality, etc). While I wrote this book with young people in mind, I sincerely believe it can be a valuable, entertaining story for men and women of all ages and backgrounds.

PART ONE

PART ONE

Chapter 1

When I graduated from college, I didn't know who I was. And I sure as hell didn't know where I was going. If you want to know the truth, I was scared. In fact, I was terrified. I was terrified because I didn't think I could survive in the "Real World." I didn't think I could be happy and successful there. I know that sounds crazy, but it's true.

Overall, I enjoyed my time in college, and I loved the illusion that I was in control of my life. For four years, I only took classes that interested me, and I only hung out with people who liked me (which admittedly wasn't a lot of people). I came and went as I pleased, and I didn't have to answer to anyone. I loved that lifestyle, and I didn't want to give it up.

Now, in the interest of fairness, I should mention that my parents were paying over $30,000 a year so I could have that lifestyle. So yes, it was definitely silly of me to claim that I was in control of my life. I wasn't in control of anything. But that was the illusion, at least. And abandoning that illusion was not appealing to me. Not at all.

Then again, I can't blame myself for feeling that way. I can't criticize myself for hating the "Real World." When I was growing up, my dad always told me that my college years would be "the best years of my life." When I was in college, that seemed true enough at the time. But now college was over. So I had a new perspective on that overused cliché. Now it meant, "Life is all downhill from here." Can you see why I was a little concerned?

Furthermore, I had no experience in the "Real World." You see, I've led a pretty sheltered life. There's no point in denying it. I grew up in the wealthiest part of the Philly suburbs. My dad was a doctor. A plastic surgeon, actually. So needless to say, money was not a huge issue in our household. I knew money would always be there for me. And I never had to work a day in my life. I'm not proud of that fact. But I'm not embarrassed about it either. I just brought it up as a partial explanation for my anxiety about post-college life. Crap, I bet you don't like me very much at this point. I probably shouldn't have brought up that whole money thing. Sorry.

But leaving personal finances aside, I'm not equipped to survive as an adult. I'm really not. It has to do with my personality. I have no real identity. I don't have a lot of confidence in my opinions, and I don't have a lot of faith in my feelings. I'm the kind of guy who won't ask the waiter for extra bread at a restaurant. I'm the kind of guy who, if another guy bumped into me, would say "sorry" – even if *he* was the one at fault! I'm the kind of guy who, if I noticed a girl staring at me, would assume that meant I had food on my face. After all, how could a girl possibly like me? I'm pathetic. I bet you think I'm being too hard on myself. But trust me, I'm not.

I remember one night – about three months before Graduation Day – I was alone in my dorm room when I started crying for no apparent reason. I was just sitting in a chair – reading a textbook or something – when I started bawling uncontrollably. I'm not even kidding. It was really weird. Looking back on that night, I think the stress of entering the Great Unknown finally caught up to me – and released itself. But I can't be sure.

Of course, I probably wouldn't have been so God damn emotional if I had actually taken the time to plan my future, like everyone else I knew. All of my friends were either going to law school (which is fine if you're into that sort of thing) or diving headfirst into the corporate world (which is a little more disturbing, but certainly understandable).

But my own future remained a mystery. I couldn't plan my future because I was too busy playing video games, reading science fiction books, and taking naps. Now, I admit, this wasn't a very good use of my time. In fact, it was a pretty *shitty* use of my time. But here's the thing: I just wasn't motivated. I know I *should've* been motivated (considering the rest of my life was at stake), but I was content to do nothing. And when Graduation Day arrived, I was fucked in the ass. I had no job. No prospects. No place to live. Nothing. It was pretty fucking depressing, I can assure you.

I was tempted to go home and live with my mother in Philly– at least for a little while. Let's face it, having my mom pay for all my bills (while I leisurely looked for a job) was an appealing option. But I nixed that idea for a couple of reasons. First and foremost, my mom and I don't get along very well. It's nothing personal. Well, maybe it *is* personal. I really don't want to get into that right now. Second, I knew that boomeranging into my old neighborhood would be a total dead end. So when my college career came to its conclusion, I drove down to Washington, D.C. to live with my cousin, Evan.

The nation's capital was a logical destination for me. For starters, I majored in political science. Plus, I'm a quintessential political junkie. I can name all the Presidents, most of the Senators, and a good chunk of the Congressmen. I don't mean to brag, but it's true. The irony is that I don't have very strong political beliefs. I think it stems from my rare ability to see things from the other person's perspective. Plus, the world is so messy and complicated, I think it's smart to keep an open mind about things. I just don't see how anyone can feel certain about anything. At least that's my opinion.

OK, I'm getting off-topic. Back to the story: Evan was a great guy to live with. Plain and simple. He was a thirty-five year old bachelor who edited a computer magazine by day and watched The Gameshow Network by night. He never pressured me to leave. In fact, he genuinely encouraged me to stay. I suppose he was lonely or something. But I felt a sense of duty to find a job and move out as fast as possible. And actually, once I put my mind to it, I found a job fairly easily.

I was hired as a researcher at America Next, which is one of the city's most prominent think tanks. If you don't know what a think tank is, basically it's a non-profit organization where a bunch of old, bearded men publish studies on just about every political issue you can think of: taxes, Social Security, energy, foreign policy, all that jazz.

I was assigned to one of the company's most boring departments – the one that investigates regulatory issues. Every day, I answer phone calls, make photocopies, and fetch coffee for a couple of middle-aged scholars. I won't try to glorify my job, because it isn't very glorifying. Any monkey can do it. But I was still happy to have it. I know it sounds quaint – and perhaps outright bizarre – but I was proud to be making a contribution to society. After a lifetime of taking and taking, I was finally *giving* something back to the world. I no longer had to apologize for my existence. My work – as humble as it was - gave me dignity.

OK, I'll stop talking about my job. Like I said, I'm happy to have it, but I refuse to define myself through my work. I learned a lot of stuff during the next year of my life – stuff that fundamentally changed me as a human being – but I didn't learn shit from filling out my bosses' expense reports.

And yes – at the risk of killing the suspense - that's what this book is about. It's about my first year out of college, and all the crazy shit that happened to me during that year. It's about how I survived, and even learned to thrive, in the "Real World." I should warn you: This book isn't just a typical coming-of-age tale; it's also a story about the power of ideas – specifically, ideas about love and faith, truth and happiness – and how those ideas shape our lives, and control our destiny. If that ain't your cup of tea, close this book immediately. But if you're like me – and you enjoy books that actually have a point - keep going. You won't be disappointed.

You know what I just realized? I haven't even told you my name yet. That's so retarded of me; I apologize for that. My name is Brian. Brian Raines. I bet you're also wondering what I look like. That's a reasonable thing to know. I won't hold anything back.

I stand a smidgen under six feet tall and weigh around 190 pounds. I have a big, round face with small brown eyes, a beaked nose, and thick lips. I own a thick mane of brown hair, which can get quite curly on a muggy day. I also have a slightly-protruding waistline, if you catch my drift. Let me clarify: I'm not fat. At least no one has ever called me "fat." At least not to my face. But I could definitely afford to lose a few pounds. In fact, I cringe whenever I come out of the shower and see my flabby body in the bathroom mirror. OK, I'm probably getting too personal now. Sorry about that. Let's just move on.

Once I started my job at America Next, I jump-started my search for a new apartment. I also needed to find a roommate to share that apartment with me. But I wasn't prepared to accept the first person I met. Call me crazy but I wanted to find someone who I genuinely liked, and could actually hang out with in my free time. If that sounds gay, or whatever, I don't care. It's too important to me.

In the first three weeks, I visited at least a dozen apartments, and met even more potential roommates, but none of them were even remotely appealing. I would chat with them for a little bit, look them up and down, and make a snap judgment about their character based on stupid things like whether or not they tucked their shirts in. And I'm sure they were they were doing the same thing to me. The whole experience was pretty sordid. Like dating, but much, much worse.

It wasn't until the first week of September that I stumbled into a bit of luck. My co-worker, Jenna, told me that her best friend's boyfriend was hunting for a new roommate. She said this kid – whose name was Mark Williams – was the greatest guy in the history of the world, and more importantly, he lived in a large, affordable apartment just across the river in Alexandria. Needless to say, I was intrigued, so I asked Jenna to arrange a time for me to come by, and take a look at the place.

She agreed, and after playing phone tag for most of the afternoon, she was able to get a hold of Mark. Apparently, Mark was in a super-hurry to find a new roommate, and wanted me to visit that night. Even though I was already exhausted from work, and would've preferred to stay home and watch *Seinfeld* re-runs, I begrudgingly accepted.

When I arrived in his neighborhood later that evening, I immediately spotted his apartment building: an immaculate twelve-story brick structure that towered over its peers. As I entered the lobby, I crossed my fingers in the vain hope that Mark was just as cool as the building he lived in.

Of course, Mark's coolness was irrelevant – unless he thought I was *equally cool*. And since I was born without the "cool" gene, I needed to put on my actor's cloak. I needed to pretend that I was "one of the guys" – someone who Mark could feel comfortable with. I needed to be fake – but not *too fake* or he would see through my fakeness. Ugh, life is complicated!

I entered the large, spacious elevator, and took it up to the third floor. When I got there, I walked down to the end of the hallway, stood in front of Apartment 316, and knocked on the door. A few seconds later, the door swung open, revealing my potential roommate. He was a shade taller than me, and quite a bit thinner too. His round face was clear and clean-shaven. He owned a mop of sandy brown hair and a pair of bright blue eyes that surely mesmerized the ladies. He flashed a huge, toothy grin that emitted both kindness and a lack of sophistication. The small gap between his two front teeth was the only chink in his physical armor. But it was also strangely charming.

"Brian!" he shouted at me, as though I was a close friend he hadn't seen in years. Surprised by the air of informality, I lamely replied, "How's it going?"

"I'm doing great," he responded. Closing the door behind me, he continued, "How are you?"

"I'm pretty good."

"Great. Can I get you something to drink?" he asked, gripping my right shoulder and staring deeply into my eyes.

"Um, yeah. That would be great. Thanks." I have to admit, I wasn't used to strangers touching me. Then again, I was kind of flattered by Mark's gesture. He seemed to have an unexplainable affection for me.

Mark spun on his heels and marched into the kitchen. Meanwhile, I decided to look around the apartment. After all, that's the reason I was here – to see if this was a good place to live. And it seemed like a *great* place to live. The living room was spacious and exquisitely furnished with a black leather couch, a rustic dining table, and a state-of-the-art stereo system. The ceiling ascended so high it was barely visible. The floor was covered by a stainless white carpet. And the entire area was naturally lighted by a pair of large windows. On opposite sides of the apartment were two closed doors, which presumably led to each person's bedroom.

"Let's see what I have," Mark murmured, shuffling bottles and boxes around the refrigerator. "Would you like some pop?"

"What's pop?" I asked.

"Sorry," Mark laughed. "I meant to say 'Coke.'"

"Oh. In that case, a Coke would be great. Thanks."

"I guess you're not from the Midwest," Mark said playfully, while throwing the can in my direction.

"No," I replied. "In fact, I've never even been to the Midwest." Ugh! I couldn't believe I had made such a stupid, smug comment. I pounded my thigh in self-disgust.

"You've got to be kidding me! Sorry to hear that, man. That's a genuine tragedy. So where *are* you from?"

"Right outside Philly."

"Oh really? I love Philly. Great town. Although I hate the Eagles, no offense," he said with a wry grin.

I chuckled. "That's fine with me. I hate the Eagles too. I'm a Steelers fan, myself."

Mark's face lit up. "Oh yeah? So am I! I'm from a small town in eastern Ohio, but it's less than an hour from Pittsburgh. So I follow all the Pittsburgh teams – Steelers, Pirates, even the Penguins."

My face lit up too. I had just stumbled into a vital connection to Mark – or any warm-blooded male: a shared passion for the same football team. Ah, the beauty of sports!

"How do you think they'll do this year?" he asked, biting his lip. I could tell he was fishing for a positive response.

"You mean the Steelers?"

"Yeah."

"I think they have a great shot. They play good defense. They don't make mistakes. If they go back to running the ball – which they didn't do last year - I think they'll surprise people."

"Yeah, I totally agree. I keep telling people that the running game is their meal ticket. If they stick to the run, they'll rack up a lot of wins. At least that's my opinion."

"I think you're absolutely right."

"Cool," he said with relief. "I'm glad *someone* agrees with me."

Now, you should know, dear reader, that I *didn't* agree with him. Basically, I just told Mark what he wanted to hear. If fudging my football predictions could win Mark's approval, and get me this awesome apartment, that was fine by me.

"So what do you do?" asked Mark.

"I work as a research assistant at America Next," I replied with caution. Most people had never heard of the place.

"That's great. I love America Next," said Mark enthusiastically. "You guys do terrific work. I read a lot of your briefings."

"Oh really? Where do you work?"

"I work on Capitol Hill. I'm a press assistant for one of Ohio's Senators."

Sweet, I thought to myself, we have a political bond – always a huge plus. I tried to milk it for what it was worth.

"Which one – DeWine or Voinovich?"

"DeWine, actually." He smiled at me. "You're smart, man. I bet most folks – even in Ohio – couldn't name one of their Senators."

"Sad but true. So how long have you lived in D.C.?"

"Not long. I graduated from Ohio State in May. Then I moved to D.C. a few weeks later. What about you?"

"Same deal," I replied. "I graduated from Middlebury in May, and I've been in D.C. ever since."

"And how are you liking D.C.?" Mark asked.

I hesitated for a moment. Normally, I'd lie about my feelings toward Washington. I had my talking points down cold: "I love this town. It's so exciting. There's such an amazing sense of energy here. I really feel like I'm making a difference." But my true feelings were quite different. In reality, D.C. was a claustrophobic, yet lonely city for a sensitive newcomer like me. In a town whose number one industry is ego, I was friendless and frustrated. I wanted to like

D.C. I really did. After all, it was my choice to come here. I honestly thought this would be the best place to have a positive impact on peoples' lives. But civic virtue was a hindrance – not an asset - in the nation's capital.

During one of my first job interviews, I told the Human Resources Director – a tall, prematurely bald guy in his late twenties – that I wasn't obsessed with making a ton of money. I said that the most important thing for me was finding a job where I could actually help people. I swear to God, he looked at me like I had just whipped out my cock and started pissing on his rug. When I foolishly asked him, "Isn't that what *you're* here for?" he proudly replied: "No!"

So, *no*, Washington wasn't a city of idealism and patriotism. It was a cynical city that chewed up and spit out kids like me. In the long-run, survival belonged to those who could sell their souls to the highest bidder, without any trace of guilt or shame.

But Mark had been so nice to me – nicer than anyone I had met in a long time – that I felt like I owed him my honest opinion. It was time to stop being fake, and start being my true self.

"Well, I think this is where I need to be right now," I began cautiously, "but there's something about this city that doesn't sit well with me on a fundamental level. It's hard to describe."

"I know what you mean," Mark said, sympathetically. "I miss Ohio a lot. It'll always be my home. I don't know a lot of folks here. And some of the folks I've met... well... let's just say I wish I *didn't* know them!"

We both shared a much-needed laugh. Once again, Mark and I were on the same page. In fact, I could imagine Mark having a similar conversation with that HR asshole – protecting his conscience from that other dude's cash. I felt more relaxed and self-assured around him. He was the real deal.

"Oh goodness," said Mark. "All this time, I've been chewing your ear off, and I haven't even shown you the room yet! Now, I should mention that the room that's open is actually *my* room. That's because my roommate, Bret, is moving out of the apartment; I'm moving into his room, which is slightly bigger."

"Why is your roommate leaving?" I asked.

Mark stared at the floor somberly. "He's going back to Ohio. He was homesick."

"I can understand that," I replied. Mark opened the door, and together we entered a large, spacious room with a bed, desk, and walk-in-closet. The place had the aura of a college dorm room, with a huge, colorful poster and an array of picture frames adorning the white walls.

There were predictable photos of Mark shaking hands with Senator DeWine, and another photo of him standing next to George W. Bush – the Republican candidate for President. But one photo, in particular, caught my eye. It was a picture of Mark sitting on a park bench, bundled up in a black pea coat and red scarf. He was happily grinning and clasping the hand of a short, unhealthily thin girl whose freckled face was partly camouflaged by her long, curly red hair. She looked like a Raggedy Annie doll.

"I guess that's your girlfriend," I blurted out, pointing my finger at the intriguing picture. I felt guilty about violating Mark's privacy, but I needed to know if I was inheriting a third roommate. At least that's how I rationalized my nosiness.

Mark's face lit up like a Christmas tree. "Yep, that's my gal," he responded. "Mary Beth and I have been together since the Ninth Grade. She's the love of my life. A gift from God, really."

I was shocked that a handsome guy like Mark was romantically attached to such a homely girl. I know that sounds superficial – and even a bit gay - but let's face it, you don't see a lot of good-looking guys hanging around with ugly women. Or vice versa. It's just a fact of life.

"Does she live around here?" I asked, probing further.

"Yeah, she followed me down to Washington. Right now, she's working at a non-profit company called Young Americans for Life."

I smiled, pretending to be interested. I really wasn't.

"How about you? Do you have anyone special?"

Ah, the inevitable question.

"No," I said wistfully, "Can't say that I do."

Mark stared at me with pity. "I'm sorry to hear that."

"I'm sorry to *say* that."

This was a touchy subject for me. Not because I'm single. There's nothing unusual about that. But what *is* unusual – and some would say suspicious – is that I've never had a girlfriend. At least not a *real* girlfriend.

No, I'm not a virgin, and I'm not gay either. If that's what you're thinking, don't bother. I have a lot of issues, but my sexuality isn't one of them. I just haven't met the right girl yet. It's hard to find her, given my situation.

And what *is* my situation? First of all, most women aren't attracted to nice, quiet, ordinary-looking guys like me. That's just a fact. I'm sure there's some Darwinian explanation for it.

Second, I'm not attracted to dumb, shallow women – which is problematic since they account for the vast majority of females. I know that sounds like a bitter remark, but it's really not. It's just an observation.

When you combine those two qualities, the outcome is a very bleak romantic life. But honestly, it's not a big deal. I don't feel sorry for myself or anything like that. So you shouldn't feel sorry for me, either.

Still, I'm sure you could see why I was reluctant to talk about all this stuff with Mark. Let's face it, no one – not even a nice guy like Mark – wants to live with a loser like me. In my rush to change the conversation, I blurted out, "I like your poster," even though I had hardly looked at it.

"You do?" asked Mark, sounding both pleased and surprised.

"Yeah, I do." Having said that, I figured I should actually *look* at the poster. It featured a large, vibrant tree with black birds flocking all around it. Above this beautiful scene was a pair of white hands holding a half-dozen tiny seeds. The text, in bold letters, read "THE MUSTARD SEED," and then followed with a verse from Scripture:

"The kingdom of heaven is like a mustard seed, which a man took, and sowed in his field. Though it is the smallest of all your seeds, yet when it grows, it is the largest of garden plants and becomes a tree, so that the birds of the air come and perch in its branches." (Matthew 13:31-32)

I always liked that passage from the New Testament, even though I wasn't quite sure what it meant. In any case, the large poster – combined with a Bible on Mark's dresser, whose pages were tagged by dozens of post-it notes – left no room for the imagination: Mark was a hard-core Christian.

I wasn't sure if that was a good thing or a bad thing. On the one hand, it reaffirmed my instinct that Mark was a decent human being. On the other hand, I didn't want to live with someone who would scold me if I opened a can of beer, or (less likely) brought a girl home for the night. My values – whatever they were - needed to be respected.

There was an awkward silence for quite a while. Finally, Mark broke the lull by warning: "I should probably be upfront with you about something."

"OK," I replied warily. Whenever a person wants to be "upfront with you," that's never a good sign.

"Actually, you probably realized this," Mark began, "but I'm a Christian. My personal relationship with Christ is very important to me. Would you feel comfortable having a Christian roommate?"

"Of course," I replied coolly. "I mean, I'm a Christian too."

"Right," said Mark, with a trace of concern. "I guess, in my mind, there are two kinds of Christians. The first kind reads the Bible every day, goes to church every Sunday, and practices the teachings of the Gospel; the second kind hangs around for the Christmas gifts."

I smiled and frankly admitted, "I think I'm in the second group."

"No problem, man," said Mark. "I totally respect where you're coming from."

I could tell that Mark's tolerance was sincere, but I still felt the need to justify myself. I didn't want Mark to think I was a bad person or anything. Because I'm not. At least I don't think I am.

"The truth is," I started to explain, "I wasn't raised in a very religious family. My parents never took me to church. They didn't give me any kind of spiritual direction. And that was on purpose. They wanted me to *choose* my faith. They thought that was the best approach."

"And was it?" asked Mark.

I hesitated. In principle, I thought it was a good strategy. After all, I'm a strong believer in freedom and individual choice. But on a psychological level, I hadn't turned out so well. So it was hard to say that my parents' approach had actually worked. Then again, people can change too.

"I don't know," I said, reflectively. "I don't think I can answer that yet. Maybe one day."

"I understand," said Mark. "Besides, what you believe – or *don't* believe – is none of my business. I'm OK with every type of religion. I just want to make sure *you're* OK with *me*. That's all."

"Yes, of course," I chuckled. "No question about it."

"Great," said Mark. "I only brought up the whole Christian thing because it's important that we're honest with each other. When people are honest with each other, they trust each another – and ultimately, trust is the foundation of every great friendship. Don't you think?"

"Absolutely," I said. "Honesty really is the best policy."

"Cool," replied Mark. "So, in the spirit of honesty, I'd like to mention one other thing. Like I said, I don't want to impose my personal views on you, or anyone else for that matter, but I really do want to keep this a sex-free apartment."

Dear reader, please re-read that last sentence. Did Mark just say he wants to "keep this a sex-free apartment?" What the hell does that mean? How do I even answer that?

"I know some people would say that's stupid," Mark continued, "but it's very important to me. Do you have any reaction to that?"

I must've stood there silently for at least ten seconds. The only words I could muster were, "So you want no sex *inside* the apartment?" Then, to reemphasize my point, I repeated, "*inside* the apartment?"

Mark nodded slowly. "Yes."

Now, dear reader, you've known me for oh, a good twenty pages or so. You know I don't get a lot of action. But still, I'd like to think that should God suddenly bless me with a hot, horny girlfriend, I could fuck her to my heart's content within the confines of my own bedroom. After all, it is *my* bedroom.

And yet, Mark's rule wasn't a deal-breaker for me. I loved the apartment, I liked the idea of Mark's friendship, and the chances of me getting any action were miniscule. Besides, if necessary, I could always go to the girl's place. Mark said he wanted a "sex-free *apartment*," not a "sex-free *roommate*." That's a pretty stark difference. So altogether, while I wasn't thrilled with the arrangement, I was also willing to compromise.

"Well," I hesitated, "if that's how you feel, I could go along with that."

Mark broke into a huge smile. "I'm so happy to hear that. I really do appreciate your honesty and integrity."

I grinded my teeth. "No problem."

"OK, here's what I'm thinking," Mark said, without skipping a beat. "I want to offer you the room. I think you're a good guy. I think we'd make terrific roommates. What do you say? Do you need to think it over?"

I was shocked that Mark offered me the room so quickly. I thought he would want to see a few more candidates at the very least. But apparently, I had made a winning impression.

"I don't think there's much to think about," I said. "I'd definitely like to move in."

"Awesome!" Mark shouted, smacking his palms together. "I'm so glad I found such a good roommate so quickly!"

"Yeah, me too," I happily replied.

"Now, I just started the process of moving my stuff into Bret's room. But that shouldn't take too long. Do you think you'll be able to move in your stuff this weekend?"

"Sure," I declared. "That works for me."

"Fantastic. This is going to be *fantastic*."

Before I left, Mark and I exchanged business cards and shook hands again. As the door closed behind me, I could hear him shout, "God bless." I wanted to say, "Thanks," but by then, the door had already slammed shut. I then began the slow trek back to Evan's apartment, where a dinner of nachos and cheese awaited me.

It's hard to describe how relieved I felt. Ever since my junior year of college, my future had been in a perpetual state of limbo. I had spent most of that time worrying about the "Real World" – and whether or not I could succeed there.

Now, my life was slowly coming together. I had jumped over the abyss between college graduation and the "Real World." I had found a good job and a great apartment too. They were the first steps in building a successful life for myself. Of course, it was a shaky foundation. It could crack at any time. But I was hopeful about my future for the first time since – gosh, I can't even remember.

One thing I needed to do was reach out to more people. I needed to find more friends in this lonely city. I'm glad I had found Mark. I didn't know if we could be friends – after all, we came from such different backgrounds – but there was reason to be hopeful: We shared some common interests (sports and politics) and I felt extremely comfortable around him. Thanks to his genuine warmth and empathy, I felt free to expose the "real me" – whoever that was. Even though we were around the same age, I sensed that Mark wanted to adopt me as a younger brother.

One other thing: While I might be in danger of reading too much into it, I felt like Mark and I shared a similar, almost unique, "sense of life." For lack of a better word, we were "seekers." We were seeking a greater understanding about life, and our place within life. This was a journey that few people wanted to take. They just wanted to "go with the flow." But we were comfortable taking a different road: the "road less traveled." And while Mark was ahead of me on that road, I was close behind.

Chapter 2

I hate moving. I hate schlepping all of my crap from one place to another. I just have too much shit – everything from my clunky PC to my filing cabinets to this enormous down comforter I've been dragging around the country for four years. Originally, it was a gift from my mom, but I never wanted it, and I've never been able to get rid of it. I mean, who needs a down comforter in the middle of July? Since it's too hot to sleep with, all it does is sit on my floor. It's just a big fucking rug.

I know, I know. I sound ungrateful. I just got this great apartment, and I'm already bitching and moaning! Typical of me! I apologize for that. I need to be less selfish, especially since my cousin, Evan, is helping me move all of this crap. Not only that, he volunteered to drive me to IKEA so I can buy a new bed, desk, and dresser.

Going to IKEA was an absolute nightmare. I was completely overwhelmed by this enormous warehouse of cheap, ugly furniture. There were just too many people – thousands and thousands of strangers stroking wood, checking price tags, and bumping into me. I hate big crowds. And do you know what was even more disturbing? Everyone there was smiling. They were actually thrilled to be there!

"I can't resist the savings!" exclaimed one emaciated blonde, clutching the elbow of her tall, tanned husband. "I know, me neither," he happily replied. Even the kids were happy. I wanted to puke!

Luckily, I had Evan to guide me through the process. Here's how it worked: Evan told me what to buy, and I bought it. Very simple. Granted, I know I should've been more proactive in picking out my furniture. After all, it is *my* furniture. But the truth is, I don't give a shit. For me, a desk is a desk, and a chair is a chair. I don't want to spend hours researching the best lamp, and how to find it at the best price. I don't care about any of that bullshit, and I'm scared of people who do.

Now that I was fully settled into my new apartment, I started to enter a predictable routine – sleeping as late as possible, waking up and running to the office like a bat out of hell, checking sports websites to pass the time at work, chowing down Lean Cuisine macaroni and cheese for dinner, and numbing my mind with video games late at night.

With a couple of exceptions, I had basically re-created my college existence. This was a remarkable accomplishment – at least for someone like me. My fears of slipping through the cracks of society had been alleviated. I had successfully crossed the bridge between college life and adult society. I was now a dues-paying member of the nefarious "Real World." On some level, this was enormously gratifying.

But it was also anti-climactic. I had labored for months – finding a new job, finding a new apartment, etc. – to essentially rebuild my previous life. The joke was on me, of course, because I never loved my previous life to begin with. I knew there was something better out there for me. Now that I had a steady job and a place to live, I intended to find it.

I thought about joining an aerobics class, but I didn't feel like getting up early (six in the freaking morning!) to get sweaty and tired, and then have to go to work for nine hours. I also thought about joining a theater troupe, since I had done some acting in high school. But the rehearsals were all-day on Saturday, and they performed every Wednesday night. I wasn't ready for that level of commitment. I enjoyed my

peaceful weekends, where I could sleep-in late, read magazines, and watch DVDs. Besides, I didn't know anybody.

I wanted to hang out with Mark, but so far he had been
surprisingly aloof. I guess he didn't want to interfere in my
personal life – not realizing, of course, that I didn't *have* a
personal life.

For the first couple of weeks, this was our daily ritual:
I'd come home around 6 o'clock and find Mark sprawled out
on the living room couch, watching Fox News. We chatted
for a little bit – usually about political stuff, nothing serious.
Then Mark would squirt away to his girlfriend's place for dinner. He rarely got back before 11, and by then, I was already
in bed watching *Seinfeld* re-runs.

Now, just so we're clear, I know Mark wasn't trying to
avoid me or anything; I know he just wanted to spend time
with his so-called "Gift from God." But still, I was disappointed he didn't make a greater effort to spend time with me.

Finally, things started to change during our second
weekend together. On Saturday night, Mark came home and
found me watching a DVD in the living room. I think he was
surprised to see me there by myself. When I asked him about
his evening, he noticeably downplayed it. "It was nothing
special," he insisted. I could tell he didn't want to pour salt
on my wound of loneliness. That was nice of him, I suppose.

Still, after a brief chat, Mark yawned: "I need to hit the
hay. Have a good night, man." I went back to watching my
DVD, but I could barely focus on the movie. I mean, it's
depressing enough when you lead a solitary life, but it's even
more depressing when other people know about it! The secret
was out. My pathetic existence had been exposed! How
humiliating!

After a short silence, the door re-opened, and Mark
came out wearing just a pair of green boxers. "Hey, man," he
said. "Got a question for you: Do you want to go to church
with me tomorrow?"

"What?"

"Do you want to go to church with me tomorrow?"

"Um, OK. Sure."

"Great. The service starts at 1 PM."

"That's a strange time." It was also a bad time, since the Steelers were playing a preseason game tomorrow afternoon.

"I know," Mark responded, completely oblivious to the conflict. "It's not your typical church. It's called 'Crossroads' and it exclusively caters to young people – teenagers and twentysomethings like us. The entire program is specifically designed for our needs."

"Hmm, that sounds interesting."

"Yeah, and it's great. Mary Beth and I have been going every week since we moved here. But she can't make it tomorrow, so I was thinking…maybe…if you want to…"

"Yeah," I interrupted, "count me in."

As I mentioned earlier, I'm not a particularly religious person – at least not in a traditional sense. I've only been inside a church three times– and all of those times were for weddings. You can credit – or blame – my parents for that. They made an early decision that I would be free to make my own judgments on God and religion.

Of course, when your family doesn't instruct you on religious issues, there's practically nowhere else to go. You're not going to learn about God in school, and you're not going to learn about morality from our shitty popular culture. Basically, you're on your own.

For me, I started to think about God after my parents got divorced. Yeah, I know I should have mentioned it earlier – but my parents got divorced when I was ten years old. It was a troubled and unhappy marriage, right from the start. My mom and dad were very different people – they were like oil and water – and it's hard to understand what inspired them to get hitched at all. They fought constantly and bitterly, which usually left me in tears. When my mom told me that my dad had moved to California, it was almost a relief.

Of course, things didn't get much better after my father left. In fact, they got worse. My mom spiraled into a deep and painful depression. She would drink herself into a stupor and lock herself in her room for a day or two at a time. In retrospect, she was probably an alcoholic – which was tough for me, especially as I entered my teen years. Sometimes I felt like I was raising myself.

Alright, enough about that. I don't want to wallow in self-pity. I know we all have our crosses to bear. I know there's no such thing as a "normal family." I only brought it up because it has to do with religion.

After my parents' divorce, I felt completely alone and uprooted. I also had no one to look up to, since my mom was out-of-commission and my dad had devolved into a West Coast ATM machine. I needed some structure and support, so I started to pray. Every night, before I went to bed, I prayed to God, asking him to take away my fear and loneliness. I asked him to make things better for me. But things didn't get any better. My downward spiral accelerated. High school was a disaster. As you can imagine, there can be a lot of hostility toward shy, overweight kids.

Anyway, I don't want to get into it. The point is, my prayers didn't work. At first, I thought that meant God didn't like me. Then I started to realize, maybe He didn't exist at all. Perhaps he was a myth people exploited to comfort themselves or dominate others (or both).

In a last-ditch attempt to salvage my fledgling faith, I started reading a couple of C.S. Lewis' books. Supposedly, Lewis was the most important Christian thinker of the 20th Century, and what made him especially interesting was that he started off as an atheist. I heard on a radio show that his books were the best medicine for skeptics like me. Since he had such an appealing background, I started to devour his books – *Surprised by Joy, The Problem of Pain, Mere Christianity*, etc.

But I have to say, Lewis' books weren't very convincing. His arguments were circular, embarrassingly simplistic, and contained more holes than a gangbang video. If this was the best the Christian elite could come up with, the search for faith was pointless. Overall, the whole experience left me feeling drained and empty inside.

By the time I arrived at college, I had settled into a muddled, dreary agnosticism. I had basically decided there was no way to know if God existed or if Christianity was true. After all, there was no proof – no tangible evidence that could convince my perpetually skeptical brain.

But at the same time, in the deepest layers of my gut, I felt God was real, and the Truth was out there, somewhere. That was my instinct. But my personal experience, sadly, *negated* that instinct. Ultimately, I stopped thinking about the whole subject, knowing I'd come back to it later on when I was emotionally ready.

Now, just so there's no misunderstanding, I didn't think that going to church with Mark would culminate in some sort of profound religious awakening. I'm not that naïve. But I wanted to experience a real church service for the first time. And if that clarified some religious issues for me, all the better.

On Sunday afternoon, Mark drove us to the "Crossroads" church in his black Jeep Wrangler. After cruising through Northern Virginia's highways for almost half an hour, we approached a large, brick church that was adjoined by a double-deck garage. After parking the jeep there, we joined a swarm of boisterous kids shuffling into the church's doorway.

Once inside, I observed the House of God with a sharp, scientific eye. As I expected, there was a central stage, a long row of wooden pews, and a cross gleaming above us. What I *didn't* expect was the rock band perched on the side of the platform. And yet, there they were: four skinny white dudes, clutching their instruments, ready to play on cue. If you couldn't see them clearly enough, you could also watch them on a pair of big-screen TVs that were shackled onto the walls. I couldn't help but think, was I at a church or a Metallica concert?

The place was packed to the brim. There must have been hundreds, perhaps a thousand, young butts stuffed into all those pews. The crowd itself was overwhelmingly white and upper-middle class. The kids were fit, well-groomed, and well-dressed. Plus, a large number of the girls wore low-cut tops, tantalizing the defenders of the faith with their most valuable possessions. They looked happy and hopeful – bearing a close resemblance to the IKEA people. In fact, they *were* the IKEA people!

Mark and I planted ourselves in the back row, next to a pair of tall, blond jocks. I sat there anxiously, waiting for the sermon (or the rock concert) to start...whatever it was. Finally, the lights dimmed and a hush fell upon the crowd. A few moments later, the silence was shattered by the band's eruption. The faithful jumped from their seats and chanted the lyrics that were helpfully scrawled onto the TV screens above us.

I sang along too, of course – although I was startled by the words that poured from my lips. I called Jesus my "Lord and Savior" and proclaimed that "my heart and soul belong to Him." I had never talked about God in such personal, intimate terms.

For me, God had always been a mysterious force – something that was far and distant from me, and could only be understood through quiet, solitary contemplation. Of course, that assumed God even existed (which was no sure thing). But these guys took a different perspective. They knew and loved God. They exulted in His love. And they were forever happy in His love. I, on the other hand, had yet to feel anything.

We sang song after song, swaying and clapping to the beat of Christian rock. I absorbed the sights, sounds, and vibes around me, while closely monitoring my own feelings. At this early stage, however, my feelings were still limited to fear – the fear of being noticed by other people and sticking out like a sore thumb.

After the music stopped, the lights came on and a short, homely woman with curly brown hair and thick eyeglasses walked up to the podium. After adjusting the microphone, she introduced herself as "Sandy" and welcomed us to the church. She then offered a "special welcome" to the newcomers and invited us to stand up.

I was eager to avoid any attention, but Mark literally propelled me out of my seat. I was joined by a handful of other men and women scattered throughout the audience. We stood there awkwardly as Sandy talked about how great it was that we were here. I didn't pay much attention to her actual words, since I was paralyzed by the gaze of hundreds of eyes upon me. Finally, I was able to slink back into the pew, and safely return to my anonymity.

Sandy then rattled off a laundry list of church announcements – a young couples' meeting on Tuesday night, a charity baseball game on Wednesday night, a church picnic on Saturday afternoon, blah blah blah. I started to check my watch.

Finally, Sandy wrapped up her speech and turned the podium over to a tall, barrel-chested man in his mid-thirties. He wore a red buttoned-down shirt, navy blue jeans, and thick brown boots. He looked uneducated and unpolished – the kind of guy you'd see carrying a lunch pail into a smoke-billowing factory.

Mark nudged me. "That's John," he whispered in my ear. "He's our pastor. He's a great guy. I mean, just a *great* guy." I nodded politely.

John twisted the microphone off the podium, gripped it in his right hand, and started to strut across the stage like a conventional talk show host.

"Good afternoon!!!" John boomed in his husky, Rocky Mountain voice.

"Good afternoon!!!" the faithful obediently replied.

"How y'all doin' today?"

"Grreeaaatt!" came the collective response.

John started to tell a rambling story about a plane trip he took to Kansas City. On his flight, he sat next to a middle-aged ad executive who shamelessly boasted about his industry's power to get people to buy just about anything – cars, clothes, homes, even a presidential candidate. John said he pitied this stranger who made a living by deceiving people, and even prayed for him during breaks in the conversation. John kindly offered the guy his bag of peanuts (which he accepted), and a ride to his hotel (which he understandably declined). Lastly, just before they separated, John handed him a brochure about a Christian charity that teaches poor children in Guatemala.

If you're confused and uninspired by this story, so am I, but according to John, it had a point.

"As Christians, we are in this world, but not of it," he declared. "That's because there is a fundamental conflict between our Christian values and the values of the world we live in. Our values come from revelation, the word of God. They are the values of faith and love and service towards others. We accept and embrace these values because we know they are true, and because they give our lives meaning.

"However, the world that surrounds us operates on a different set of values. Their values come not from above, but from within. They come from the ego, the part of the brain that feels separation from others, and constant fear. These are the values of selfishness, greed, and quite often, hate and destruction.

"This clash of values comes from a contrast of visions. The fallen world has, shall we say, *near-sighted vision.* It sees only what's right in front of it, and no further. It sees greed rewarded with wealth, and charity punished with poverty. It sees separation rewarded with freedom, and unity punished with responsibility. It sees violence rewarded with power, and pacifism punished with death. Worst of all, it sees death as final. The end of everything for everyone.

"When a person sees the world in this way, is it any wonder that they yield to the selfish commands of the ego? Of course not. Their behavior is understandable. Sad, but understandable.

"What is *not* understandable, however, is why they persist in this vision once they see how unsatisfying it is. The consequences of their vision are swift and inevitable: frustration, anger, depression, and despair. That's what it's like to live with near-sighted vision."

That got a brief chuckle from the crowd.

"These folks are leading lives of 'quiet desperation' and yet they never bother to find an alternative. They're so convinced they see the world 'the right way.' And they're so suspicious of people who see it differently. I'm talking about people like *you and me.* They dismiss us as dreamers and schemers, cranks and crazies. But are we? *Are we?"*

The crowd shouted in unison: "NO!!!!"

John smiled. "That's right! No! We just have better vision." For dramatic effect, he whipped out his eyeglasses and wrapped them around his head. Then he continued, "Our vision has been corrected by our Savior. When we accept Jesus into our life, it changes our entire perspective. We can see the unseen. We can see the loving purpose that God has for each and every one of us. We can see the sanctity and unity of all of God's children. We can see our final destination – at the right hand of God in the Kingdom of Heaven.

"Jesus changes our vision, and he changes our hearts. He changes our entire way of life. He fills us with peace and joy, and we are then empowered to share that peace and joy with others.

"Now, you're probably asking yourselves, 'How can we share the message of Christ with those who refuse to see His glory, and refuse to accept Him into their lives? How can we repair their vision and inspire them to embrace Christ as their Savior?'

"As always, Jesus has shown us the way." John cleared his throat. "Jesus opened the Kingdom of Heaven by performing small acts of compassion and healing. He planted tiny mustard seeds of faith inside the hearts of his lost children, which as the Book of Matthew tells us, gradually grew into powerful trees of conviction. Jesus never engaged people in great intellectual discussions. He knew that logic alone would never persuade anyone to change their vision of the world.

"What *could* change their vision, however, was these daily acts of kindness and courage. They would force people to look deep within themselves, see the beauty of God's Earth, and witness the redemption of mankind. Over time, this self-reflection would propel the lost children of God to find their way into the Kingdom of Heaven.

"Brothers and sisters, we must plant mustard seeds of faith inside the souls of all of God's children."

John raised his voice and starting pumping his fist into the air. But if he was trying to hold my attention, his gesture failed miserably. I have to admit, I get bored pretty easily. It's just part of my nature.

I started thinking about the Steelers. Were they winning? Were they losing? The suspense was killing me. It was a shame they couldn't post a box score on one of those big TV screens above us. Even if it was for just a moment. What a fucking shame! Ehh, sorry for swearing.

I zoned out for a few more minutes, until I finally heard a cry of "Yes!" from the faithful. That recharged my attention.

"Make no mistake about it," John continued, "no one should think we do these things by accident; no one should be under the illusion that we perform these acts randomly or out of habit. We need to show them there's a principle behind it. We need to show them there's an entire worldview that sustains it –the Christian worldview.

"That's why I gave David, that man I met on the airplane, a brochure for the Christian Education Fund. I wanted him to know that my character – which he embraced – was dependent on my surrender to Jesus. You too, my friends, must take the initiative for Christ.

"And let's be clear about this. Some acts of compassion require no sacrifice, like when I offered Henry that bag of peanuts. Some acts will require a tiny amount of sacrifice, like when I offered to drive Henry to his hotel, even though it was miles from where I was living. But, as Christians, there may come a time when we'll need to sacrifice everything – and I mean *everything* - to spread His gospel and redeem the world. Folks, we must be prepared to answer Christ's call, whenever and wherever it comes. Because it *will* come."

John concluded his sermon and asked us to join him in prayer. I have to admit, I was disappointed by his speech. I mean, it started out alright. I was impressed by his admission that Christianity isn't really compatible with how the world actually works – at least from the perspective of a novice like me. By acknowledging this inherent problem with his faith, he gave me some hope that he owned a solution.

No such luck. Instead, John's speech dived headfirst into a morass of mysticism. It all began with his ridiculous assertion that Jesus couldn't convert people through "intellectual conversation." I mean, shit, that's precisely what I *wanted*: an "intellectual conversation." I *wanted* someone to challenge my mind and possibly change it. Instead, I was encouraged to surrender my mind and passively receive a "mustard seed" of faith. Sorry, dude, my soul can't be bought with a big bag of peanuts; it just doesn't work that way. The worst part of all was when he urged me to "sacrifice everything" for Christ. I mean, come on, man, you know I ain't ready for that shit!

I felt so incredibly sad and lonely. I was surrounded by hundreds of happy people who shared a beautiful dream of unconditional love and eternal peace, untainted by doubt and death, whereas I sat there quietly, a prisoner of my own mind and experience. I wanted to mute my mind and share their dream, but I lacked the willpower to embrace it. I couldn't escape from the idea that my stubborn brain should be the *only* arbiter of truth. Reason was my misplaced pride; my fatal weakness. God, how I hated my mind!

The piercing silence was shattered by the rattle of the band, and everyone instinctively jumped up to join the chorus. I closed my mouth in a silent act of protest. I couldn't fake my unhappiness anymore. But the words they sang – "Jesus, I love you, and I know you love me" – gave me pause. I peered at the cross above me. I felt embarrassed for having such a cold, impenetrable heart. I imagined Jesus standing in a sea of clouds with His arms outstretched and tears streaming down His face – and here I was, standing far away, refusing His embrace. Jesus just wanted my love, and I was too stubborn and selfish to give it. God, I'm such a pathetic loser!

These thoughts nearly threw me over the emotional edge. I could feel my throat tightening, and my eyes moistening. I needed to distract myself (and I needed to do it fast)!

I told myself to stand strong and resist the siren's song of Christian rock. So I condemned the chanting voices, the clapping hands, and the instrumental noise as a dangerous temptation – a temptation to surrender my mind for a purely sensory experience. Armed with these thoughts, I started to calm down.

Overall, the last few minutes were a jarring experience – a total emotional roller coaster. First, I condemned myself for lacking the courage to embrace faith. Then, I condemned faith itself for being a dangerous temptation. And yet I have to say, there was a strange consistency to it all: I wanted to feel the presence of God, but I needed to do it on *my* terms. I didn't feel comfortable in this cultish atmosphere. I needed to find an alternative route to Him – whatever it was.

Once the music ended, Sandy briefly reappeared to wish us a safe drive home. At that point, we were basically free to leave. But Mark wanted to say "hi" to the annoying pastor. So I reluctantly joined him as we waited in line for our chance to speak with him.

Finally, John got around to talking to us. In fairness, he was quite friendly to me, although he was totally gaga over Mark.

"Mark is a wonderful human being," John beamed. "One of the best I've ever known. But I'm sure you already know that."

"Yeah, I do," I replied.

"I don't deserve that kind of praise," Mark interjected.

"Sure you do," replied John. "You never give yourself enough credit."

Mark was eager to change the subject. "What did you think of the service?" he asked me.

"It was good," I mumbled back. "I really enjoyed it."

John whipped out his business card, and proudly handed it to me. "If you ever need anything – anything at all - don't hesitate to contact me. I'm here for everyone."

"Thanks," I replied. "I'll keep it handy." If you want to know the truth, dear reader, I had no intention of talking to John ever again.

Finally, Mark and I left the church and walked towards the jeep. By his standards, he was surprisingly quiet. So I felt the need to say something.

"That was a good experience," I declared matter-of-factly.

Mark snorted. "Be honest, man."

"What?"

"Be honest. I know you didn't like it."

"I *did* like it," I replied defensively. "Look, I said it was a *good* experience. And that's true. I mean, you know my background with all this religious stuff. I'm just not at a point where I can say 'Christ is King' and truly believe it. Maybe one day. I just don't know."

"What do you want out of life?" Mark asked me point-blank.

"Excuse me?"

"Oh, come on, man, you heard me. What do you want out of life?"

I couldn't remember the last time someone had asked me that. In fact, I'm pretty sure *no one* had asked me that. Still, I felt like Mark deserved an honest answer (and so did I, for that matter).

"I think I want what everyone wants: to be happy."

"Fair enough. So, are you happy?"

Mark was treading into personal territory, and I wasn't sure how to respond. I mean, yeah, I was unhappy, but I didn't like admitting it to other people. I'm a big fan of honesty, but not when it makes me look bad. I think Mark realized my dilemma, so he artfully rephrased the question.

"In your life, *when* have you been happiest?"

"Gosh," I said, stammering for time. Once again, Mark was sniffing around for intimate info, but in this case, I could give a candid answer without hurting myself too much. "I guess I would say when my parents were still together."

"Why do you say that?"

"Back in those days, I felt loved by my parents. And I was sure their love for me would last forever."

"Did it?"

"Not really. I guess that's what happens when your parents get divorced. I mean, one day, you're living a perfect childhood, and the next day, your dad's moving out to California, your mom practically becomes a shut-in, and you're forced to deal with your problems alone."

"You don't think your parents love you?" Mark asked, oozing with pity.

"Well, they're my parents. I'm sure they *think* they love me. But they barely know me anymore. Shit, they don't know anything *about* me. We have our own lives now."

"You don't feel loved by anyone else?"

"No," I replied bluntly. "Where are you going with all this?"

"You said it yourself, man: Love is happiness. If you want to be happy, you need love. Now, here's my question: Do you want to know where to find that love?"

"Um, sure."

"God!" he proudly announced. "When you open your heart to God, you will feel bathed in His love, which is a stronger love than anything you could possibly imagine, and it lasts forever." Mark put his hand over his heart. "Trust me, Brian: God's love is a one-way ticket to happiness."

"And that's been your experience?" I asked skeptically.

"Absolutely," he replied. "It's not just my experience; it's the story of my life. From the time I was a little kid, my parents raised me to open my heart to Jesus, and keep Him close to me at all times. And that's exactly what I've done. Let me tell you, I can feel His Love in every breath I take, protecting and comforting me. And when I feel His love, I hear his call to serve and sacrifice for the betterment of mankind. It's the only way to live, Brian. And that life is open to you if you want it."

I folded my arms, and sighed. "I'm sorry, Mark, but I don't think that attitude works for me. I'm a compassionate person, but I'm also a skeptical person. I can't open my heart to something that as far as I know, doesn't even exist. And I can't sacrifice for other people unless I know they're worthy of that sacrifice. I'm open to faith, but I have to stay faithful to the facts. If that means I can't be truly happy, well..."

"God is not a mathematical equation," Mark interrupted.

"Yes, I know that," I said with a chuckle. "John summed it up very nicely: Basically, I can't find God through intelligent conversation. I can only find Him by blindly accepting the words of other people."

Finally, Mark started getting annoyed. "Dude, you completely misunderstood John's message. He didn't say you *can't* have an intelligent conversation; he's said *there's no point* in having one. Let's face it, your brain is a useful tool (after all, you need it to survive) but it can't connect you to God. In fact, your brain's rigid logic can hurt your relationship with God. You need to take a different approach. Be like a child again and open your heart to God's love. I can assure you, it's a transformational power."

I cleared my throat and responded: "I have a big problem with that: it doesn't jell with my experience. Years ago, I *was* a child and I *did* open my heart to love. But later, that love was taken from me. I've already adopted your approach, and it doesn't work. Plus, I know my experience isn't unique; it happens to people all the time."

"I see you have a nasty habit of misinterpreting things," said Mark with a playful smirk. "When you were a kid, your parents might have stopped loving each other, but God *never* stopped loving you. You know, it's a shame nobody told you that at the time. I guess it's understandable why you closed your heart to God. But I'm here to tell you today, God's love is eternal, and you need to reopen your heart to Him again."

"So it can get hurt again?" I replied sarcastically.

"Keep God close and you will never be hurt again," Mark whispered soothingly.

"Well, it's an interesting concept – and I'm inclined to go along with it. But I still don't have enough information to make a real commitment. I need to know for sure that He exists, and that He's good. And right now, I can't say that. It's a big hang-up for me."

"I've already told you, it's not helpful to think of Christianity in that way. I wish you could see how your cynicism is hurting you. I want to help you change that. In fact, I'm going to make this incredibly easy for you. I only want you to do one thing: Give God permission to love you. Can you do that?"

"How? I don't even know what that means!"

"Come on, man. You said you wanted to be happy, right?"

"Yes, of course. But I want to be happy for the right reasons. Call me naïve, but I want to have a *happy* life and an *honest* life."

"That's not naïve at all," Mark replied. "But the only way to find that life – and to actually *live* it - is to give God a chance."

I figured Mark was right about that, even though I couldn't shake my skepticism that he could actually get me there. Still, I was ready to hope for the best. "Fine," I murmured, "I will God give a chance."

Mark smiled. "Good, you've made the right decision, my friend. You won't regret it. But please be patient. This is an ongoing process, and you can't expect immediate results."

"I'm in your hands," I said, succumbing to Mark's steely self-assurance. This marked the end of our lengthy debate – perhaps the deepest, most spiritual conversation of my life. My roommate, perhaps humbled by his new responsibilities, entered the jeep, started the engine, and remained silent for the entire ride home.

I used the silence to reflect on the whirlwind I had just survived. Basically, the entire evening was a microcosm of my life – the fierce conflict between reason and emotion, the schizophrenic embrace, rejection, and return to faith, and the ultimate triumph of hope over experience.

I held a vague hope that Mark's life-changing formula (which could be summarized by the classic song, "All you need is love") might actually be helpful to me. I was willing to keep an open mind, but only if I could *keep* my mind. I was never gong to surrender my better judgment, even for the promise of happiness. Shit, if I wanted to be happy at all costs, I'd be a God damn heroin addict, or something.

I resented Mark's opinion that a lot of my unhappiness could be traced to the relationship I had with my parents. While there's a kernel of truth there, the source of the problem is larger (and more complicated) than that.

Think about it: All of those kids at church were fundamentally different from me. They were born with a gene, or something, that I could never possess. They enjoyed coming together in a mass lobotomy. They liked being the puppet of an imaginary friend. But I couldn't concede that kind of authority. By nature, I am too fiercely logical and independent. I've always been that way. And I'll always be that way. To be honest, I'm proud of that. If that means I'm a lost cause – and that I have to remain a perpetual loner doomed to eternal doubt - well, so be it.

Even so – despite it all - I am keeping my faith in faith. And I am cautiously hopeful that Mark can reward that faith. As I watched the sun set beneath the horizon, I couldn't help but feel that a benevolent, mysterious power governed the universe – a power that cried out for explanation. From now on, I will be seeking that explanation.

As we approached the apartment building, Mark parked his jeep on a nearby street and turned off the ignition. Before I could open the door, he leaned towards me, and whispered:

"God always has you exactly where you need to be."

Chapter 3

In the early hours of the following morning, I was having a nice, pleasant dream (fucking some hot blonde from behind), when all of a sudden I heard: BEEP! BEEP! BEEP! A few moments later, I realized it was the God damn alarm clock, jolting me out of my peaceful slumber. I stumbled out of bed, smacked the snooze button, and dived back into bed again.

Five minutes later, the alarm clock started freaking out again. BEEP! BEEP! BEEP! Dear reader, I have to ask: Is there a more annoying sound in the entire universe than a fucking alarm clock? I considered grabbing another helping of "snooze," but I was already running late, as usual.

I sprinted through my morning routine - brushing my teeth, taking a shower, and getting dressed as fast as humanly possible. I hate running in this stupid God damn marathon every day. It always puts me in a shitty mood!

That hassle is followed by my daily subway ride – a dark, hellish trip in which I'm squeezed like a sardine between scores of other sleep-deprived zombies. For almost half-an-hour, I have to endure the sting of flinging elbows and the stench of body odor. It has to be the most diabolical form of transportation in the world.

After emerging from the underground, I briskly walk to work, where I have the unenviable duty of reading dozens of federal regulations. I study them page-by-page for nine hours a day, five days a week. Yep, it's one hell of a job! And one hell of a life too!

I'm not sure if you remember, but there was a point – not so long ago – when I actually *enjoyed* my job. I honestly took pride in "contributing something to society." Now, my day is a joyless grind from start to finish.

It's funny how things work. During my senior year, I was always anxious about whether or not I could find a job. Any job! The constant fear of falling through the cracks of society made me miserable. Now I'm a full-time member of that society – flushed with a small, steady paycheck – and I am still equally miserable. I guess it's all part of the "life cycle."

Still, I trudged on – quietly hopeful that I could either accept my fate, or somehow improve it.

This sleepy Monday should have been like any other. But shortly after 10 a.m., our HR Director – a short, petite brunette named Melissa – approached my cubicle.

"How's it going, Brian?" she asked me.

"O.K.," I replied.

"I have some good news," she promised. "I know you've been very busy lately, so I've decided to get you some help."

"What do you mean?"

"I've hired another research assistant for your department. His name is Troy Dawkins, and he just graduated from Harvard with honors. I think he'll be a major asset to our team."

"Cool," I replied. In a lot of ways, this was a big breakthrough for me. First, like Melissa said, having another body in the office would diminish my workload. But just as importantly, I was no longer the "new guy" in the office. Now some other rookie would own my slot at the bottom of the corporate pecking order. It was about freaking time!

Melissa smiled blankly. "I was hoping you could show him the ropes – you know, teach him the basics about working here and stuff - so I put him in the cubicle next to you. I trust that's not a problem, right?"

"Nope. No problem at all." In fact, I enjoyed the prospect of having an office buddy – someone I could work with on a regular basis. As of now, I'm completely isolated from all of my co-workers. I have virtually no exposure to any of them – besides some brief banter at the water cooler. No conversation ever survives more than ninety seconds – and the topics are usually limited to the weather and weekend plans (on Monday and Tuesday, they ask, "What did you do last weekend?" On Thursday and Friday, they ask, "What are you *going* to do this weekend?" Wednesday is always murky).

Since I started working at America Next, nobody – not a single person - has invited me to do something after work. Not a happy hour. Not a ballgame. Not a movie. Nothing. I can only reach one sad conclusion: no one wants to be my friend. Heck, I don't have a single friend in this entire city, with the possible exception of Mark. Knowing that, I bet you can see why I craved some company.

"So when does the new guy start?" I asked.

"Well, today is his first day. Right now, he's filling out some paperwork in my office, but he should be wrapping up pretty soon. In any case, I hope you can take him out for lunch - assuming you don't have other plans."

"That's fine," I replied. "But he better pay for himself."

Apparently, my attempt at humor flew straight over Melissa's head. She replied curtly, "I'll have him swing by at noon." Then she spun on her heels and left.

Once again, I was free to resume my work – reading and writing emails with the much-needed aid of some coffee. One of the emails I received was a CNN "breaking news" alert. According to the alert, there was an escalating political protest in Downtown Washington.

Literally thousands of protestors were gathering in front of the International Monetary Fund – a major international organization that provides loans and economic advice to poor, developing nations. The protestors were angry because (according to them) the IMF's policies led to a cycle of debt, dependency, and poverty. For that reason, they were trying to close down its annual meeting. But they hadn't succeeded so far – probably because they were trying to accomplish it through "non-violent" means. Overall, I was disappointed by their pussyness. After all, a healthy dose of violence could shut down the whole city (and enable me to leave work early today). Oh well! So much for that! I hit the delete button.

A short time later, I received another email – a cheerful message from Mark. I smiled when I read the text...

"I'm so glad you came to Crossroads with me, and I really enjoyed our conversation afterwards. Next Sunday, Mary Beth will be back in town, but I hope you'll be able to join us for the sequel. God bless."

I have to give Mark a lot of credit. Of all the people in that congregation, I bet he was the only one who could've truly "enjoyed" our discussion. I hate to say it, but most of those brain-dead zombies would've either ridiculed me, or simply ignored me. But Mark felt invigorated by our bull sessions, and hankered for another one. So did I, for that matter.

I hit the reply button, and wrote, "Sure, count me in." I was one second away from sending it, but then I noticed some guy staring at me.

"Where are we going?" he asked me.

"Excuse me?" I replied, extremely confused.

"Where are we going *for lunch?"*

"Oh, you must be..."

"Yep, I'm Troy Dawkins."

As we shook hands, I looked him up and down. The young kid was very tall (about 6'3), wiry (but not athletic), with a mane of straight black hair on top of his square-jawed face. His bright hazel eyes were softened by a pair of chic

eyeglasses. His thin lips curved upward and outward in a perpetual smirk. Overall, he looked like a self-confident, self-
absorbed intellectual, without even a trace of warmth or
empathy.

"It's great to have you on board," I said.

"Are you sure about that?" he replied, cryptically.

"Hmm," I smiled playfully, "Maybe not. After all,
you're a Harvard grad. Everyone who went to Harvard is a
snotty know-it-all."

"Ha!" Troy shouted. "Why do you say that?"

"I'm just joking, dude," I said, grabbing my wallet, and
stuffing it down my pants.

"Every joke contains an ounce of truth," he replied.

"Well, this one didn't," I said, defending myself.

"Oh, *come on.* You can say it."

As I led us toward the elevators, I cautiously replied:
"Well, all those Ivy League schools seem to have a bunch of
snotty know-it-alls." I shrugged my shoulders. "I hate to say
it, but it's true."

Troy nodded. "Yeah, I hate all those phony pricks too. I
wasted my whole life with them. Trust me, I'm not like them
at all."

"What do you mean - you wasted your life with them?"

The elevator opened and we jumped inside.

"Well, I come from the Upper West Side of Manhattan –
which is a smug, obnoxious community where all the little
rich kids, shortly after they're born, are herded into the best
pre-schools and best private schools - so one day, they can get
into the best colleges and receive the best jobs. Basically, it's
a gigantic breeding and training program for the country's
elite." Troy shook his oversized head. "The whole thing is
sickening. I can understand why all those folks in 'flyover
country' resent us so much. I mean, Christ, I feel resentful
too."

"You're resentful? Why?"

"I resent being associated with such a corrupt institution like Harvard – with all of its pious, conformist elite bullshit. Come on, dude, you brought it up after knowing me for barely five seconds."

"Stop, you're being ridiculous," I complained. "I know Harvard isn't a corrupt institution. In fact, it's one of the best universities in the world. If someone busts your balls about it, just shrug it off. Don't waste your time worrying about what other people think about you."

"Dude, let me tell you something: In my whole life, I have *never* worried about what other people think of me. And I've been afraid to say what I think. If I have a problem with Harvard, it's because I hate any institution that's afraid of self-expression."

We walked out of the elevator, past the lobby, and onto the sidewalk. "Look, I'm an honest, independent guy," Troy continued. "If you have a problem with that, we can't work together, and we certainly can't be friends. OK?"

Clearly, I have a talent for saying the wrong thing at the wrong time. So I cleared my throat and tried to make amends. "I respect where you're coming from," I began. "If I said something to offend you, I sincerely apologize. I honestly didn't mean to do that."

"Listen, man, it's impossible to offend me. I love having spirited, no-holds-barred conversations. I crave new ideas, and I detest conformity. I used to have an English professor who called me an 'intellectual arsonist,' and I take pride in that label. So yank the broomstick out of your ass, let loose, and tell me what you *really* think!"

I released a painful laugh, which inspired Troy to laugh too.

"I like your approach, man," I remarked.

"Cool, dude. But right now, I'm starving." Troy rubbed his emaciated stomach. "Where are you taking me?"

"We're almost there," I assured him.

Eventually, we arrived at an upscale, jam-packed sandwich shop called "Xanadu." I usually come here for a meatball sub twice a week, and I always eat by myself – although last Monday, I spotted some of my co-workers eating at one of the tables. Not long after, they saw me and waved me over, but it was so incredibly awkward. I mean, if they wanted to eat with me, they would've invited me in the first place, right? Since then, I usually sit in the corner to avoid repeating that embarrassing scene.

For today, I chose to ditch the meatball sub in favor of a salad. I sure as hell didn't want a "straight-shooter" like Troy asking me about my weight problem. Of course, I soon discovered that Troy bought his own meatball sub. I guess the joke's on me.

We put our meals on the table, and sat down face-to-face. As we devoured our food, there was silence for a long time. But silence makes me uncomfortable, so I decided to provoke the "intellectual arsonist."

I cleared my throat. "So why is Harvard a 'corrupt institution?' I want to hear specifics."

"It's not just Harvard," he grinned, revealing a mouthful of half-chewed meat. "The entire education system is corrupt - from kindergarten through twelfth grade, all the way through college."

"Fine, but what does that mean?"

"Let me begin with a simple premise: Our schools are not virtuous temples of learning, where students are given the tools to craft a meaningful life for themselves. Rather, our schools are crude instruments of social control, whose mission is to groom pliable workers for our economy. I know that sounds harsh, but it's true, right?"

I constructed a balanced response. "I think that's a cynical assessment, but I'm willing to go along with it for now."

Troy smiled and continued: "The education system has crushed the spirit of our generation. Before entering school, we are naturally curious and happy creatures. We follow our instincts – the instincts Nature has graciously bestowed upon us – without fear or judgment. We explore the world with enthusiasm. With each experience, we gain a sense of independence and a streak of self-confidence. We love life. We *lust* for life. But as we navigate through the school system – year after painful year – all of that pleasure gradually melts away. By the time we reach Graduation Day, life is no longer an adventure to be enjoyed; rather, it is a burden to bear. Now tell me, Brian: hasn't that been *your* experience?"

I ruminated over my gloomy school days. "Well, I guess I *did* become unhappier as I grew older - but that could be for many reasons. Why do you blame the school system?"

"I don't blame *the schools,* necessarily," he said, pulling out a pack of cigarettes. "I blame *us.* We're the ones who accept their pre-cooked 'knowledge'– the filtered facts we need to become cogs in their machine. Why do we do it? The answer is obvious: We succumb to the temptation of status – the age-old hunger to be 'better than our peers.'   After all, if we 'apply ourselves,' we can be part of the economic elite, and then we can feel superior to those working-class stiffs forever. For that privilege, we will gladly surrender our souls!

"But it's a fatal bargain," Troy continued. "Later – in high school and college– we are exposed to the *ultimate* knowledge – which is that life itself is meaningless."

"Wait a second," I interrupted. "What are you talking about?"

"Ever since the days of Darwin, science has been stripping away humanity's illusions about God and love and happiness. We – as human beings – are *not* made in the image of God. In fact, there *is no* God. Every religion is a fraud, and every code of morality is a deception. We are simply animals, and like all animals, our mission in life is simple: eat, shit, fuck, and procreate. Even now, some people can't accept our animal heritage. They insist that 'love' is the reason people get married and raise children. But 'love' is just a firing of neurons and hormones with a single purpose: to pass our genes into the next generation. Overall, we are selfish creatures with no hope for redemption.

"Let's face it, Brian: Each of us is completely and utterly alone – trapped in a mortal coil, highly conducive to pain and suffering – in a random and meaningless universe. When a person eventually understands this truth, the hope for happiness is vanquished. Once that happens, we can go on for many, many years – but we're never quite the same. Psychologically, we're fit for the grave.

"But thankfully, our educators – in their infinite wisdom – have found a great way to distract us (at least temporarily). It's called the SAT. If you study real hard for the SAT, you can get into a great college and then earn a shitload of money. Then, maybe, *maybe*, you'll be happy again."

Troy crammed his cigarette into his paper plate.

"But of course, you can never *truly* be happy again – because even if you reach the pinnacle of your profession – you are burdened with a tremendous feeling of guilt. After all, the source of your status – your intelligence – is also a parasite on your soul. In a very real sense, you are 'the man who knows too much.' When it comes time to buy stuff – like a house or a speedboat or a diamond bracelet - that intelligence is a gift (since it's the root of your wealth). But deep down, it remains a guilty burden.

"Now, eventually we can assuage that guilt, and there are three ways to do it. First, we can dedicate ourselves to humanity – sacrificing our miserable lives in service to 'others.' Take a look at those kids who are boycotting the IMF. They're a great example. They're just a bunch of spoiled rich kids – haunted by the guilt of their own intellectual superiority. They hate their own lives – so they sabotage their lives by 'serving others.'

"But their service is an illusion – because they not only hate their own lives, they hate life itself. They secretly hate the people they claim to 'serve.' Overall, it's a fucked-up system that creates grief and misery throughout the planet. But what can you expect? This is what happens when you crush a child's instincts, replace it with 'knowledge,' and then say knowledge itself is meaningless. The consequences are always deadly.

"The second option is to embrace the poison. Do you know Nietzsche?"

"Nietzsche? The German philosopher? Yeah, a little bit."

"I consider myself to be a Nietzschean in some ways. It was Nietzsche who proclaimed that 'God is dead,' and if He is dead, everything is permitted. I agree with that, and I think we should celebrate it. We should aspire to be the 'superman' who lives only for himself – without fear, or guilt, or shame. But as Nietzsche pointed out, this transformation is never simple. In fact, it requires a great deal of willpower, because our society loves to kill the creative spirit of the rebel. So the rebel must learn to harness his willpower – his most basic animal instincts of survival – and if he does that, he will succeed.

"The final way to cope with life is the least satisfying, although sadly it is the path of most people - those who - in the words of Thoreau - 'lead lives of quiet desperation.' They muddle through life, carrying the vain hope that no one will notice their pain - not even themselves.

"So that's what our education system has done to us, Brian. Can you see why I call it a 'corrupt institution?'"

"Hmm," I muttered loudly, stroking my chin.

"I suppose you disagree?"

"Well, I'm mulling it over. So let me get this straight – you think happiness comes from 'following our instincts?'"

"Yes. In my lifetime, I've witnessed only one form of authentic happiness – the happiness of children. Their happiness comes from following their most basic instincts, and indulging in them without any shame or conscience. We should all be like children again."

When Troy said those words, I remembered yesterday's church service, and Mark's identical plea to "be like a child again." Of course, Mark was referring to a child's heart (not his ego).

I pressed Troy on that issue. "Some people say that a child is happy because his heart is open to the world, and overflowing with love. Isn't that true?"

"No way!" Troy exclaimed. "The child has virtually no understanding of love – not even love for his own parents. He is a huge egoist. He is completely concerned with his own needs, and barely concerned with the needs of others. *That's* what makes him happy."

"Fine," I said. "Let's assume you're right. There are millions of people who just graduated from college, including the two of us. What can we do to be 'like children again?'"

"We should follow the path of Nietzsche – silencing the voice of our minds, and pursuing pleasure for its own sake. For years, that's how I've lived my life, and it's the only healthy way to live, my friend. I can assure you, it definitely beats the alternative: a life of 'quiet desperation.' I bet that describes your life, doesn't it, Brian?"

I sat there quietly for a few seconds. "I don't know. I can't say that for sure. If it does, I'm working to change it."

Troy took a long drag on his cigarette. "I know where you're coming from, man. I know you're a seeker. But take it from me, you need a new approach. You need to find your one true pleasure and indulge in it – without feeling any doubt or guilt."

"Well," I hesitated, "I will keep an open mind." Then I repeated: "I will keep an open mind."

"If you do *that*," Troy said with a suspicious grin, "I know you'll make the right choice."

I checked my watch. "I hate to cut this short," I confessed, "but I think we need to head back."

"Sure," Troy replied, "but first, let's hike to the IMF Building. We can watch all those phony protestors swarming outside."

"What?" I asked, incredulously. "Why?"

"Don't worry, we'll be back in plenty of time."

"But what if it's dangerous?"

"Dude, stop being a pussy!" After such a nasty rebuke, I had no choice but to follow him.

A couple of blocks later, we were confronted by a row of barricades, guarded by several police officers. The streets and sidewalks were virtually deserted, and it was eerily quiet too. I began to wonder if the protest had faded into oblivion. But as we skirted past the barricades, we could hear an undecipherable murmur in the distance. The strange noise reached a crescendo as we approached a barren intersection.

Once we weaved around the corner, we saw a huge swarm of people – perhaps two thousand folks in all - milling in front of a black, ten-story building. They were chatting with each other (and on their cell phones, too). A few of them held up cardboard signs – "Stop Global Warming!" "End Racism!" and "Workers of the World, Unite and Fight!" But there wasn't much fighting going on.

Instead, every few minutes, a protestor would carefully cross the barricade blocking the building's entrance – an illegal act that triggered a prompt (and polite) arrest by the cops. As the cuffs clicked behind their backs, a clique of friends would snap photographs – presumably to record this courageous act for posterity. The picture was a prized possession – certifiable proof of the rebel's brave clash with authority. I would later learn that the rebels were driven to jail, and then immediately released.

The crowd was dominated by college kids, although there was a healthy serving of middle-aged hipsters. Nearly everyone was unkempt, ungroomed, and unpolished (the men could've used a razor; the women could've used some make-up). Their clothes were plain, dreary and drab. Their faces were stern, and their bodies were stooped. The collective mood was serious in purpose, but sullen in spirit.

The IMF folks were different from the IKEA people I had seen (and ridiculed) earlier in the summer. The IKEA people felt comfortable in the hyper-consumerism of modern society. They valued pleasure, not goodness; convenience, not morality. If they thought about morality at all, it was as a means to an end – and the end was getting more "stuff." The pursuit of morality for its own sake was a waste of time that could be better spent at the mall.

The IMF folks, on the other hand, prized morality. They knew the capitalist system was morally wrong, so they renounced it, and joined together to destroy it. They performed their duties with conviction, but without pleasure. The heavy burden of self-righteousness erased all smiles, and silenced all laughter. But heck, what's the difference? After all, happiness is so bourgeois!

Troy scoured the depressing scene - apparently searching for something by the barricade.

"I see her," he proclaimed.

"Who?"

"Come on, follow me."

We elbowed our way past a swarm of ponytailed punks, and an overweight gal whose pink t-shirt shouted (without any trace of irony): "End world hunger!"

Finally, we caught up with a short, skinny brunette, staring silently at the corporate tower. Troy greeted her with a loud slap on her bony ass. The startled vixen spun around and smiled.

"Well, this is a surprise. I didn't expect to see *you* here," she said, playfully jabbing her finger into Troy's chest.

"Why's that?"

"I thought you were selling out by joining the workforce today."

"I *am* selling out. But I'm also taking a long lunch break. That's my way of sticking it to 'The Man.'"

"Ah, I see. And who is sticking it with you?" she asked, glancing in my direction.

"Oh yeah. Brian, this is Julia. Julia, this is Brian."

"Hi," I said.

"Hi" she replied, swinging her hair behind her shoulder. She was surprisingly attractive – with her pale blue eyes, petite nose, and prominent cheekbones– but she hid her beauty behind baggy, grey clothes and a bandana.

"In case you're wondering, I'm Troy's girlfriend," she explained.

"Oh, did you go to Harvard together?"

"Yeah, although we didn't meet until our senior year. In fact, we met in a very strange way," she said, pulling out her Virginia Slims. "One day, I was driving through Cambridge when I saw a cute kid squatting on the side of the road, struggling to replace a flat tire. So I pulled over to help him."

"In my defense," Troy interjected, "I'm from New York, so I don't have a ton of driving experience."

"Well, in any case…we hit it off immediately – and the rest, shall we say, is history."

"Are you living in D.C. now?" I asked.

"Yeah," she said, lighting her cigarette. "I'm renting a studio a few blocks from here. Then next month, I'll start law school at Georgetown. I wanted to stay at Harvard – which has a much better program – but I couldn't leave Troy here by himself. I know it's a sacrifice, but it's worth it. At least I hope it is."

"Aww, isn't she sweet?" Troy said sarcastically.

"Shut up, you prick," she replied. But she obviously liked it.

"So, what's happening here?" Troy continued. "I see a lot of talking, but no action. I thought you were going to chase these fascists out of here."

"We want to eliminate the IMF – and, if possible, the entire capitalist system – but it has to be done through persuasion, not violence."

"Hah! Good luck with that!" Troy chuckled.

"Look, honey, you can't expect immediate results. This is a long-term project that demands patience. The most important priority is raising public awareness – and that's precisely what we're accomplishing today. There is a ton of journalists here. I was interviewed by both the *New York Times* and the *Washington Post*. The local TV stations are filming dozens of arrests. I know everyone here is very proud of themselves, as they should be."

"Why do you want to eliminate the capitalist system?" I asked innocently.

"Well, for starters, it's fundamentally immoral. I don't think that's a controversial point anymore. But more importantly – and what people don't realize – is that capitalism is a disaster for humanity – creating war, poverty, and ecological destruction all over the world."

"Do you really think capitalism is responsible for all that?" I humbly retorted. "The institutions that created capitalism – banks and corporations - have existed for barely a few centuries, but poverty and war have been around for thousands of years. Think about it."

"I don't need to think about it," she barked at me. "I studied economics at Harvard, so trust me, I'm very knowledgeable about the history of banks and corporations. Those institutions didn't create capitalism; they are the consequences of it. If you really want to understand capitalism, you need to see it as a form of religion."

"Come on, capitalism is *not* a religion," I corrected her.

"I know it's not *precisely* a religion, but it's useful to see it as a *form* of religion. In fact, I would argue that capitalism

– or if you prefer the term "consumerism" - has been the dominant religion in America for decades – even if people don't openly subscribe to it.

"What do you mean?"

"Let me back up a bit. By our very nature, we – as human beings – need to have a purpose to our lives. We need to have a mission to provide structure and meaning to our existence. When science killed God, and crushed the hope for paradise in the next life, it created a huge void inside of us – a void that needed to be filled – by something, anything.

"Capitalism has filled the void by promising fulfillment through consumption, and a paradise of 'stuff' in this lifetime, here on Earth. This new religion provides you with a code of ethics to acquire the most 'stuff,' but its code is premised on two radical, and destructive ideas.

"The first idea is that it's natural – and in fact, beneficial – for people to value their own needs over the needs of others. The second idea is that people should suppress their spiritual needs and focus exclusively on their material needs (best of all, through buying a lot of 'stuff').

"The high priests of capitalism – the captains of American industry – sell you their 'stuff' and reap the profits accordingly. What is the purpose of all this stuff? Basically, it's to look better on the outside, and hide your ugliness on the inside. But nothing can be hidden forever. Every dollar you spend for a sexier body, or fancier clothes, or a more luxurious car is ultimately wasted – because there will always be a newer product in the store tomorrow that everyone will simply 'have to have.' From there, the Rat Race accelerates, draining your wallet, and ultimately, draining your soul. The whole process is so unfulfilling.

"Every day, you think to yourself: 'I know something is wrong. I know I'm not happy, and yet, I don't know what's causing it.' Sadly, it never occurs to you that the source of happiness isn't the 'stuff' you buy – it's what's *inside* of you

– the *best* part of you - constantly repressed, but yearning endlessly to express itself: your innate love for humanity.

"This should be obvious, but you've never made the connection. After all, you've been trained to seek joy through toys – and so you continue to hope that the next toy may bring you the pleasure you've been promised – although it never keeps that promise. As a lifelong member of the Rat Race, you've become a pitiful creature of consumption.

"Meanwhile, back in your community, and in communities all across the world, people lack the basic necessities of life – food, clothing, shelter, medicine. Their suffering is undeniable – although we surely try to deny it. We offer every possible excuse for their agony – it's the fault of the victims, or an error of fate – without ever bothering to look at the real culprit: The person you see in the mirror. Yourself."

I instinctively resisted that idea. "Sorry, I can't blame myself for someone starving in Ethiopia; I simply can't accept that."

"I know you can't accept it," Julia smirked. "Only a few people on Earth are willing to accept that level of responsibility. So the game goes on." She sighed and repeated: "The game goes on."

"So let's say – for the sake of argument - you're right. Let's say capitalism is a religion of greed and exploitation. What would you replace it with? Do you want to go back to Christianity?"

Julia unleashed a torrent of laughs. "Hell no!" she answered. "Christianity is a plague upon humanity – a parasite that enslaves the believers, and slaughters the unbelievers. Besides, it's already been scientifically disproven – so it's never coming back. I say good riddance.

"This is what we need: We need a new code of values – a new code based on the single, fundamental truth: that our personal happiness depends on the well-being of others. We need to stop this constant obsession with ourselves, and give equal consideration to the needs of other people. We need to stop caring about 'me' and 'my,' and start caring about 'we' and 'ours.' We need to be like children again - opening our hearts to everyone."

In the past two days, I had heard three people say "we should be like children again," although each person had a different reason for saying it.

"This is how we must live in the 21st century – if we plan to live at all," Julia continued. "The challenge of global warming is forcing change upon us. The constant rape of the Earth – to support our selfish, greedy lifestyle – has become unsustainable. We have to submit to a smaller, healthier lifestyle – and make sacrifices for the good of all. Actually, we don't have a choice in the matter. We must love each other, or we will die."

I cringed when I heard that. I've never been a big fan of sacrificing for things I can't understand (whether it's Jesus Christ, or Mother Earth).

"Well," I said, "even though *you* don't care about 'stuff,' there's a lot of folks who do, and they're not going to sacrifice it without a fight."

"There won't be any fighting," Julia said, clearly annoyed that I hadn't bent to her will. "Right now, people understand the system isn't working, but they stay inside it – and even protect it – because they can't imagine an alternative. That's why all of us are here today. That's why we're raising our signs and marching in the streets. We're raising awareness about a better way of living. We have faith that, over time, people will wake up and see the light. Eventually, they'll realize that capitalism doesn't serve their interests, and they'll join us in destroying it."

I couldn't help but notice a slight contradiction in Julia's sermon. "So your plan is to replace capitalism – a system based on self-interest – by appealing to people's self-interest?"

Julia stood silently for a few moments. She was apparently stumped. Then she spouted: "I think people's understanding of their self-interest can change over time – until eventually they lose their self-interest completely." I could barely work up the energy to respond to such a lame comeback.

"I think we have to leave," said Troy, much to my relief. "I'll look for your photo in tomorrow's *Times.*"

"Call me!" Julia pleaded.

"I will," Troy replied blandly.

"It was nice meeting you," I said, although Julia could barely bring herself to nod. I walked briskly out of the pseudo-protest, with Troy at my side.

"So that's your girlfriend?" I asked.

"Yeah, I guess you can say that. Why do you ask?"

"I'm just a little bit surprised, that's all."

Troy stopped dead in his tracks. "Why? You don't think she's hot?"

I chuckled at Troy's obliviousness. "No, man, I wasn't talking about the way she looks. I was talking about her values! I'm just surprised you would date a woman who has such a radically different values system. Let's face it, she's the very definition of that self-sacrificing, guilt-ridden sloganeer you hold in such contempt."

Now it was Troy's turn to laugh at *my* obliviousness. "Look, dude, have you ever been in a relationship?" he asked.

Christ! I definitely didn't want to chat about *my* relationship history. I sputtered and simply said, "Maybe."

"Well, you should know that relationships aren't based on values; they're based on needs. I have something that *she* needs, and she has something that *I* need. It's as simple as that."

"So what does *she* have that *you* need?"

Troy shook his head, and smiled. "Gosh, you're a nosy bastard, aren't you?" I smiled, but refused to respond. Then

Troy confessed, "Well, we have very good *chemistry*, if you know what I mean. Basically, she let's me do whatever I want." After some more awkward silence, he continued, "Also, her dad is the Chairman of Chevron. It's nice knowing that – if things get serious – we'll be well-taken care of."

"Whoa, her dad is the Chairman of Chevron? How is that possible?"

Troy enjoyed another hearty laugh at my expense. "Dude, I already explained all that stuff to you. These kids are drowning in the guilt of their privileged childhood. It makes *perfect* sense!"

"I suppose. But what do *you* have, that *she* needs?"

"Shit, I don't know," he responded, with genuine amazement. "That's always been a mystery to me. I sometimes wonder what inspired her to sacrifice her career and move to Washington with me."

"You should ask her."

"Yeah, right. Come on, man, be reasonable here. If I did that, she'd realize she doesn't need me. Then she'd break up with me."

"Alright," I sighed, "if you say so."

We returned to America Next, and hopped onto the nearest elevator.

"I'm afraid to look at my watch," I said.

Troy didn't have that fear. He checked the time and shouted: "Crap, I was supposed to be in Melissa's office fifteen minutes ago."

"Well, just blame it on me," I said.

"No way, man. I'll take the heat."

The elevator doors opened, and we stepped onto the fourth floor.

"I think you should see Melissa now," I warned.

"Yeah, definitely."

"OK, well, I'll catch you later."

"Listen, man, thanks for lunch. Next one's on me, alright?"

I never expected to be thanked – but it was nice to be appreciated, anyway. I nodded and simply replied: "You got it."

As I walked back to my cubicle, I thought about all those crazy protestors, standing in the streets and preening in front of the cameras. I wanted to admire their idealism, but if you want to know the truth, I pitied them. After all, they seemed so miserable. I mean, if they wanted to recruit people like me to join their cause, their visible display of anger and despair was a shitty marketing tool. Their entire lifestyle held no appeal to me.

I couldn't help but think, "what the hell are these kids going to do with their lives?" Then I stared blankly at my computer monitor, and leafed through my copy of the *Federal Register* – and asked, "what the hell am *I* doing with *my* life?" I suppose we all have our crosses to bear.

The only person who seemed to have it figured out was Troy. This guy was surrounded by insecure conformists (whether at Harvard, America Next, or outside the IMF), and yet he radiated a powerful aura of self-confidence. He knew who he was – and quite frankly, he *liked* who he was – and he wasn't going to change for anyone. Period.

I admired his strong, forceful personality, and his raw, independent intelligence. But was he *happy*? The theme of his philosophy was: "If you objectively analyze the world, there is no *reason* to be happy." But did he believe his own philosophy? Could anyone *truly* believe it? Granted, I usually believed it, but my conviction was tempered by hope – the hope that I *could* be wrong, and maybe, just *maybe,* there was purpose to my life.

But what if the "Real World" robs me of that hope? In that case, perhaps Troy was onto something. Perhaps I needed to "find my one true pleasure and indulge in it." After all, it seemed to work for *him*.

Honestly, I didn't know what to think. I promised Troy that I would keep an open mind. And I will keep that promise. To be fair, I will keep an open mind for Mark too.

Chapter 4

Well, it finally came. When I returned home on Friday afternoon, I immediately discovered a foot-long cardboard package lying on the carpet. I grabbed a pair of scissors and tore the box right down the middle, and after weaving my fingers through a sea of Styrofoam, I retrieved the object inside: my college yearbook.

I was supposed to receive my yearbook shortly after graduation – which was literally months ago – but a "printing error" delayed its shipment to our class. I was excited to receive it – perhaps because I thought it could provide closure on a significant chapter in my life. No pun intended.

I walked into my room, jumped onto my bed, and immediately started scanning through the yearbook. I quickly found the page with my name and photograph on it. In the picture, I stood in a large field of grass, with my arm draped across a wooden gate. Overall, it was a pretty decent photo – especially when you consider that I took it myself. I never felt comfortable asking anyone else to take it for me.

As you would expect, most of the graduates inserted a couple of quotes on the bottom of their page – representing a cornucopia of stale and overused clichés. In contrast, I simply wrote, *"to be continued..."* I know that line isn't very creative or inspirational, but it nicely summarized my attitude as I prepared to enter the "Real World."

For one thing, I have always felt a compulsive need to be completely honest (at least with myself) about everything. I can't pretend – like most people – that my life has been an exciting and enjoyable adventure. By choosing the words, *"to be continued,"* I reluctantly acknowledged that my life hasn't been memorable, or even pleasurable – for the most part. Even after twenty-two years, I can't brag or boast about anything at all.

However, those three little words revealed another, brighter aspect of my personality – my sense of optimism. I bet I don't strike you as an optimistic person, but it's true! Even though I'm a naturally skeptical guy, there's always been a stream of optimism running throughout my life. I've constantly kept my head afloat – despite everything that's happened to me – by clinging to the hope of a better tomorrow. In the closing days of college – when the abyss opened up in front of me – I kept that hope alive (albeit just barely).

And I believe that hope has been rewarded. I think there's been genuine progress in my life over the past four months. First, I found a pretty decent job in my field. I know it's not an exciting job, per se, but it pays the bills and it could propel me into a better job in the future. Overall, I'm pretty satisfied with it.

Second, I found a great apartment at a reasonable price – instead of moving into one of those over-priced shitholes that are abundant in this area. In fact, I really couldn't ask for a better place to live (at least at my salary).

Lastly, I've made a couple of new friends – my nice, compassionate roommate, Mark, and my smart, provocative co-worker, Troy.

I wasn't the only kid at America Next who enjoyed spending time with Troy. On his second day there, a couple of the corporate veterans (i.e., the guys who had been out of college for at least a year) invited Troy out for lunch. I wasn't invited, of course, so I returned to my usual routine of eating alone in the back of the sandwich shop.

However, when he came back from lunch, Troy said he was disappointed that I hadn't tagged along. I honestly couldn't remember the last time someone had said something like that. I was forced to explain that I hadn't been invited, and probably wouldn't be invited in the future, either.

"Well," he said, "let's get together for lunch tomorrow – just the two of us. Those other guys are cool, I guess, but they're boring as shit."

I burst out laughing when I heard that. I felt an immediate kinship with Troy – another outsider who was wearied by what passed for serious conversation in our generation – basically the pros and cons of each bar in town, and the plusses and minuses of each alcoholic beverage (they were all pretty good, apparently).

During the next three days, Troy and I had lunch at Xanadu, and we resumed our engrossing discussions, especially about sports and politics.

I thought I knew a lot about both subjects, but Troy had me beat by a country mile. His mind was like an interactive encyclopedia, rattling off names, dates, and statistics for baseball players, football games, congressional races, and presidential administrations. Just about everything.

But he was personally detached from such hot-button topics; he didn't have a favorite sports teams, or a preference for either political party. If I had to guess, I think he frowned upon the conceit that one team or one party could be inherently better than another one. In his mind, his fierce objectivity was his defining virtue. I could relate to that in some ways.

However, when it came to religious matters, Troy was a passionate advocate – an advocate for atheism. He ridiculed any person who believed in God – or as he put it, the "imaginary friend for adults." When I asked him for proof that God doesn't exist, he fired back, "I can't prove it, but I don't need to prove it. By definition, I can't prove a negative. Think about it: Can you prove the Easter Bunny doesn't exist? The same principle applies to God. The burden of proof belongs on all those hillbilly Bible thumpers. They need to show *me* the evidence. And they have none."

I wanted to challenge Troy – in the same way I had challenged Mark in the parking lot of the church – but it was futile. Deep down, I shared Troy's attitude about faith. We didn't need to prove our beliefs. The believers needed to prove *theirs*. And they hadn't. Yet.

Despite our blossoming friendship, I really didn't know Troy on a personal level. I had a good sense of Troy's intellect, and his thoughts about the world, but I knew almost nothing about his overall character. The only way to fix that was by seeing him in a venue outside of work.

As if on cue, earlier today Troy invited me to a house party hosted by his old college roommate – some guy named Keith. Apparently, Keith had just moved to Washington, and wanted to have the local Harvard alums (and their friends) over at his place the next night.

I was happy Troy invited me, but if you want to know the truth, I was reluctant to accept. In college, my house party experience was pretty limited, and mostly unfavorable (yes, I'm in the minority on that one). Here's my problem: By nature, I can't find pleasure by wallowing around in a drunken stupor. The same instincts that restrained me from church – the instinct to remain in touch with reality at all times – restricted my exposure to one of the supposed perks of college life: drunken house parties.

But the college days had come and gone – my life was "to be continued" – and so, just as I had agreed to go to church – I accepted the house party invite. This time of my life was dedicated to new experiences. And perhaps it was time to find "my pleasure," as Troy had recommended.

When Saturday rolled around, I began the day by taking a walk around the Washington Mall, and then I did some shopping around the neighborhood. When I returned to the apartment around mid-afternoon, I found Mark sitting on the living room couch watching a baseball game.

I have to confess that I was secretly avoiding Mark. Ever since he gave me that homework assignment – the whole "give God a chance" thing – I've been trying to avoid his disapproving gaze. As you probably expected, I've been a delinquent student. And if you want to hear my excuse, here it is: As a practical matter, I don't know *how* to "give God a chance." Is it something you meditate to, like a Buddhist mantra, or is there a specific course of actions that go with it? The answer wasn't obvious to me.

My only deliberate action came yesterday morning. As I walked from the subway to the office, I noticed a small, sickly, dirty young man – probably no older than me - sitting on a rug on the edge of the sidewalk. He stared at the ground, with nary an expression on his face. Overall, he exuded despair and hopelessness; the complete annihilation of a man's spirit.

Next to him was a hand-written cardboard sign – a sign that became clearer as I approached him. I started to make out the words: "Hi, my name is Blake. I have AIDS. My parents threw me out of…"

I quit reading the sign to prevent my heart from aching and bursting in sympathy for this genuine victim of the world's cruelty. Sadly, not a single person stopped to give him some spare change. Not one! I could only wonder, "Did they even notice this kid? Did they feel any sympathy at all? Why couldn't they help just a little bit?"

As for me, I couldn't be so indifferent to human suffering. So I walked toward Blake, and discretely dropped a dollar into his collection plate.

Incredibly, I didn't receive a "thank you," or any form of acknowledgement, and I was *really* pissed off by it. I know that sounds awful, but I thought he should be grateful that I donated my hard-earned cash to save his sorry ass. Instead, the fag just sat there silently and motionless. Sorry, I shouldn't use that word. Sorry.

I kept walking along – but I didn't feel any better about myself, or the world around me. Instead, I was haunted by doubts. "Did the kid really have AIDS, or was he a liar? Even if he had AIDS, couldn't he have found a job? And why am I such a schmuck for worrying about this shit?"

This act of compassion – which was supposed to open my heart, and make me feel happy – ended up making me feel guilty. And to assuage that guilt, I donated a dollar to Blake every time I walked past him.

So anyways, that represents my bold attempt to "give God a chance," and open my heart to a stranger. A mondo disappointo, no? I'm sure you can see why I was keeping Mark at a safe distance.

But in our brief conversation, Mark avoided the topic of religion altogether. Instead, he focused on the newest hot-button political issue: a Congressional bill that would ban assisted suicide throughout the nation, even in the few states that had chosen to legalize it.

I could see that Mark was trying to lure me into a discussion about morality, but I wouldn't take the bait. I had more important things to do, like take a shower and get dressed for the house party. So I humored him for a little bit, while desperately searching for a discrete way to maneuver into my room.

I didn't get very far. Just when I thought the conversation had come to a close, Mark said, "By the way, you never responded to my email."

I was confused. "What email?"

"I sent you an email a few days ago, asking if you wanted to go to church with me and Mary Beth tomorrow."

Finally, I remembered what he was talking about. "Oh my goodness," I said, smiling at my own stupidity. "I'm so sorry. I totally forgot about that. I was all set to respond, but someone interrupted me at work, and I guess, after that, it slipped my mind."

"No problem," Mark assured me. "So do you want to come with us tomorrow?"

"Sure. Count me in."

I wasn't sure what a second trip to Crossroads would accomplish. I was pretty confident I got the message the first time, and it wasn't a very compelling one. Still, I owed it to myself (and to Mark) to give it another chance – even if it meant waking up early on another weekend.

After enjoying a long, hot shower and spraying myself with cologne for the first time in ages, I squeezed into a light green polo shirt and a pair of blue jeans. It was the best out-fit I could come up with, under the circumstances.

After that task was finished, I stared at myself in the bedroom mirror, striking different poses and flashing differ-ent smiles at multiple angles. I looked bad in all of them. There's no way around it, I'm simply *not* an attractive person. It's a shame I have to feel so insecure about something I can't control. I stepped away from the mirror before I felt the urge to smash it.

After grabbing my keys and wallet, I walked out of the apartment and headed toward the nearest metro station. Then I spent the next half-hour riding the subway to a place in Downtown D.C. called Dupont Circle.

When I came out of the Dupont station, I immediately discovered Troy, wearing a blue and white striped shirt, and a pair of beige khakis. Leaning against the façade of a steel building, he puffed away at a freshly-lit cigarette. Overall, he was the perfect blend of a preppy and a rebel. I guess you could call him a "preppy rebel."

Finally, I got his attention.

"Hey," he muttered.

"Hey," I replied. "What's up?"

"Same ole shit, man. What about you?"

"Nothin much, I suppose. Do you know where this place is?"

"Yeah, it's just a couple of blocks from here. Let's get movin."

We barely made it past the first block before Troy's cell phone started ringing wildly. He stared at the number flashing on the screen.

"This God damn thing is an electronic leash!" he bellowed. Then he put the phone against his ear and shouted, "What is it, Julia?"

I tried not to listen to the details of their conversation (see, what a nice guy I am!), but it was obviously filled with tension.

Finally, after a few minutes, Troy ended the conversation with a sharp "Fine, good bye," and then jammed the phone back into his pocket.

"Sometimes, I wonder if she's worth the trouble," he whined.

"What's the problem?" I asked.

"Well, I won't bore you with all the details, but basically, she's withholding sex from me until I sign some stupid animal rights petition.'

"Huh?"

"Exactly. It's crazy, right? This woman won't be happy until she sees all suffering – both human and animal – totally abolished. She's obsessed, and *I'm* the one who has to pay for that obsession."

I was so stunned by the weirdness of this argument that I was literally speechless. So I kept silent until we arrived at a four-story brown townhouse on the side of a narrow street.

We climbed a short set of stairs to reach the lobby. Luckily, Troy knew the electronic code to enter the building. Once we were inside, we walked up to the second floor, and then made a bee line to Apartment 203.

After a few knocks from Troy's fist, a mysterious bald dude in a wifebeater opened the door for us.

"Come on in," he said. And so we did.

The place was a tempest of human activity – jam-packed with loud, sweaty young men and women, alternating between shouting at the top of their lungs over the blare of formulaic rock music, and swallowing the beer filled to the brim of their plastic cups.

I felt overwhelmed by the horde of strangers relinquishing all contact with reality, along with the responsibility that comes with that contact. I wanted to run away immediately, but I felt an obligation to stay.

"Let's find the beer!" Troy screamed in my ear.

"O.K!" I shouted back. I'm not sure if he heard me.

I followed Troy as he squeezed through a pack of people. The guys wore way-too-tight shirts in order to flatter their arms and chest. Meanwhile, the girls wore even tighter shirts that magnified their cleavage, and exposed their belly buttons. Incredibly, they all managed to pull it off. Their fitness stood in sharp contrast to my slothfulness.

We bumped and grinded our way to the kitchen, where a gigantic keg was resting comfortably on the floor – sitting like a Buddha statue, as its wide-eyed worshippers gathered around to partake of its nectar.

I reached down to fill my cup with the golden liquid. As you could probably guess, I'm not much of a beer drinker, but a thirst for alcohol was mandatory in this setting. Now don't get me wrong, I certainly don't think that drinking is immoral or anything like that. I'm just not a huge fan of the taste (personally, I would rather have a can of Coke or a Sprite). It's really that simple. In any case, I took a few swigs of beer from my cup, symbolizing my solidarity with the rest of the congregation.

After that, Troy filled his cup to the brim. But before he could enjoy his first sip, a big burly dude – wearing a colorful Hawaiian t-shirt and a backwards baseball cap – suddenly tackled him from behind. Both guys landed on the floor, with beer spilled all over them.

"What the *fuck*!" Troy shouted in anger. But once he spun around and saw the perpetrator, he broke into a huge grin. "Fuck man! Why are you such an asshole?" he shouted, readjusting his eyeglasses.

"It's my nature, genius," the nameless thug replied, reaching his arm to help Troy off the floor. Then they embraced.

"How are you, man?"

"I think you know the answer to that," Troy responded. "And how are you?"

"I'm great. I mean, *absolutely* great."

I quietly observed this exchange until Troy recalled my existence.

"Keith, this is my good friend, Brian. We just started working together. Brian, this is – well, you know the drill."

Keith instantly grabbed my hand, and inflicted it with a painfully firm handshake. Damn it, I really hate those kind of handshakes!

"Cool to meet you, Brian," he beamed. He looked like he had just stepped off the fratbot assembly line – with his sandy hair, chiseled jaw, ripped arms, and ever-so-protruding beer belly. But he seemed very nice and friendly. Of course, that could just be the alcohol talking.

"This is a great party!" I shouted, lying between my teeth. "How do you know all these people?"

"This is my hometown," he proudly replied. "I was born and raised in DC. I know a lot of these kids from back in the day. There's also some Harvard guys here, like Troy."

"What do you do now?" I asked.

"I work in the research division of the Pentagon, but I won't be there for long. Next year, I'm going to Emory University to study biochemical engineering."

"Wow!" I said. I couldn't believe this red-faced, speech-slurring drunk was smarter than me - way smarter than me, in fact. "That sounds awesome."

"What about you, man?" he asked. "Are you going to grad school?"

"Gosh, I don't know," I sighed. "I really just - "

At that moment, another fratbot barged into our discussion, completely ignoring me and Troy. Apparently, our conversation was officially over.

"Keith is a dim-witted jock asshole," Troy matter-of-factly whispered to me.

I laughed at my co-worker's bluntness. "Come on, Troy, tell me what you *really* think!"

"Well, if you really want to know," said Troy, slurping the last sips of his beer, "I think I need to get laid."

By now, I should've been numb to Troy's blunt language, but I wasn't immune to it yet. I simply replied, "What?"

"I need to bone a girl."

"What about Julia?" I asked, nursing my beer.

"What about her? She's a dumb cunt for withholding sex from me, and for the lamest of reasons. She needs to take responsibility for her actions. Besides, I just want a girl for *one* night. It doesn't mean anything."

"If it doesn't mean anything, why do it at all?"

"God, you're naïve! Do you even have a cock?"

"What? Of course I do. I'm trying to…"

"I know where you're going with this, man, but here's the thing: For me, there's nothing moral or immoral about sex. Sex is sex – and I hate those people who think sex is either a mortal sin, or a wonderful spiritual experience. They have no idea what they're talking about. They're projecting their psychological issues onto a simple task: plugging a hole. Sex is a biological urge – just like eating or drinking or taking a dump – and like all of those urges, it feels *really* good when you do it. The pleasure is all that matters. So why stop it? Why try to control it? Why condemn yourself for wanting more of it? Have you ever watched the Discovery Channel? Those animals have the right idea. They just do it. So please, spare me a lecture about the immorality of it all. If it's natural, it can't be immoral."

"But we're *not* animals," I protested. "In fact, that's what separates us from the animals – our ability to be morally responsible."

"What the hell does that mean – morally responsible?" Troy asked while he refilled his beer cup. "Our only responsibility is to ourselves, and our own needs. Everything else is an illusion. A dangerous illusion." Then he took another sip. "Besides, I *know* you must've thought about bringing a girl home tonight."

Actually, it never crossed my mind. For starters, I had already promised Mark that I would keep our apartment "sex-free." But more importantly, the prospect of bringing a girl home with me seemed practically impossible.

Then again, it *had* happened once before. OK, I'm going to be completely honest with you about my sexual history – even though it's quite brief and not very flattering. I've avoided the subject so far – but I can't avoid it any longer. Besides, you deserve the truth.

I suppose I should start with puberty itself – back in junior high, and high school. I was pretty lonely during that time – very lonely, in fact. I never had a girlfriend. I never even had a real date.

I think there were a couple of reasons for that. First of all, I really didn't like any of the girls in my neighborhood. They were super-spoiled upper-class princesses, purely fixated on material things, and constantly snickering at people beneath their status. Their bodies were primped by the city's best stylists and trainers, and their brains were bolstered by private academies and personal tutors, but their souls were an empty void. If you wanted to peel off their masks and see their true spirit, there was no "there" there. They were nothing.

At least that's what I told myself at the time, and looking back at those days, I still think that's an accurate assessment.

But to be completely honest, there was another thing holding me back – namely, myself. I was simply too shy and too God damn chubby to elicit any interest from girls. From their perspective, I might as well be dead.

The rest of the guys, on the other hand, were very much alive – and they were spreading their seed around town like dandelion dust in the wind. While I was playing video games, they were screwing nearly every chick in sight. By the time we graduated from high school, I was probably the only virgin in my class – which was very frustrating to me, as you could probably imagine.

Remarkably, I lost my virginity in my second week of college. I went with my roommate to a sorority party, where the alcohol was flowing, the music was blasting, and the women were trashy – just like tonight.

I was approached by a short, overweight sophomore with long, curly brown hair, huge knockers, and a surprisingly sweet smile. I wasn't attracted to her, but she was definitely attracted to me for some peculiar reason. I instinctively saw the hook-up potential, and I kept feeding her shots – which she willingly swallowed until she was completely plastered. As the party wound down, she escorted me into someone's bedroom, where she plopped down on the bed, with her legs spread open.

As she laid there mindless and motionless, I immediately got to work – removing my jeans and boxers, and stripping off her shorts and panties. I climbed on top of her big body and eagerly entered her.

As I rocked us back and forth, her fat jiggled up and down and her eyes struggled to stay open in a drunken stupor. Even so, I kept thinking to myself, "Yes! Finally! I'm doing it! I'm having sex!" With every thrust, I felt years of shame shedding from my body.

Since I didn't wear a condom, I came out and ejaculated on her stomach. After cleaning up my mess, I put her panties back on, and lifted a blanket on top of her body. By this point, she was fast asleep and snoring like a wildebeest. I took my cue and left. I was now a man.

As the days passed, however, my self-confidence melted into self-loathing. For so many years, I had prided myself on being a "good guy," who treated women with utmost respect. Now, I was just like every other guy – a horny prick who exploits women for his own gratification.

The festering guilt gave me a fresh appreciation for the Christian dogma of saving sex for marriage. This is why I accepted Mark's dictum of keeping our place a "sex-free apartment." The logic was straightforward: If you can't do it out of love, don't do it at all.

So there you have it – my pathetic and disgusting sexual exploits. I'm sure you don't think very highly of me now – if you ever did.

Anyway, returning to tonight's event, I innocently told Troy that I had no intentions of bringing a girl home with me. It was the truth.

"Well, suit yourself," he barked, taking a swig. "In the meantime, I'm going to chat with *that* chick."

"Who?" I asked.

Troy pointed at a smoking-hot blonde who was chatting with a few of her girlfriends in the corner. She was arguably the prettiest girl at the party.

I smiled at the absurdity of it all. "If you think *that* chick is gonna talk to *you,* you're *nuts."*

"My friend, with beer, all things are possible."

With those famous last words, Troy abandoned me to hunt for pussy. I started walking around the apartment, hoping to give the impression that I was heading somewhere important. Like a shark in the sea, I needed to keep moving to stay alive. Otherwise, the strangers around me would see the dark truth – that I was a loser.

During my sprint around the apartment, I kept an eye on Troy's progress with the hot blonde. I was hoping my new friend would fail spectacularly. I wanted him to be humbled by the opposite sex – just like I had been humbled throughout my life. It was only fair.

"Excuse me!" I heard a woman shout. I looked ahead of me and beheld a short, cute blonde with solid, but unspectacular, cleavage.

"Yes?" I asked, afraid that I was in trouble.

"Where are you going?"

"Um, what do you mean?"

"I keep seeing you walking around, but you're not talking to anyone."

I was totally busted. "Well, I'm just waiting for my friend to finish his conversation."

"Oh, who's your friend?" she asked. I scanned the room for Troy, and found him chatting with Keith. I suppose his pussy hunt had gone poorly, and he was now re-strategizing with his buddy. I showed Troy to this strange woman who was (gasp!) actually talking to me.

"I see," she said, with a touch of playful sarcasm. "Can you talk to anyone else in the meantime?"

I laughed. "Absolutely. I'm Brian. What's your name?"

"I'm Sarah," she said, smiling. I could've been totally mistaken, but she seemed to be checking me out – and she was both cute and (relatively) sober.

"Where are you from?" I asked.

"Well, originally I'm from Indiana, but I went to Vanderbilt University. I just graduated last May. I'm still not sure what I want to do with my life. I'm still finding myself, I guess you can say. So I'm living with my older sister, who rents the apartment across the hall. That's how I got to know Keith. What about you? What's your story?"

I dutifully explained my story – my trek from Philadelphia to Vermont to Washington. She listened attentively, seeming to hang onto my every word. I felt a real connection to her – another uncertain soul struggling to stay out of the abyss. I thought she was simply wonderful.

Then she blurted out, "Can you introduce me to your friend?"

"What's that?"

"Can you introduce me to your friend – you know, the tall guy with the glasses?"

"Oh. Sure," I said, completely flummoxed. "Come on."

I walked up to Troy, and introduced him to Sarah. They seemed smitten with each other, with Troy towering over her, and Sarah fidgeting with her long blonde hair. I hung around briefly, pretending to be a part of the conversation, but after a while, I got the hint and quietly walked away.

I visited the keg, and poured myself another cup of beer. After quickly downing that serving, I refilled my cup, and plopped down on the sofa to watch Troy and Sarah conduct their mating ritual.

I felt so disgusted I walked into another room, where I promptly sat down on another couch. I stayed there alone, except to occasionally refill my beer cup. At this point, I didn't care who saw me there. I was a loser – an utter reject – and I could no longer pretend otherwise.

Near the end of the night – way past 1 a.m. – I fell asleep, only to be re-awoken by a heavy nudge on my shoulder. I saw Troy sitting next to me on the couch – completely shit-faced.

"What's up?" he asked.

"God, you look awful," I said. You drank *way* too much!"

"Relax!" he shouted. "I know my limits."

"Fine, whatever. Are you ready to leave? I think we should take a cab. I drank too much as well."

"Nah," he said, perking up. "I'm headed to the next apartment."

"What do you mean?"

"I'm headed back with Sarah, that girl we were talking to, remember?"

I couldn't believe what I was hearing. I knew Troy was hungry for pussy, but I never thought Sarah would give it up so easily. I mean, she was a sweet girl – or at least she seemed that way. I guess she was a fraud. She used me to get to Troy right from the start. I wanted to be angry at her – but I couldn't be too upset. After all, I could see why any girl would choose Troy over me. He was much better looking. Heck, it wasn't even close. And I couldn't be too mad at Troy, either. I mean, the dude didn't know I was interested in Sarah. It wasn't his fault. Still, the whole thing hurt like a bitch. Finally, I made one last-ditch attempt to sway Troy from his nectar.

"What about Julia?" I asked.

Troy flashed his classic, mischievous smile. "I won't tell if you don't." Then he stood up, stretched his legs, and towered over me.

"Is everything OK, man?" he asked.

I sat there silently for a few moments, not really sure how to respond. I desperately wanted to explain the situation to him, but at this point, it wouldn't do any good. I couldn't deny him "his pleasure" – especially if it bore no impact on me. It was a lost cause.

"I'm fine," I stated. "Really, I'm fine." This satisfied Troy, who smiled and walked away – presumably to leave with his whore.

I stuck around for another half-hour, downing more and more alcohol. I lost count of how much I drank. I know it was a lot. I wanted to be in a state of mindlessness, to dull the pain of my existence.

Finally, I got up, brushed myself off, and left the apartment. After a few minutes standing on the curb, I hailed a cab and jumped in.

The cab driver was a big black guy with a thick Jamaican accent. He kept trying to lure me into a conversation, but I could barely concentrate on what he was saying. I felt terrible about it. I probably seemed like one of those snotty rich kids who thought they were too good to chat with a cab driver. But frankly, I was too smashed – and too sick – to be friendly at this ungodly hour. I just needed to get to bed as soon as possible.

After handing the driver an extra-large tip (hopefully, that softened the blow), I stumbled into the apartment, and dived straight into bed. I conked out almost immediately.

After several hours of very deep and much-needed sleep, I heard a constant knock on my door. I ignored it for as long as I could, before finally moaning, "Come in!"

My roommate opened the door – fully dressed and primped with a worried look on his face.

"I thought you were coming," he said meekly.

"What?" I asked, still lying in my bed.

"I thought you were coming to church with me," he repeated. It took me awhile to comprehend the situation.

"Oh!" I finally said. "I, I, I can't. I feel awful. I have a throbbing headache, and my body just feels terrible."

Mark nodded, barely disguising his disappointment. "I understand," he said. "Do you want some medicine?"

"No," I squawked. "I just need to sleep it off."

"Don't be silly," he resisted. "Let me get you something." Before I could resume my protest, Mark strode into the bathroom, rummaged through the cabinet, and returned with a pair of Advil and a plastic cup of water. He sat on the edge of the bed, and handed me the medicine.

"Thanks," I said meekly. I placed the pills on the tip of my tongue and swallowed them quickly with a swish of water.

"I'm going to head out," Mark said, reclaiming the cup. "Feel better, OK?"

"Yeah, I will. I'll be OK."

"Alright," said Mark, "I'll be back." He rose from the bed, and opened the door to leave. However, a pair of words remained to be said.

"I'm sorry," I shouted.

Mark spun around and smiled faintly. "Don't worry about it," he said, "it's not a big deal." And with that, he closed the door and left.

But nonetheless, I couldn't fall back asleep. I felt too upset and ashamed about everything that happened. I had been tempted by Troy to "find my pleasure" in the loins of a woman simply because it "felt fucking good." But the hunt for that pleasure had exposed, not eliminated, my greatest vulnerability – my pitifully low regard for myself as a person. The single-mined pursuit of selfishness had ruined, not inflated, my self-confidence. The reckless drift into mind-lessness had pushed me further than ever from the path to happiness.

I respected Troy for his intelligence and charisma and for the strange fact that he seemed to like me too. But his moral philosophy was anathema to me – an intriguing idea, in theory, but a poor one, in practice. Worst of all, the ill effects of that God-forsaken party had forced me to abandon my friend Mark, even as he sought to salvage my soul on this Sunday morning. What a disaster, from start to finish!

I had been led astray by Troy, who seemed to offer noth-ing to me now. I wanted to renew the spiritual journey with Mark. I just hoped it wasn't too late.

Chapter 5

I've always been an outsider. I simply can't relate to other people – whether it's a saint like Mark, or a playboy like Troy, or anyone else for that matter. Everybody seems so comfortable with their place in the universe (except for me). I think that comfort comes from knowing and mastering the rules of life. But no one ever gave me a copy of the rulebook. I bet – sometime, long ago - it was delivered to everyone's doorstep (like the Yellow Pages) but my edition was lost in the mail. So I have to spend the rest of my life in a state of confusion – acting and improvising to survive.

I'm not sure how this happened. I guess a psychologist would say it's a combination of nature and nurture. First, the "nature" part. Let's face it, I'm not biologically wired to thrive in the social jungle – where brain-dead conformity is rewarded, and independence is punished. There must be some mutant gene coursing through my veins.

Next, the "nurture" part. Basically, I was raised in a pretty shitty family. I think my parents were too busy fighting amongst themselves to raise me with any kind of value system, and then – eventually - they simply abandoned me. In fact, the more I think about it, the more I see a family connection to my current problems.

If I'm being too harsh on my parents, perhaps it's because Thanksgiving is rapidly approaching. For most people, this holiday represents a celebration of family and heritage – but, for me, it's an anxious reminder of the failures of both. During this annual ritual, I inevitably have to choose between visiting my mother in Philly, or my father in California. I hate having to choose between them. I always feel guilty about rejecting one parent, and then I feel even worse when I'm actually spending time with the other one. If it was up to me, I would avoid the decision altogether.

Luckily for me, I eventually found a way to solve the problem – thanks to the kindness of my roommate. Sometime in early November, Mark entered the living room, and asked me about my holiday plans. "Are you going home for Thanksgiving?" he wondered.

"I'm not sure *where* my home is," I replied cryptically.

"What do you mean?"

"Well, it's complicated," I replied dismissively, hoping to end the conversation. It didn't work.

"Well, if you want, you can always come to Ohio with me. We always have a big Thanksgiving dinner with lots of friends and family."

Suddenly, a new option lay before me – a fresh way to bypass the family controversy altogether. If I went with Mark to Ohio, I didn't have to choose between my parents. I could reject them both equally.

"Do you think your parents would mind?" I asked haltingly. "I certainly don't want to impose on anyone."

"Don't be silly," he replied, with a brush of his hand. "We'd be thrilled to have you. Come with us."

I certainly wasn't going to argue with Mark's generosity – and so we made tentative plans for our road trip. On the day before Thanksgiving, I left work early – right around noon – to get a head start on our voyage. As I waited on the street corner, a black jeep Wrangler pulled up beside me. Staring through the windshield, I noticed Mark sitting in the drivers' seat, with his ugly girlfriend riding shotgun.

This was my first time meeting Mary Beth – the freckled girl whose photo caught my eye during the apartment hunt.

"Hi, I'm Brian," I said, planting my butt on the back seat.

"Hi," she said, stifling a yawn. She didn't seem too interested in me – which was fine, since I wasn't too interested in her, either. I simply sat quietly, as she and Mark discussed a host of trivial (and boring) topics. Every now and then, Mark tried to include me in the conversation – but my role usually died quickly thereafter. I simply had no position on church bake sales, laundry detergent, or Aunt Peggy's pregnancy. So I fell asleep.

During the seven-hour trip, I alternated between the Real World and the Dream World, until eventually the two worlds converged. The small towns that peppered Eastern Ohio were trapped in a half-century time warp. These plain, rural communities were a relic of the 1950s – completely immune to the dramatic changes of the modern era. And yet it was strangely comforting to know these places still existed.

As dusk settled over the countryside, Mark triumphantly announced from the driver's seat: "Welcome to Palestine!"

"What's Palestine?" I asked, groggily.

Mark laughed. "It's where my family lives."

"Mine too," Mary Beth chimed in.

After navigating through a few empty streets, we eventually parked in front of a one-story, white house fortified by a small, green lawn. We exited the jeep, retrieved our luggage from the trunk, and lumbered toward the front door. Mark eagerly rang the doorbell, and impatiently waited for a response. Finally, the door opened – and with it, came a huge eruption of hugs, kisses, and smiles.

The woman who lived there – presumably Mark's mom - was probably in her mid-40s. She had a long, lined face and a short crop of blond hair, sprinkled with a few grey strands. She wore a tight green sweater and a pair of old blue jeans over her tall, frail frame. She seemed like a wholesome, yet slightly weather-beaten, woman.

"I bet you're Brian," she said, in a thick country accent, wrapping her warm arms around me.

"I am," I smiled. "Thanks for inviting me to Thanksgiving."

"Oh, I'm so glad you're here," she said, finally releasing me from her suffocating hug. "Did y'all have a good trip? Let me fix y'all somethin' to eat."

I followed Mark's mom into the kitchen, which was inundated with a wide variety of vegetables, pies, and desserts for tomorrow's meal. The upcoming feast looked great, and smelled even better.

"Do y'all want some hamburgers?" she asked politely. "I can fix 'em for y'all real quick." Everyone stared at me, so I compliantly replied, "Sure, that would be great. Thank you."

While Mark's mom prepared the burgers, her son transformed the living room couch into a pullout bed, and foisted some sheets and pillows upon it. Just then, the front door slammed, and two guys sprang from behind the corner. They looked at me suspiciously.

"Hey," the alpha dude bellowed in a gruff voice. He was probably a few years older than me (mid-twenties) and quite a load at 6'4" with a stocky, football player's build. He wore a large white hoodie and a pair of baggy blue jeans over his massive frame.

His partner was younger – probably still a teenager. He was around my height, but much skinnier with pale white skin and a crew cut. His oversized red hoodie looked patently absurd on his narrow, rail-like body.

I broke the ice by introducing myself. "Hi I'm Brian," I said. "I'm Mark's friend."

"Oh yeah," said the alpha dude. "How are you, bud?"

"I'm good," I responded. "How are you?"

"Eh, I've been better," he sighed. "I just got my butt whipped at the arcades by this little guy over here." The little guy – once stiff and silent - broke into a huge grin over his victory.

Finally, Mark reentered the living room with a fistful of blankets. Once he spotted the two guys, he flung the blankets onto the bed, and raced to embrace them in a group hug. There was a chorus of "It's so good to see you; I missed you; I'm so proud of you." I stood there awkwardly by the side, but it was a heart-warming scene, nonetheless.

Once the hug dissipated, Mark finally explained who these dudes were: they were his brothers. The elder bro, Luke, toiled at a driveway paving company, and lived in a one-bedroom house just a few blocks away. He was engaged to his high school sweetheart, Lisa, an aspiring pharmacist who planned to come to dinner tomorrow.

The younger bro, Matt, was a high school senior who was working part-time at Safeway while applying for community college. He also had a girlfriend named Tammy, who was paralyzed from the waist down, and was confined to a wheelchair.

The boys disappeared once dinner was served, and Mark, Mary Beth, and I devoured our burgers with reckless abandon. From start to finish, the meal was delicious.

Once our meals were safely in our stomachs, Mark's mom joined us at the kitchen table. She seemed exhausted from several days of cooking, but she still did her best to make us feel comfortable.

"Have you ever been to Ohio before?" she asked me, kindly.

"No, as a matter of fact, I haven't."

"Well, there's not much to see here, I suppose – except a lot of rusty small towns like this one." I wasn't sure how to respond, so I kept quiet.

"But we like it here," she continued. "Our family has lived in Palestine for generations, and we have so many friends and neighbors who we can rely on for help. I honestly couldn't live anywhere else. Heck, I don't *want* to live anywhere else."

I nodded my head slowly. "I really admire that," I said candidly. "I wish I had grown up in a place like this. But I didn't."

"Where are you from?" she inquired.

"I'm from the Philly suburbs – a sterile community of faceless strangers. The entire atmosphere was phony and isolating. If you want to know the truth, I hated it, and I never want to go back."

She stared outside the window and reflected, "I think it's important for every person to have a real home – a real community – a piece of Earth where they feel loved and connected to God, and His children." Staring back at me, she concluded, "I think that's the key to happiness, right there."

"I agree," said Mary Beth. "But if you're not born into that kind of community, it's almost impossible to find it."

"No, that's not true," Mark corrected her. "It's never too late."

After our conversation ended, we retrieved our suitcases and began to unpack. The plan was for Matt and Luke to share the pullout bed in the living room, Mark and me to sleep in separate beds in the boys' room, and Mary Beth to sleep alone in the guestroom. It was a complicated maneuver – expressly designed to keep Mark and Mary Beth from sleeping together – although let's face it, they didn't want to, anyway.

As I jammed my socks and underwear into an empty drawer, I noticed a framed family photo sitting on top of the dresser. Every person was recognizable – Mark, his mom, his brothers, and Mary Beth – except for one unknown person. In the middle of the picture was a smiling, middle-aged man with grey eyes, coke-bottle bottom glasses, and a dark hair combover wearing a green and white plaid shirt and khakis. The most reasonable conclusion was this was Mark's dad –

but if it was Mark's dad, where was he now? Was he stuck at work on the night before Thanksgiving? Was he a deadbeat? Was he…um…dead? Nobody had bothered to mention it.

I slept pretty well in the new bed, although Mark inadvertently woke me up several times with his surprisingly loud snoring. When I awoke the next morning, the sunlight was scorching me from the window, and I heard a commotion coming from the kitchen.

I stumbled to put my jeans on, brushed my comb through my messy hair, and entered the kitchen where I found the whole gang chatting amongst themselves.

"Good morning, sleepyhead," said Mark's mom. I stared at the clock, which revealed that it was almost noon.

"Come on," said Mark, dribbling a basketball. "Get ready so we can play some two-on-two."

I went ahead and brushed my teeth, took a shower, changed my clothes, and ate a big bowl of Corn Flakes, before marching down to the local basketball court with Mark and his brothers.

"I should warn you, I'm a pretty lousy basketball player," I said.

"Don't worry," said Luke, "we're just playing for fun. In fact, you can be on my team."

"OK," I said. That seemed appropriate – considering Luke's size and strength, and my lack of it – not to mention my total lack of ability.

The game started predictably – with me throwing a bad pass that landed out-of-bounds. I immediately apologized to Luke, who casually shrugged it off. "No worries, bud," he said with a twinkle.

The rest of the game wasn't much different. I continued to miss wide-open layups and jumpers, enabling my opponents to dash right past me for easy scores. But through it all, Luke kept on encouraging me – which made my performance a little more bearable.

After a while – once I started to realize that the point of

the game was to have fun – I started to, um, *have some fun!* I enjoyed the camaraderie of playing with the guys, and I loved the sight, smell, and touch of the Earth itself – the wind sweeping across my face, the beads of sweat dripping down my forehead, the thick dirt covering the palms of my hands. We were like oversized children – playing for no other reason than good, old-fashioned fun. It was a nice break from the rat race of my normal life.

After an hour of hoops, Luke said we should head back home and get ready for Thanksgiving.

When we arrived, I took another shower and changed my clothes again. Then I helped Mrs. Williams delicately place all of her food in the trunk of her car – so they could be safely transported to her brother-in-law's house, where the family was gathering.

Once that task was complete, Mrs. Williams drove her station wagon onto the highway, while her son, Mary Beth, and I trailed in the jeep behind her. We traveled about ten miles, drove past a series of barns and cornfields, and then finally arrived at a surprisingly large (but very old) house with more than a dozen cars and trucks parked in front.

We jumped out of the jeep, collected the food from the trunk, and then waddled carefully toward the front door. After we rang the bell, we were greeted by a very overweight woman wearing a radiant smile – perhaps because she was attracted by the smell of our food.

"Oh, hello Cheryl," she said to Mark's mom. "Those sweet potatoes smell delicious!"

"Thank you, Sally. That's because they're made with love." The two ladies shared a laugh, as we followed closely behind them.

Once we were inside, Cheryl introduced me to Aunt Sally and her husband, Charlie, who was a frail, soft-spoken man with a thick mane of grey hair and a huge mole on his right cheek.

The introductions continued as I met with a whole host of grandmas and grandpas, aunts and uncles, cousins, friends, and girlfriends. Overall, they were homely, unsophisticated folks – with the notable exception of Mark, and perhaps his mom, who might have turned some heads in her day. Even so, they were the happiest group of people I had ever met.

They were happy because they shared their lives with the people they loved. The purpose of their lives wasn't to climb the career ladder, or chase some tail, or mull the mysteries of the universe. Rather, their purpose was to live for each other – to support and care for one another, now and always. Their web of friends, family, and neighbors kept the angst of life at bay.

Best of all, these folks treated me like a part of their family. Everyone seemed so glad to see me, and chat with me, and hug me. From start to finish, it was a welcome change from the cold isolation of Washington, DC. Their enthusiasm was infectious – even for a normally-cynical guy like me.

A little after 3 o'clock, we all gathered around the dining room table – except for four little runts who sat at the "kiddie table." It was a wholesome scene – right out of a G-rated movie - and now I was living it. Finally.

Uncle Charlie sat at the head of the table and proudly wielded the carving knife. But before he could slice the simmering turkey, he cleared his throat and announced, "I'd like to say grace."

Everyone fell silent and bowed their heads as Charlie declared: "Heavenly Father, we thank you for this wonderful meal – shared with our loving family, old friends and *new* friends. We pray that you will continue to bless us with good health, happiness, and a renewed sense of purpose to serve you, oh Lord. Please also bless the soul of my brother Henry – who I'm sure is proudly watching his wife and three sons today. We will keep Henry in our hearts, and we will keep *You* in our hearts as well. In Jesus's name we pray. Amen."

After a chorus of "Amens" reverberated throughout the room, there was silence for a few moments, until Uncle Charlie ordered: "Let's eat!"

As people passed around their plates of pumpkin pie, I ruminated about Charlie's blessing of this unknown person named Henry. I naturally concluded that this person was Mark's father – and, therefore Mark's father was dead. Strangely, Mark had never bothered to mention this before. It was a stark omission from someone who seemed so honest.

The meal itself was delicious – truly made with love as Mrs. Williams had promised. The turkey was tender, the sweet potatoes were scrumptious, the string beans were bursting with flavor, and the chocolate cake was to die for. Sorry, that probably isn't the best phrase to use at this point.

After we devoured our food, we brought our dirty plates to the kitchen where Sally and Cheryl led the all-female clean-up crew. Then I joined Mark and the rugrats in a game of hide-and-seek. None of them were very good at it. They kept making a lot of noise so it was very easy to find them. But it was still a lot of fun – and I enjoyed entertaining the kiddies.

Finally, we joined most of the men who were watching the football game in the living room – sprawled out like beached whales on the ancient, turd-colored couches. Since there was no room available, I lied down on the floor, and a short time later, my bloated stomach pulled me into Dreamland.

I slept for what must have been a few hours – until Mark rocked my shoulder and whispered that it was time for us to leave. I rubbed my eyes, rose onto my feet, and started the round of goodbye hugs to people like Grandpa Bill, Aunt Peggy, Cousin Lou, and Coco the Dog. Each of them (except for the dog) said it was wonderful to meet me, and that I should come back again next year. For what it's worth, I wanted to come back too.

On the ride back, Mark seemed quieter than usual – although perhaps he was just fatigued from the food. When we returned home, the family gathered again to watch some TV in the basement, before finally deciding to call it quits for the evening.

"Good night, y'all!" Cheryl shouted, as she trudged up the basement steps. Luke and Matt followed soon thereafter.

"So what do you want to do now?" asked Mark.

"I think I want to go to bed," said Mary Beth, unleashing a mighty yawn. She kissed Mark on the cheek and followed the rest of the gang upstairs. Now Mark and I were alone.

We kind of stared silently at each other for a few seconds until Mark piped up and asked, "Do you want to go for a walk?"

"Um, sure," I replied. It was a weird suggestion, but whatever.

"OK," he said, "but put a jacket on. It's freezing out there."

After I followed Mark's instructions, we left the house, and entered the cold, eerily quiet night. As I shivered along the sidewalk, I looked up at the sky above us, which was brightly lit by a full moon and a dazzling quilt of twinkling stars. The sky itself was beautiful. *So* beautiful.

"So how was your Thanksgiving?" Mark finally asked.

"Oh, it was wonderful," I boasted. "Simply a wonderful combination of great food and great company."

Mark laughed. "So my family didn't overwhelm you or anything?"

"Not at all," I said. "In fact, they are very kind, generous people. I wish I had a family like that."

Mark smiled but remained quiet. We walked silently for a few hundred yards until we reached a flowing stream on the outskirts of town. The sound of rushing water smacking against the rocks had a soothing effect on the two of us, so we sat down to soak it in.

I felt like Mark was struggling to tell me something, and by coming here late at night, he was trying to create the right atmosphere for an honest discussion. Finally, it worked.

"I'm sorry," he said, pressing his knees against his chest.

"Sorry for what?" I asked.

"Sorry for not being honest with you – about my dad. I just never found a way to bring it up. That's all."

"You have nothing to be sorry about, Mark. It's none of my business. Whatever happened, I'm just sorry it did. I really am."

Mark stared whimsically at the sky. "I loved my dad with all my heart. We all loved him. He was the anchor of our family: a strong, kind man of faith who took good care of each of us. He was the best father a boy like me could ask for.

"One night, when I was fifteen years old, I came home late at night after a track meet. The entire house was pitch black – except for a single, small light coming from a room deep inside. There was no sound at all. Absolutely none. I knew something was terribly wrong.

"I opened the front door, walked towards the light, and found Luke sitting in a brown chair in the kitchen, staring into the void. Once Luke saw me, he slowly rose from his chair, buried me in his arms, and whispered: 'Dad's dead.'

"I started to cry so much I could barely breathe. I felt like my world had suddenly collapsed around me. My dad was only forty-two years old – a victim of his first heart attack. It didn't make any sense. It seemed so unjust. So unfair. I just couldn't comprehend it all.

"A few days later, when I was at the funeral, I was crying more than ever. I was a total mess. Finally, my Uncle Charlie wrapped his arms around me and said, 'It's OK to cry. In fact, it's good to cry. But cry for us – we the living – who must go on without your dad. At least for now. Don't cry for your dad, for he is in a better place.'

"Those words re-centered me, and renewed my understanding of God's plan for each of us. In retrospect, it was selfish of me to want my father all to myself – when the Father of All of Us had already called him home. As children of God, we have to accept our loss. And we must be thankful for the short time we have with each other."

Mark stared at me with small puddles of saltwater underneath his eyes. I stared back sympathetically. I wanted to say something – anything – to comfort him – but no words could come out of my mouth.

"I suppose I was lucky," Mark continued. "My mom and dad had already raised me with a strong faith in Christ – so when the crisis struck, I was still in His hands – where I remain today. If my parents hadn't raised me right, I probably would have wilted in the heat of adversity – cursing God for His cruelty, or damning myself for ever believing in Him. But thanks to my parents, I *do* believe in Him, and I have never been surer of his goodness than I am right now."

"Why do you say that?" I asked.

"Because you're here with me – and together, we can turn our separate suffering into shared healing. That is God's plan."

"What do you mean? What suffering?"

"You lost your father too, right?"

When I heard those haunting words, "you *lost* your father," I felt like I was stabbed in the heart. Suddenly, the tables had turned; this was no longer about Mark's pain; this was about *my* pain.

"I guess you could say that," I mumbled. Inside my head, I flashed back to the day of my parents' divorce – seeing my father drive away in his Mercedes – never to see him again.

"In some ways, my dad feels dead to me," I continued. "But the fact is: He *is* alive. Meanwhile, your dad is *actually* dead. I think that's a big difference. You've suffered a lot more than I have."

"You think so?" he inquired.

"Yeah, I do. In fact, up until today, I always assumed you were immune to suffering. Ever since I met you, you've always seemed like such a nice, easy-going guy, without a care in the world."

"I *am* an easy-going guy," Mark protested with a smile.

"I know – and that's my point. Despite the death of your dad, you've managed to be a spiritual rock for me – and yet, here I am, in much better circumstances, struggling to find peace and happiness in the world. I've spent most of my life alternating between anger and despair – blaming and pleading with God to release me from the trauma of my own emotions. Then, of course, I condemn Him for His silence. I simply can't move on from my suffering. The pain still feels real to me. I feel like I'm tied up in knots – a prisoner of my own refusal to forgive a Force that seems indifferent to me in every way." I started to choke up a little bit. "No one understands how I feel. I feel so alone. Sometimes I feel like the loneliest person on the face of the Earth."

"My friend, you are *not* alone. And God is *not* indifferent to you. God loves you. I am here to help you understand that. I am here precisely for that purpose."

"Why do you say that?" I asked, as a tear dripped down my cheek.

"Because nobody comes to God alone," he answered. "In the same way my family supported me in hard times, I want to support you, if you'll let me. No one can enter Heaven unless they bring somebody with them."

I'm not sure what happened next – but somehow the image of me entering heaven - an image that hadn't occurred to me since I was a small child – triggered a huge outpouring of emotion. I was crying loudly – wailing, actually - and Mark came over to console me. He was crying too.

"I just want to be loved," I whispered. "That's all I ever wanted – just to love and be loved. Why is that so God damn hard for me?"

"Remember what I told you, Brian: Lose your fear and open your heart. Therein lies the key to happiness."

I wiped away the salty tears and snot from my face. "I think I opened my heart to you and your family today. I can't remember the last time I felt so loved, and accepted."

"And were you happy?" asked Mark.

"Yeah. I was happy."

"See? Now you have a model for when you come back to Washington. Just keep opening your heart and you'll be amazed by the beautiful things that will come *into* it, and *out* of it."

"What about God?" I asked.

"What about Him?"

"What can I do to know *God's* love?"

"Keep opening your heart, my friend – and you will find Him there." For some reason, those words triggered another torrent of tears – even fiercer that the last round. Somehow, this one-on-one conversation had struck me in a powerful way that the inspirational sermons and hypnotic music of Crossroads never did – and never could. The wall of reason – which had separated me from God – was blowing away in a tidal wave of emotion. I felt a strange stirring in my soul for the very first time – an indescribable feeling of being safe and taken care of, like a young child in the arms of his father. For the first time, Mark's words – and not the constant drumbeat of negativity from my own subconscious – seemed real and truthful. This was a turning point in my meandering, pathetic life. No question about it.

"I think I want to go to Crossroads with you again," I said to Mark.

"Sure," he smiled. "Anything you want."

We sat there silently for a few more minutes – absorbing the beauty of nature even at this late hour. Finally, Mark stood up and tapped me on the shoulder. "Come on," he pleaded, "let's go home."

After we walked in the dark silence and returned to an even darker household, I changed into my PJ's and jumped underneath the covers of my bed. I stared outside the window and gazed at the same glorious stars that had enchanted me earlier. I decided to pray.

"Dear God, it's me, Brian. I know I haven't talked with You in a very long time. I'm sure You know my reasons. But those reasons aren't important now. I'm willing to chart a new course. I'm ready to start a new beginning. If You'll let me.

"I forgive myself for everything I've said and done in the past. None of that stuff matters now. I can proudly say, I'm not the man I used to be. I choose to be something different. Something better. I choose to be Your son again.

"I hope You'll provide me with enough time to make this transition, because I know it won't happen overnight. But I'm committed – with Mark's assistance – to walking across the abyss, and landing on the other side into Your out-stretched, loving arms. I promise not to abandon You, if you promise not to abandon *me*. So please don't. Please, *please* don't.

"I believe Mark when he says I am exactly where I need to be. I believe I was destined to be here tonight – praying under this gorgeous night sky. I am thankful for this special moment. And I'm excited for what awaits me in the future. Peace unto all. Amen."

I closed my eyes and rolled onto my side – somewhat surprised by the words that cracked through my lips. But every word was true. At least for now.

The ultimate question was whether this newfound faith could survive my daily life in the "Real World." That, of course, remained to be seen.

Chapter 6

The end of Thanksgiving marked the beginning of a new, livelier, and much more expensive holiday – the countdown to Christmas. Everywhere you turned there was a scene of wreaths and decorated trees, the smell of scented candles, and the sound of Salvation Army bells – all heralding the encroachment of Christ's birthday.

When I was a young boy, this transformation was the highlight of my year – the apex of my existence. Every fiber of my being revolved around that snowy, late-December morning when I would wake up at the crack of dawn and dash into the living room, where a huge crop of presents awaited my eager claws. Then, after duly waking up my sleepy parents, I unleashed a storm of shredded paper, proudly displaying each gift before the flash of my father's camera.

In retrospect, I'm almost embarrassed that I took such pleasure in what was essentially an orgy of materialism, but I forgive myself, because my joy wasn't just rooted in receiving toys, but in receiving love – the love of my family, and perhaps even the love of a higher power. The entire holiday season was a validation that I – as a child– mattered, and my happiness mattered, not just to the people around me, but also to the powers above me. It was a happier time. A better time. A more innocent time.

Now, at the age of twenty-two, those Christmas symbols trigger a flood of overwhelming sadness – because that happier, better, and more innocent time is gone forever. The prison of the Real World leaves no room for such stupidities as Santa Claus.

Still, I remain fascinated by children – and even though I really don't understand them – I still feel compelled to help them – so perhaps one day their rendezvous with reality won't be as traumatic as mine.

Therefore, when Mark suggested that I volunteer for Big Brothers Big Sisters (as part of my recharged effort to "open my heart") I thought that was a great idea. Since the spoken word alone couldn't create positive feelings – as my initial trek to Crossroads proved – this new concept of "learning by doing" seemed much more promising. I couldn't just sit back and listen to some middle-aged preacher. I needed to go out and actually *help* people (and by doing that, I could help myself).

The plan was for me to join Mary Beth – who tutored students at a public school in Anacostia – probably the poorest part of Washington – for a few hours every Saturday afternoon. Early in the week, she dropped off a couple of ninth-grade textbooks at my apartment. By re-reading those textbooks, I could refresh my knowledge of math and science.

Flipping through the pages, I was surprised by how much I had forgotten in less than a decade. I felt sorry for those kids who had to forfeit their weekend – and probably their self-esteem too – in order to learn something they would never need in the next stage of life. Oh well!

On Saturday, Mary Beth picked me up in her silver Saturn shortly before the stroke of noon. I saw the car ride as a chance to get to know her better, even though she seemed vaguely uncomfortable around me.

"So where do you work again?" I asked, as she steered onto the highway.

"Young Americans for Life," she replied, without elaboration.

"Is that an anti-abortion group?" I ventured.

"Well, it's a pro-life group," she corrected me. "We fund programs that spread the pro-life message at colleges and universities. Lately, we've been funding sex-ed classes that promote abstinence as the best method to avoid this tragedy."

"They teach abstinence to college students?" I asked, incredulously.

"Only in some places, but we're trying to make it more mainstream. So far, it's been quite a challenge."

"I bet," I replied, fighting the urge to laugh.

"Why do you say that?"

"Well, it's hard to convince college kids to refrain from sex. It's their instinct."

This triggered a sharp response from Mary Beth. "Sex might be an instinct, but that's irrelevant. Let me remind you that murder, rape, and theft are instincts too – but they can be overcome by remembering that we are children of God, and that we have an obligation to lead moral lives."

"Do you really think sex – as long as it's consensual – is on the same level as murder, rape, and robbery? I mean, sex creates life, whereas the others destroy it."

"No, you're wrong about that," she sighed. "The consequences of premarital sex *do* destroy life – not only the life of the unborn child (in the case of abortion), but our own lives. Look around you. Look at the problems of our society –the nihilism, the despair, and the violence that corrupts our culture – and if you study them carefully, you'll see that the root of those problems comes from a preoccupation with sex."

"What are you talking about?" I asked.

"We live in a society that worships sex and laughs at God. We think that choice has no consequences. But disobeying God's law always has consequences. The ethic of sex – "if it feels good, do it" - doesn't stop at the bedroom door. It infects everything. Just ask the women of Anacostia. They get pregnant around 17, 18 years old. And then, when the father inevitably leaves, the mom is forced to raise her child alone. But since she is ill equipped to raise and discipline him properly, the kid eventually finds a substitute family by joining a gang. When he enters adulthood, he lacks any practical skills – not even the ability to distinguish between right and wrong. So he is unleashed onto society – where he creates all sorts of mayhem – specifically, the murder and robbery you think has no relationship to sex.

"So yes, premarital sex is a real evil – and because of its growing acceptance, we're facing a total societal breakdown within a generation. Once the collapse of the family reaches a critical mass, the collapse of our civilization will follow shortly thereafter. Of course, Young Americans for Life is trying to prevent that from happening - but we're facing quite a challenge. As you point out, it's hard for people to fight their instincts."

"I see your point," I replied, "but if the problem is out-of-wedlock births, isn't the solution actually abortion? I mean, it's harsh – but wouldn't abortion eliminate many of the problems you're talking about – by basically eliminating the source of the problem?"

I could practically see the steam rising from Mary Beth's head.

"No," she insisted, "because abortion is the taking of a human life, and the unborn child shouldn't be punished for the sins of his parents. Nearly all of the kids you're going to meet today are the product of poor, single-parent families, and right now, they're struggling to overcome the temptations of the ghetto. I'm not prepared to say to these kids, 'Your mom should've killed you when she had the chance.' And when you meet them, I think you'll agree with me."

"Wait a second. I wasn't saying…"

"The solution to revitalizing our culture is this: People should remain abstinent until they're married, and then they should *stay* married. If they do that, their children will be happier, and the rest of us will live in a better, healthier country.

"I know that's what I want for myself. In a few years, Mark and I will move back to Ohio, get married, and raise a family of our own. Yes, it's old-fashioned, but that's our dream – and the world could use a few more dreamers like us."

I compliantly nodded my head, hoping to prematurely end our conversation. I had heard enough propaganda from my friends' girlfriends – first Julia, now Mary Beth – about how the world will ultimately collapse unless we radically readjust our lifestyles to fit their rigid ideologies. I just wanted to help some kids, for Christ's sake.

As we pushed further into the city, the quality of the neighborhoods dramatically declined – becoming older, dirtier, and much, much bleaker. The people on the street seemed shifty, desperate, and vaguely menacing. Mary Beth locked her car door, and I followed suit. This wasn't a safe place for us – or anyone else, for that matter.

Finally, we arrived at the school. We abandoned the car and fought the blustery winter wind to enter the front door. Once inside, Mary Beth approached the security guard – a tall, heavy-set man with a scowl.

"Hi, we're with Big Brothers Big Sisters," she said, pleasantly.

"Second floor, Room 210," he replied robotically.

We duly marched up the steps – which smelled like stale piss – and walked past a carved note on the wall, which advised: "Eat shit and die." I felt welcome already!

When we entered the room, it was completely empty, except for a frail, elderly woman named Mrs. Jones who offered us apples and orange juice. I scarfed them down immediately.

As we waited for the kids and other tutors to arrive, I floated around the room, which creaked with every step I took. I spotted a large poster on the side on the left wall (called "The Evolution of Man") which showed the transition from apes to full-fledged humans in the course of a few million years. In the back of the room, I studied a life-sized skeletal model of the human body with replicas of our organs – including heart, lungs, and stomach. Finally, on the right wall, there was another large poster, featuring photos of three separate people - a businessman carrying a briefcase, a doctor using a stethoscope, and a general standing in front of a tank. Below those pictures was the motto: "Knowledge is Power."

For some reason, I flashed back to Troy's diatribe against the school system. The premise that schools crushed our spirit (after all, we're nothing more than a bag of bones descended from apes) and then lured us into the Rat Race by playing on our vanity ("Knowledge is Power") seemed more plausible now.

But before I could delve into the matter, the room started to fill up with a half-dozen high school kids, along with a collection of middle-aged mentors. I just stood against the wall – absorbing the scene – until Mrs. Jones approached me.

"Brian, I want you to come with me," she remarked.

"OK," I responded. Then I followed her toward the back of the classroom, where a tall, thick, caramel-skinned young man sat alone, bopping his head to the beat of his walkman.

"Chris, this is Brian," she said, holding onto my elbow, "he'll be your tutor today."

"Hi," I said, "how are you?"

"Failin," he said, removing his headphones in displeasure.

"Failing? Well, I'm here to help with that – hopefully."

"Good," said Mrs. Jones, smacking her bony hands. "Start by reviewing Chris's science homework from last week, and then prepare him for next week's assignment. If you have any questions, see me." Then she left us alone so we could suffer with each other. I tried to break the ice in my usual way: by bringing up sports.

"Do you like any teams?" I asked.

"What?" he asked, incredulously – as if I was speaking another language.

"Do you like any sports teams – say, like the Redskins?"

Chris shook his head violently. "Don't bother, man," he replied dismissively. "I don't need a friend; I need you to teach me science – or whatever this shit is - so I can get these parole board bitches off my back."

I swallowed nervously at this setback. Even if my heart was open to the world, it seemed like everyone was determined to close it again.

"OK," I said, pretending that everything was normal and pleasant. "Do you have those homework assignments from last week?"

Chris chuckled at my earnestness. "Sure, bro, I got those stupid papers for ya." Then he whipped them out of his bookbag – each assignment blazed with an "F" in red ink. I scanned the first homework question: "Please describe the theory of sexual selection." I then read Chris's answer: "Sexual selection is the process by which bros compete with each other for the things bitches crave (such as cash, pecks, and power) in order to screw the most bitches (and feel better about themselves)."

Then came the second question: "What is an example of sexual selection?" Chris answered: "When a dude closes a drug deal and buys a new BMW, it's a signal for the bitches to run over, unzip his pants, and try to have his baby."

"Hmmm," I said thoughtfully.

"What's wrong with those answers?" Chris asked.

"Well, I think you misunderstood the spirit of the question. I'm pretty sure your teacher wasn't referring to human beings; she was referring to animals."

"But we're animals, right?"

"Well, we're a kind of animal, but I think for the purposes of a ninth grade science class, you should focus on other animals – say, like a spider or a cheetah."

"Who cares about some dumbass cheetah? I'm trying to use real-life examples here. Why should I be punished for that?"

I respected the kid's stubborn independence, but I felt obligated to defend his teacher's decision to strike out his bold answers.

"I think if your teacher was here, she would say: we shouldn't associate our own behavior – as people - with the behavior of wild animals. After all, we've built a highly-sophisticated civilization."

Chris grumbled at my phony explanation. "Look, bro, if anyone thinks the rules of evolution don't apply to us…well, they're just living in a fantasy world. I've sat in this classroom for years, and I've absorbed the truth, even if other kids choose to ignore it. If the truth earns me an 'F' in school, that's fine; because I'll get an 'A' in the Real World. And that's the only place where any of this shit matters."

For emphasis, Chris kicked the chair in front of him, and hurled it forward by at least six feet. The noise forced everyone in the room to stare at us. Somewhat embarrassed, I smiled and waved at the crowd, as if to say, "Carry on, folks. There's nothing to see here."

"Let's move onto math, shall we?" I suggested in desperation.

So that's what we did for the next hour – study math - until finally, Mrs. Jones gathered the kids together and led them into the schoolyard for a thirty-minute recess. I wanted to stay behind and chat with Mary Beth, but I couldn't find her anywhere. She had seemingly disappeared.

Finally, I saw her run into the classroom, looking extremely frazzled, and even kind of scared.

"Brian," she said, huffing and puffing, "I need to leave for a while."

"Why?"

"This kid I normally tutor – a boy named Danny – was picked up by the police for questioning – something about beating up another kid with a baseball bat."

"Yikes!" I said.

"I know, but he didn't do it."

"How do you know?"

"Because he wouldn't do something like that. I've looked into his heart, and there's no darkness there. Trust me. This whole thing is just a huge misunderstanding. That's why I'm driving down to the police station: to clear things up, and hopefully, get him released."

"Should I go with you?"

"No, I'll be fine. Once I help Danny get released, I'll come back here and pick you up. OK?"

"Yeah, sure."

"Alright, I'll see you later," she said, marching toward the classroom door. Then she spun around and pleaded: "Wish me luck."

"Good luck!" I shouted, and with that, she vanished again.

I decided to visit the schoolyard and watch the kids play a game of hoops. They seemed to be having a lot of fun, shooting and rebounding, and running up and down the court. Then Mrs. Jones strode beside me.

"What do you think of Chris?" she asked.

"Um, I don't know yet," I replied, thoughtfully. "I suppose he's a bright kid, but right now, he's unfocused and undisciplined."

"Bingo!" she shouted, gripping my elbow. "A lot of these church folks come here and think all these kids need is love and compassion. But in reality, they need some discipline, and perhaps even a good kick in the ass."

I bristled at the old lady's harsh language, but she continued: "If you want to succeed with Chris – or anyone, really

– you can't rely on your *heart* alone; you have to use your *head* too. I wish some of those church folks – like Mary Beth - would understand that."

Before I could respond, Mrs. Jones blew her whistle and ended the basketball game, which, of course, heralded the start of more studying.

Chris and I returned to our desks, and launched an in-depth review of pre-algebra (always one of my favorite subjects). Once again, my pupil was bored, restless, and even slightly annoyed that I was wasting his time with such worthless nonsense.

"I hate this shit," he muttered at one point.

"I know," I replied, sympathetically, "but let's just get through it, OK?"

"Why do you care so much?" he asked, curiously.

After thinking about it for a few seconds, I answered firmly: "Because you deserve a chance. And I want to give you that chance."

Chris stared at me – strangely sad and vulnerable. I suppose those words touched him in a deeply personal place. For the first time, my open heart had reached him – and perhaps, changed him too.

We started to plow through the pre-algebra problems – but this time with more focus, determination, and eventually, success.

"I'm starting to get the hang of it," he smiled. I smiled back – revitalized in my faith, and happy to be an agent of God's will.

Shortly before 5 o'clock, Mrs. Jones strolled to the front of the classroom, and announced that everyone was free to leave.

Now that the tutoring session was over, Chris stuffed his books into his bookbag and shot up from his seat.

"Later, man," he mumbled.

"Later," I replied. I watched as he waddled out of the classroom, trailing a pack of boisterous teenagers. As he turned the corner, he extended his arm and gave me the thumbs-up sign. I happily returned the signal, but by that point, he was already gone.

The only person left was Mrs. Jones herself. She rapidly erased the blackboard and asked me: "Do you have a ride home?"

"Yeah. Mary Beth is going to pick me up in a little bit."

"Good," she asserted. "Let's wait for Mary Beth in the lobby. I need to lock this room up, or I'll get in trouble."

After Mrs. Jones locked up the classroom, we walked down the stairs and caught a second glimpse of my favorite greeting ("Eat shit and die!"). Honestly, it's a shame no one cared enough to remove it.

"Do you know when Mary Beth is coming?" she asked.

"No, but let me try her boyfriend's cell phone number. Perhaps he can give me her number, and I can reach her that way."

I dialed Mark's phone number, but nobody answered. I tried again a few minutes later, but still, there was only silence.

"I'd give you a ride, sweetie, but I don't own a car. I live just a couple of blocks away."

"I understand, Mrs. Jones. Thanks anyway."

She patiently waited with me while I tried Mark's number every few minutes – all to no avail. Finally, Mrs. Jones had a solution.

"Let's walk together toward my apartment – and then, from there, you can walk by yourself to the metro station. Sound ok?"

By instinct, I wanted to decline her offer. I hated the idea of walking alone in a dangerous neighborhood – especially at night. Then again, I couldn't be sure if Mary Beth would ever come back. Even more importantly, I didn't want my heart to be closed by baseless fears. I wanted to stand strong for God's love.

"Sure," I said, with a tinge of hesitation.

We walked through the cold dusk, striding past abandoned, burned-out buildings, doped-up bums, and the frightening sound of laughter in the far distance. I have to be completely honest: I was scared. Scared shitless.

"Are you coming back next week?" she asked.

"Of course," I replied.

"I'm really glad to hear that, because I think you made a lot of progress with Chris today."

"You think so? Thanks," I said with a humble smile. "Hopefully, today was a turning point." And not just for Chris. For me too.

Eventually, we arrived at Mrs. Jones's apartment – where she instructed me on how to find the subway station. "Keep heading straight for two blocks, then take a left at the next block, then take a right at the last block. That's where you'll find it."

"O.K., thanks," I said. I wasn't sure if I should shake her hand or give her a hug – so I smiled, waved, and spun away. I thought I heard her shout, "God bless you," but I couldn't be sure because I was too busy repeating her directions in my brain.

Now that I was all alone, I picked up my pace and focused like a laser on every sound or sight that penetrated my senses. I could feel my heart racing, and small beads of sweat forming on my forehead – even though the temperature was way below freezing.

Suddenly, I realized that I should be praying for God's protection, and to release me from this primitive, unnecessary fear.

"Dear God, please keep me safe as I travel through this valley of shadows. I choose to be an agent of your love – even in the darkest corners of Earth – now and always. Amen."

I kept repeating this prayer as I briskly walked to the subway station. I felt better once I realized that no harm could come to a true believer in the Lord's goodness.

As I turned the corner, I heard a commotion from far ahead – but I couldn't see anything in the pitch-black streets. The noise of young, teenage boys shouting over one another – mixed with occasional heaves of laughter – brought chills down my spine.

"Oh God, I'm fucked," I thought to myself.

Finally, over the top of the hill, I could see the poorly-defined image of four tall, well-built boys, sporting baggy clothes and gold chains – with the kid in the middle carrying a heavy sports bag.

I thought about scurrying over to the other side of the street, but I didn't want to reveal my fear and vulnerability. If I seemed afraid, it might tempt these teenagers to take advantage of my perilous situation.

As we continued on our collision course, the commotion dissipated and was replaced by an eerie, uncomfortable silence. I suppose I had caught their attention – and they decided to be silent, for whatever reason. I kept marching straight ahead – refusing to make eye contact, struggling to keep a blank expression, and constantly repeating my prayers to the Lord.

"Dear God, please keep me safe as I…"

The silence was shattered by a single chuckle – which nearly gave me a stroke. In spite of my newfound faith, I remained overwhelmingly scared – which was strange because there was nothing to be scared about. I mean, why would anyone want to bother a normal, innocent kid like me walking alone in the dusk? Looking at the situation objectively, it didn't make any sense; the only rational course was a seamless crossing, free of any incident.

And that's exactly what seemed to happen – as the distance between us shrank from 20 yards, to 10 yards, to 5 yards, and finally, to zero.

I breathed a huge sigh of relief as the four teenagers passed to my left - and our frightening collision was effortlessly avoided.

"Thank you, *God*," I murmured in gratitude.

But then, a few seconds later, I heard a piercing zipping sound, followed by a loud thump, and then a few muffled laughs. I stoically marched forward – clinging to the hope that I could avoid a confrontation.

Finally, I heard a torrent of footsteps racing toward me – a sound that forced me to sprint as fast as I could. But it was already too late. By my second stride, I felt an excruciating, stinging pain as the head of a metal bat whipped into my lower back.

"AAHHHHH! I screamed, plummeting toward the pavement.

This provoked the batsman to continue beating me with his stick – one hit after another, on my back, then my leg, then my back again. I curled up in a fetal position, covering my face, and wailing in torment. I was in so much pain - and I feared that one lethal strike could literally kill me.

"STOPPP! PLEEEAASE! STOPPP!" I cried. But he wouldn't stop. Instead, he kept hitting me over and over again – spurred by the laughter and cheers of his buddies, who circled me like wounded prey.

"WHAT DID I DO?" I screamed. "WHAT DID I DO?" I could feel my bones crunching with every thrust into my mutilated body.

"Look up bitch!" the batsman shouted. I stayed in my curled-up position, but that didn't faze him.

"LOOK!!! UP!!!" he shouted again, kicking me in the stomach. To avoid his wrath, I removed my elbows from my tear-soaked face and stared at his cold brown eyes.

Once our eyes locked, the agent of death lifted the bat over his head, and marked his target: the front of my skull. But before he could hammer it down, his buddy pushed him and shouted: "Come on, Danny, let's go!"

"Fuck you!" Danny shouted, pointing his bat at his friend.

"Grab his wallet, and let's get the fuck out of here!"

After a brief staring contest, Danny bent down and ripped my wallet from my jacket pocket. Then they fled – yelping and cheering, as I laid stricken on the sidewalk, swollen and throbbing, with blood dripping from my open mouth.

After waiting for a few seconds, I sought to stand up – but my broken legs couldn't support my weight. I returned to my fetal position and launched a fresh flood of salty tears.

"Please help me!" I wailed. "Please, please someone help me!" There was no response. I was alone in my suffering – both in body and spirit. The all-powerful God was absent in my hour of need – not because He was indifferent, but because He didn't exist at all. I stared at the same starry sky that had enchanted me in Ohio – but all I saw tonight was the void, the chasm, the abyss that makes atheists of us all – if given enough time.

I felt a fresh burst of pain from the front of my skull – the skull that should have been shattered by a madman and ended my pitiful existence.

The pain poured through my brain – shocking me into sleep – but not before I released a final whimper: "God, why have you forsaken me?"

Then came the darkness.

Chapter 7

I was trapped in a hazy netherworld, caught between life, sleep, and death. I couldn't feel a single part of my body, my mind was foggy and disoriented, and my soul had rotted away, like an oak tree torn asunder from its roots, lying helplessly on the cold ground.

In the void, I could hear voices – low, unintelligible whispers encircling me. I strained to open my eyelids, eager to take stock of the situation. I couldn't feel my eyelids, so I remained imprisoned in the darkness. I tried to open my eyes again, but yet again, I failed. This triggered a full-scale panic. Finally, on the third attempt, I focused all of my energy on rolling back my eyelids – and this time I was successful.

I was alive. At least I thought I was alive. I could see the lower half of my body resting motionless on a large, elevated bed, wrapped in a gurney and several layers of sheets. I could see a couple of machines and monitors, closely guarding my heart rate and brain waves. Surely, I was in a hospital.

The rest of the room was freshly-painted white, and completely sterile and barren, with the exception of a tiny plant resting comfortably on the heater, and a poster of Babar – the elephant of children's book fame – hanging crookedly on the wall in front of me.

Perhaps most importantly, a couple of people were hovering over me – chatting amicably, completely oblivious to my existence. On the left was a tall, middle-aged doctor with a full moon face and a red, but receding, hairline. On the right was a short, slightly tubby nurse, who was just a smidgen over thirty. She was the first to notice I had awoken from my stupor, and she signaled to the doctor with a wave of her hand.

The doctor leaned toward me and asked: "Brian, can you hear me?"

I tried to speak normally, but no words could exit my mouth. So I harnessed all of my energy, and this time I managed to whisper: "Yes."

"How do you feel?" the doctor asked.

"I'm not sure," I candidly answered. I was certainly tired and weak, but I didn't know if I was badly injured or injured at all. I lifted my head off the pillow with nary any difficulty. I wiggled my arms and hands, again with little trouble. But when I tried to shift my back I was pulverized by a pulsating, scorching pain. "Ohhhahhh!" I moaned. Fighting back a fresh round of tears, I grunted through my teeth: "My back!"

"O.K., we'll take care of that," the doctor casually answered. Then he stared at his subordinate: "Let's get him some more tranquilizers."

As she left the room, the doctor brought his focus back to me. "So what happened to you?" he asked with phony concern.

"What do you mean?" I replied.

"How did you hurt yourself? An elderly man found you lying motionless in the middle of the sidewalk with blood dripping out of your mouth. He called an ambulance which brought you here. But you've been unconscious up until a few minutes ago."

I stared silently at the Babar poster – digesting the doctor's new information. It's funny, up until that moment, I had completely ignored the circumstances that brought me here. Now, the memories of that fateful night came chasing me.

The scalding pain of a baseball bat against my back. The whooping, hollering, and laughing of pathological thugs. The cold, icy stare of a smiling angel of death. My heart sank as the past re-entered the present.

"There were a bunch of kids," I answered, somewhat embarrassed over my sad fate. "They beat me with a baseball bat. Over and over again."

"Do you know those kids?" he asked.

I shook my head. "No, I never saw them before. Ever."

The doctor squinted his eyes in another round of fake sympathy. Then he continued: "Those kids – whoever they are – did a lot of damage to you. In a couple of days, you'll need to have surgery to replace a couple of broken disks in your back. In addition, you'll need to have casts placed on both of your legs to heal a few broken bones. But don't worry too much. In the long run, you'll be fine. After a few weeks here in the hospital, and several months of regular physical therapy, you'll be back to normal again. Do you have any questions?"

I had a million questions – but none that he could answer. Only He – the creator of us all – could answer them, and He was an illusion. Nonetheless, I did have one remaining concern – justice in this world – if there was any.

"Are the police investigating?" I asked.

The doctor – still nameless, after all this time – pressed his chin against his chest. "Absolutely, and now that you're awake, I'm sure they'll want to speak with you – probably sometime tomorrow."

"Good," I said, with a sad smile.

The doctor cleared his throat, but his reply was interrupted by the nurse, who returned with a needle and some sort of watery package. She grabbed my left arm, cleaned a piece of my skin, and shot me up with a fresh dose of tranquilizer. Then she stood next to the doctor, and together they watched me like a lab experiment.

"Now," continued the doctor, "you'll probably fall asleep in..." and just like that, I was back in the darkness.

I remained there for countless hours, completely oblivious to everything and everyone around me. Finally, I reawakened for no apparent reason only to find a new person monitoring my condition: Mark. There he was - sitting in a steel armchair, flipping through the pages of *Christianity Today.* I was ambivalent about seeing him. I appreciated his sincere friendship, but I was also resentful - even angry - toward him.

After all, he was the one who lulled me into this false faith – embracing a loving God, eradicating all restless doubts, and opening my heart to everyone (even if they didn't deserve it). The whole endeavor was a failure – a painful catastrophe that redirected my emotions from hope to anger to despair. I wanted Mark to know my despair – to know, just once, the feeling of being inside the abyss – alone, helpless, utterly crushed. This was my life. This was my future. There was no escape.

I started to cry again – ever so quietly, at first. But inevitably, my muffled wails broke the silence, and Mark realized I had returned to reality.

"Brian!" he shouted, rising to his feet. "Are you O.K.? What's the matter?"

I tried to look away from his blue, innocent eyes, to hide my shame and embarrassment. But it was no use.

"I'm fine," I whispered, through a verklempt throat.

"No, you're not," he insisted, clasping my hand. I looked away again, too choked up to respond. "Do you want me to get the doctor?"

"No!" I noisily grunted. This beckoned Mark to return to his seat, where he remained quiet for oh, a good ten seconds or so. But inevitably he pestered me again by rephrasing the question: "What's wrong, Brian?"

I stared straight ahead. Shit, if he was going to keep asking me the question, I might as well answer it – even if he didn't like the answer.

"This wasn't supposed to happen," I said through tears and snot.

"What? What do you mean?"

"I promised to change. I promised to be a better person: to be a child of God, to obey His will. And I thought God would keep his promise to me – to give purpose to my life, to make me happy. Last month, when we were in Ohio, I felt His presence; I felt a greater sense of peace than at any other point in my life. I truly believed that I was where I needed to be, and that God would protect me, assist me, and love me. But now the covenant is broken. I guess it had to break at some point since it was held together by lies – and all lies are inevitably exposed by the painful nature of reality."

I twisted my head to gauge Mark's reaction. He looked like a man who had been suckerpunched in the stomach.

"God is not a liar," he finally replied, not in anger, but in sympathy. I was unfazed by Mark's comments.

"If there was any validity to this Christian crap, I wouldn't be lying in this God damn hospital bed, hobbled by a broken back and crippled legs. I'd be at home, eating dinner, and watching TV, just like any normal person."

"Brian, are you listening to yourself? Did you really think that nothing bad would ever happen to you again – that you'd always be protected from any form of suffering? Frankly, Christianity is *all about* suffering – coming to peace with suffering, and accepting it as part of God's plan."

"You're not listening to me, dude. I never thought I was protected by some sort of supernatural force field. I'm not *that* stupid. I simply expected a grace period – some small block of time where I could immerse myself with the faith, and accept it unconditionally in my mind, body, and spirit.

"Think about it: I had already made the commitment (praying, going to church with you, volunteering at that school, etc.). I just needed a short period of time to close the deal. I honestly didn't think I was asking for much. I was just asking for a simple act of fairness. But there was nothing fair about what happened to me: getting beat up with a baseball bat.

"Objectively speaking, that's not the outcome you'd expect from a loving, compassionate God. But it's definitely the outcome you'd expect from a random, meaningless universe. I guess that's the universe we live in. Knowing that, I will never make any kind of religious commitment again. Even when my body heals, my soul will never be able to recover."

I was shocked that Mark had allowed me to speak for so long, without even the slightest interruption. Finally, he chimed in with his own thoughts.

"Brian, I think you're misinterpreting this very powerful experience. First of all, you're *alive* —so we should be thankful to God for that. The Lord obviously has something good in store for you – provided you keep an open heart and learn the necessary lessons. Don't give up on Him yet."

I rolled my eyes at this newest plea to open my heart – just a day after it was nearly stopped by a heartless thug. Still, Mark could not be deterred.

"I'm going to pray for you," he said. "If you'd pray *with* me, I'd be forever grateful."

I didn't respond, but once Mark's eyes closed, I reluctantly followed suit. After all, I couldn't reject a prayer on my own behalf.

"Dear Heavenly Father," he began, "I feel so profoundly blessed to be here with my friend, Brian, who has courageously survived a painful, challenging ordeal. Through Your…"

Suddenly, we were interrupted by a familiar voice. "What the hell is going on here?" he asked.

I opened my eyes and found Troy standing at the foot of my bed, carrying a full plastic bag, and cringing his face in unmistakable disgust.

"Excuse me?" Mark asked.

"Why are you praying?" Troy pressed.

"Because God has spared Brian from death, and we're expressing our gratitude. Why do you care? Who are you, anyway?"

"I'm Troy Dawkins; I'm Brian's friend."

"Well, I'm Mark Williams, and I'm Brian's friend too."

"I see," said Troy, as he pulled up another steel chair. I could only watch with horror and amusement as these two men – who had never met, and yet had been so influential on my thinking– were now meeting for the first time, perched on each side of me, squaring off for the rights to my soul.

Troy fired the opening shot. He smugly announced, "That's quite a racket your so-called God has."

"What do you mean?" asked Mark.

"First, God allows Brian to be nearly bludgeoned to death, and yet you shower Him with praise and affection for his callousness. I wish I could come up with a crazy scheme like that."

"Look pal, as I'm sure you've heard, the Lord works in mysterious ways, and it's not our role – as human beings – to question His will. We can only accept it, and be thankful for the opportunities to learn and grow on His Earth. If we lash out and blame God for every cut, bruise, and setback we experience, we'll be ugly, angry creatures, and love and happiness will be beyond our reach."

Troy flashed one of his trademark smirks. "I'm not blaming Him. I'm saying we should ignore Him. Because He doesn't exist."

"How can you say that?" Mark asked, flabbergasted. "Do you have any proof that He doesn't exist? If so, give it to me. I'd like to see it."

"I *can't* prove it, but *I don't need* to prove it. In a situation like this, *I* am the one who is entitled to the benefit of the doubt. I'm not obligated to prove a negative; I'm not required to prove that Santa Claus, or the Easter Bunny, or your imaginary friend (God) doesn't exist. It's you guys who need to prove it. It's *your* responsibility to show me the evidence – *any* evidence - of God's existence. But you have none. And you never will."

I had pressed Mark for such evidence months ago. Back then, he dodged the question by appealing to the hopes of my heart, rather than the logic of my head. I had given Mark a free pass at the time, but I doubted Troy would be as kind today.

"If you're searching for evidence, you're probably looking in the wrong place – looking outward at the material world, instead of looking inside of yourself. I, for one, don't see God; I *feel* Him inside of me. I feel His love and His grace with every thought and action of my body."

I have to admit: I envisioned my roommate squatting on the toilet, misinterpreting the rumblings from his stomach as God's love, and expressing thanks for each turd that squeezed through his ass. I know that's a revolting image, but I never claimed to be a good, spiritual person, and at this point in my life, I'm less apologetic for that fact.

"I'm sorry," said Troy, "but your feelings don't come from God. Some other person (probably your parents) put those feelings in you, and over time, you've accepted them, and adopted them as your own. I'm afraid you're just another nameless victim of too much Sunday school, Bible study, and the last, dying remnants of our Christian civilization."

"How do you know?" Mark protested.

"Because if you could feel God, I'm sure I could feel it too – but I don't feel shit, and trust me, I've tried, just like I'm sure Brian has tried too." For the first time, Troy was suggesting that he was once a spiritual seeker – and not just the proud atheist he was now. Then he continued: "It's time for each of us to understand and embrace the truth about the nature of reality."

"What truth?" Mark asked. "What reality? What are you talking about?"

"I'm talking about the cold, hard facts that you've been seeking to avoid for your entire existence. Basically, each of us is condemned to a nasty, solitary life in a meaningless universe, and our destiny is permanent death. I tried explaining that to you, Brian. I know you didn't want to believe me, but now you have the proof etched in your broken back." I found myself nodding as Troy confirmed all of my worst fears.

But Mark wasn't prepared to accept defeat – not by a long shot. In fact, he pleaded with me to see things from his perspective.

"Brian, this is a beautiful world – and life itself is a glorious gift – but only if you choose to believe it. God has given you the power of choice. If you choose to use this experience for healing and peace, then that's what you'll receive. If you choose to use it for hate and separation, then *that* is what you'll receive. If you choose to believe in God, you will see the truth. The *real* truth. The choice is yours, my friend. Only *you* have the power!

Troy thrust his fist into the air, and shouted, "*You got the power*!!" But his parody of the early-nineties dance song went over like a lead balloon.

I sat up in my bed, and spoke up for the first time in a while. "I'm not in the mood for slogans," I reminded them. "The fact is, I've never felt more powerless in my entire life. I'm lying here in this bed, practically unable to move, awaiting not only surgery, but probably months of rehabilitation. This isn't a positive experience for me - and there's no point in pretending that it *could* be a great experience 'if *only* I *choose* to believe it.' I've tried that crap before but it doesn't work. I'm not trying it again."

I wanted Mark to fight back – to finally convince me I was wrong – but he needed to do it in a sensible, logical way. Instead, he stayed silent.

"Come on Mark, please help me understand. How could God allow this to happen? How could He allow those evil thugs to hurt me? I didn't deserve it. Honestly, I didn't deserve it."

I was offering Mark one last chance to renew the debate, and this time he seized it.

"Brian, people have been asking those questions since the beginning of time: If God is a just and loving creator, why does He allow His children to suffer – especially the children who serve Him best? In other words, why do bad things happen to good people? I won't pretend that I have a final, all-encompassing answer, but I'd like to offer a theory…

"I think it all comes back to the nature of free will. As I mentioned earlier, God has given us the power of choice – and inevitably some people will make the wrong choice – choosing hate instead of love, pain instead of joy, violence instead of peace. Sadly, in some cases, the repercussions of that wrong choice are shared by innocent bystanders – folks like you - helplessly caught in the crossfire. A single incident – such as what happened to you – can be described as grossly unjust, but taken as whole, the system itself - *life itself* - is totally just, because it preserves free will as the only means to love our Father."

I shook my head. "So what's stopping people from making the wrong choice, when they don't have to bear the consequences of that choice?"

"I think they'll eventually realize – mainly through trial and error – that hurting other people also hurts themselves. This is because we're all children of God - a single Being of Love made in the image of our Creator."

"Huh?" Troy and I asked in unison.

"Do you know the story of the frightened wave?" Mark continued.

"A frightened wave?" said Troy disdainfully. "This should be good."

"What's the story?" I asked.

"It's a story my dad told me when I was a boy. Once, there was a little wave, bouncing along in the sea, enjoying a wonderful day. Suddenly, the little wave notices that he is about to crash into the beach – and so he begins to cry and scream as loud as he can.

"'What's wrong?' asks the wave rolling next to him.

"'Don't you see that we're going to crash into the beach and die!' the frightened little wave yells.

"'Don't you realize," says the other wave patiently, 'that you're *not* a wave. That you're a part of the ocean.'

"The reason we hurt each other is because we don't see who we truly are. We think we're separate waves – but in reality, we're all part of the ocean. We may live in separate bodies, but we're also part of a greater whole. We may be individual human beings, but we're also - *all of us* – a single being within Christ. We are *one* family here to love each other, help each other, heal each other, and redeem the world."

"Oh give me a break!" Troy spewed, releasing his venom. "Do you live in the same world that I do? Do you have any connection to reality at all?"

"What now?" asked Mark in exasperation.

"Once again, you're offering cheery slogans over facts. Let's face it, when Brian got busted up, I didn't feel a God damn thing – and neither did you. The only person who felt anything was Brian – suffering alone in the cold darkness. So much for your stupid wave theory."

"But you're looking at it from a narrow, materialist per-spective," Mark protested.

"You're God damn right I am!" shouted Troy. "Sorry for the rude awakening, buddy, but materialism – matter – that's all there is." Smashing his fists together, he repeated, "that's all there is."

"The nature of matter is to struggle – to fight with other matter in a Darwinian battle for survival. We are in constant conflict with each other – fighting for resources, whether it's a piece of steak, or a piece of ass. It's easy to forget that in our modern, high-tech society with our CD players, DVDs, and free Internet porn. But every now and then Reality intrudes onto our cozy paradise. The mask of civilization comes off, and all that's left is the naked truth. Brian, you've seen that truth. It wasn't some harmonious 'ocean.' It was a bunch of assholes swinging a baseball bat."

Mark rose from his chair, and began to pace around the room, searching valiantly for the right words.

"I didn't say we were *literally* part of an 'ocean' – at least not in this lifetime. I'm talking about the next stage of life – the hereafter. If we make the right choices today, God will reward us with an eternity of happiness tomorrow. The pain of the present is worth every penny if it takes us to a better place – namely, Heaven."

"A better place?" asked Troy, rising from his seat. "I don't think so. I'd encourage you to think about every form of life – from amoebas to plants, from animals to humans – and consider how they handle their own mortality. All of them cling to life and fight the approach of death with every ounce of strength they possess. There's a reason we're biologically conditioned to fight off the Grim Reaper – because even though life can be a bitch, it's still preferable to death. Death is worse. So to say there's some glorious afterlife – or any afterlife – goes against our most basic instincts. Death is the end." Then he returned to his seat, and playfully waved, "Buh-bye."

But Mark remained standing, with his hands locked on his hips. "The choice is yours," he said to me. "Only *you* can decide."

Both guys stared at me, patiently awaiting my verdict. I collected my thoughts and spoke with as much candor and conviction as I could muster. "I think you're partly right, Mark. The choice *is* mine. If I choose your perspective, I could be a happy wave in the ocean. But if I did that, it would be a lie, because there is no ocean. I refuse to surrender my mind any longer. I will make another choice. I will choose the truth. The truth is, I am alone. I am in pain. There is no God to hear my cries. My life is meaningless. Everything is meaningless."

Mark kneeled by the side of the bed, grabbed my forearm, and stared into my foggy eyes. "I know you're angry and depressed right now. But don't allow your despair to consume you." I felt like he was a doctor – but instead of trying to resuscitate my body, he was trying to resuscitate my soul. "Please try to forgive your assailants. There's an old proverb, 'to understand all is to forgive all.'"

"Why are you guys always so eager to forgive evil?" asked Troy, shining his glasses. "I think I know the reason. It's because the presence of evil is the greatest impediment to faith. Evil exposes the concept of a just and loving God as a fraud – and you guys know it. So you choose to ignore evil, and place the responsibility solely on the victim by crying, 'Forgive! Forgive!' But the evildoers have no interest in forgiveness. In fact, they sense your weakness, and exploit it, becoming even stronger.

"The only way to stop evil is through force. The sins of slavery in America and genocide in Europe weren't eliminated through forgiveness, but through violence – raw, righteous, and total violence. Look, even Jesus himself could never have spread his message had it not been for those blood-thirsty souls who used the sword to conquer in His name. If the Good wants to survive, it must be the Evil sometimes. If a religion refuses to understand evil, it can't fight evil and is eventually doomed to fail, causing even more suffering in the end."

"So what's your point?" I asked.

"Never, ever forgive. Bring those cocksuckers to justice."

"Let me remind you," said Mark, "it's smart to forgive, not only for the other person's sake, but for your own sake. If you forgive, you will move forward with confidence, and you'll be better equipped to learn the right lessons from this experience."

"I can't forgive anyone unless they ask to be forgiven," I concluded. "And I can't believe in God because He doesn't exist."

"Please don't say that," said Mark, sadder than I had ever seen him. With those words, I had just abandoned my best friend, along with my loftiest hopes and dreams. But I really had no choice in the matter. "I'm sorry," I said, fighting back another burst of tears. "I'm truly sorry."

Mark rose from his knees, dusted off his pants, and looked away. "I need to head out," he said, stoically. "I'm meeting Mary Beth at the mall to do some Christmas shopping."

"O.K.," I said.

"I'll pray for you," said Mark, grabbing his hat, jacket, and magazine. "Something good will come out of this. You'll see. Don't give up, Brian. Don't ever give up."

I nodded politely, but I didn't bother to smile.

"It was nice meeting you," he said to Troy, exhibiting his usual class.

"Later, man," said Troy, with a grimace and a quick wave.

Now that we were alone, Troy rummaged through his plastic bag and whipped out a six-pack of beer. He tossed me a can, and then opened one for himself.

"So I guess that's your roommate?"

"Yup."

"God, what a douche!"

"Nah, he's a good person, and a great friend - but he's just plain wrong about some important stuff."

"Hey, I'm a great friend too. After all, I bought you a beer."

I laughed for the first time in ages. "Yes," I said, taking a swig from the can. "You're a very good friend too. Thank you."

"So was I right about everything?"

"What do you mean?"

"Dude, you know what I mean, so just come out and admit it. I was right about everything – God, society, how to live, etc."

"Hmm, not really," I said, rubbing my nose.

"Fine, don't admit it. But I really believe this experience will make you a stronger, better person. By smashing your illusions, you'll be a more complete individual and less inhibited about pursuing your pleasures. Remember: 'without God, all things are permitted.'"

I thought back to the night of Keith's party, and I remembered how a life committed to the pursuit of selfishness and pleasure could never appeal to me. Despite the numerous temptations, it was a path to mindlessness and misery, and I wanted to avoid that fate again.

"I just want to get out of here," I whined.

"I hear ya, man. This sucks ass."

"It's funny," I mused. "I really thought I had turned the corner. I really thought I had chosen the right path for my life. I really believed I had felt the presence of God. But it's simply not logical at this point. It no longer jives with my experience of the world. So the jig is up, so to speak, and I have nowhere to go. It's a shame reality is such a bitch."

"I know dude, but things will get better. Trust me."

"Thanks," I said, sucking the last few sips from my can. I really had nothing left to say, so I burped.

"Alright," said Troy, wrestling his jacket from the back of his chair. "I need to head out too. I'll leave the rest of the beer with you."

"Cool," I said, complacently.

Then he raised his fist and summoned me to raise mine – and we jabbed them together in a slightly depressing ritual of male bonding.

"Keep it real man," he said, as he roped around the bed. But before I could respond, he was already gone.

I spent the next couple of hours watching TV (including a couple of *Seinfeld* reruns) while munching on a salad and a jello pudding snack brought up from the cafeteria. Eventually, as the clock struck midnight, fatigue set in – so I flipped off the TV, adjusted the mechanical bed into a comfortable position, and closed my heavy eyelids.

I thought back to those crazy days right after graduation – when I was anxious and scared about entering the "Real World," completely unequipped to meet its challenges, and deathly afraid of failure. I had tried so hard to stay afloat – and for a while I *did* stay afloat – finding a decent job, locating a terrific apartment, and creating a pair of close friendships.

But despite all that, I never managed to silence the demons of my own mind – the self-loathing, the insecurity, the paranoia – that had traveled with me since my late childhood. I had weighed a couple of philosophies – the first represented by Mark, the second by Troy – but I found both of them wanting, in their own unique ways. Neither of them could save me from the abyss – where I was stuck right now.

I had truly fallen into the lowest pit of despair – in a physical, psychological, and spiritual sense. I wished I had never been born; I wished I could just disappear forever. Poof! Just like that!

I no longer believed in God, but I was still angry at Him. Does that make any sense? No, of course not. But still, that's how I felt. I wanted to scream at Him, punch Him, kick Him in the balls. I wanted Him to know what a colossal fuck-up He was – so I decided to pray (or actually, vent) at God for perhaps the last time in my life.

"Dear God,

I hope you're happy. I really hope you're fucking happy. I'm a good person - not a perfect person, perhaps - but still a damn good person, by any standard. I am always nice to people, I never steal from anyone, I never do any drugs, and I've only had sex once (even though I'm not sure why You're so hung-up on sex, but whatever). The point is, if this world was supposed to make any sense at all, somebody like me would be happy, self-confident, well-liked, and maybe even slightly-protected from some of the dumb bullshit you choose to impose on humanity.

But no! NO! NO! NO! In fact, it's been the complete opposite. I have spent most of my life in abject misery. I have become, through these experiences, a middling imbecile, constantly groping for some greater meaning to my existence. Not so long ago – shit, it was less than 10 freakin days ago – I looked up at the sky, and thought maybe, just *maybe*, there was a purpose to all this crap…and maybe, just *maybe*, a better future awaited me.

Incredibly, you didn't see this epiphany as a chance to help me; to take me under Your wing. Instead, you saw it as a chance to smash me into the ground, literally. God damn it, what the fuck are you trying to accomplish? Not just with me, but with this whole God damn world? I mean, there is something fundamentally screwed up with this world. Don't you realize that? There is just too much pain and suffering, and nobody has a good answer for it.

For most of my life, I have given You the benefit of the doubt, but no longer. I'm sorry to say it, but I *hate* You. I really do hate You. And I have nothing left to say. Good night. Good bye. Brian."

I felt a little better now, so I rolled onto my side, entered the fetal position, and prepared to fall asleep. But after a few minutes, I remained somewhat uncomfortable. I had left something unsaid, so I opened my eyes again, and whispered:

"If You still want to help me, I will accept Your help."

Then, after a few more seconds, I concluded:

"God, please help me."

PART TWO

PART TWO

Chapter 8

I didn't want to talk to my mom about everything that happened, but at the same time, I still felt obligated to tell her. After all, she was my mother! Sure enough, when I called her, she was completely devastated, and after hanging up, she was on the next train from Philadelphia to Washington.

She popped into the hospital around mid-afternoon on Wednesday, and instantly started nagging me with ridiculous questions.

"Why were you walking in such a dangerous neighborhood all by yourself? Do you have a death wish or something? What are you eating these days? You look a little thinner, but not thin enough. Now that you're confined to a bed, you might want to start studying for the LSATs. It's not like you have anything better to do. Do you want me to order some law school brochures? How are...?"

I closed my eyes and counted backwards from twenty – a strategy that kept me calm when I was a kid. But now, her constant pestering was driving me crazier than ever. On the bright side, she wasn't drunk. At least not yet.

A few days later, I finally went under the knife, as a team of doctors replaced a couple of disks in my lower back. The surgery was successful, but I still needed to recuperate in this God-forsaken hospital for a few more weeks. Even worse, my mom insisted on staying by my side, even though she annoyed the crap out of me.

Finally, one day, she left the hospital around mid-afternoon, and returned late at night in a drunken stupor, crying and shouting for her own mother (my grandmother) who had died of lung cancer before I was born. Curled up and sobbing in the hallway, one of the security guards asked her to leave – which is precisely what she did. Early the next morning, she called me and said she was returning to Philadelphia. Somewhat relieved, I said that was fine with me. So she left.

Unfortunately, her absence was filled by more annoying people– namely, my co-workers, and of course, my boss. I mean, I thought one of the perks of being in a hospital was not having to see those Rat Race runners. I know this sounds harsh, but seeing those guys made me sick.

Mark and Troy stopped by a few more times (although never at the *same* time, thankfully). We shrunk the topic menu from God and the meaning of life to safer subjects, like the football season and the 2000 election saga (George W. Bush and Al Gore were locked in a bitter recount in Florida). Even so, my roommate always left the room with the same parting words: "I'm praying for you." I usually salvaged enough energy to say, "Thank you." I might have lost my faith, but I hadn't lost my manners.

I never spoke with my father about the incident, but he did send me a fancy "get well" card with a $1,000 check wedged inside. No, I'm not joking about that. I'm sure you think he's a prick, but the truth is, I'm glad he did that. At this stage of our lives, the less contact between us, the better. Besides, I could use the money.

I also had the pleasure of being visited by a couple of short, stocky police officers who were conducting their investigation. They hovered over me, and peppered me with questions about that awful night. I gave them a physical description of my assailant, his likely name ("Danny"), and the theory that it could be the same "Danny" that Mary Beth tutored.

The Danny she knew had a recent line-up photo, and when I saw it, I confirmed it was the same person who had assaulted me. The police started hunting for him - searching his home, his school, and the streets around his neighborhood. But he had apparently vanished – probably to start trouble in a new city. The cops promised to keep the case open, but they weren't optimistic about solving it. I grew disillusioned, as well. I figured that justice would never be served.

I should mention that I had another pair of visitors. In fact, I saw them every day, every few hours – a couple of silent, dutiful immigrants who scrubbed my body parts with a washcloth, and administered my bedpan.

I never spoke to them (or even made eye contact with them), since I felt too embarrassed about my condition. I felt embarrassed for them too – since they had to deal with all of my shit (literally), and probably couldn't aspire to anything better in life. Despite my pity, I still *needed* them to survive. And I guess they needed me too – at least for their minimum-wage paycheck. In any case, this emotional swing between pity and gratitude was wreaking havoc with my sanity.

When Christmas Day arrived, my room was as bare and empty as it had always been. If you didn't have a calendar to mark Christ's birthday, you would think it was just another cold and miserable day.

I was completely drained of the Christmas spirit, but I still felt like I should pretend to have it. So when the two lower-level hospital workers arrived, I mustered the strength to say, "Merry Christmas." Unfortunately, my words were greeted with silence – total silence. I guess it's possible they didn't speak English, or perhaps their superiors had warned them not to chat with their patients. But most likely, they deliberately chose to ignore me.

After all, who was I? I was just the kid whose cock they had to clean, and whose crap they had to haul out – just like some mindless animal in a zoo. I could be safely ignored, just like so many people had ignored *them* over the years – comforted by the notion that they didn't have any feelings, and they didn't deserve even the slightest trace of compassion. And so, in half a second, another potential human connection was lost forever.

But physically, at least, I was slowly getting better, making noticeable progress week-by-week. By the middle of January, I was cleared to leave the hospital. I could walk (albeit with a slight limp) but I couldn't run, or bend over to touch my toes. I was prescribed a steady diet of painkillers, instructed to wear a brace around my lower back, and required to visit a physical therapist every Tuesday and Thursday for the next few months.

On my final day, I was given a routine physical, including a chance to step on the scale, and check out my weight. Because of the shitty hospital food, I had shed 15 pounds in six weeks. This brought my total weight loss – since I arrived in Washington – up to 25 pounds. I haven't been this thin since…shit, I can't even remember. Right now, I no longer have to cringe when I see my naked body in the mirror. In fact, I kind of excite myself.

But enough about that. After packing my suitcase, I filled out the necessary paperwork, darted to the first floor lobby, and called for a cab.

I rested comfortably in the center of a long row of steel chairs, facing another row of chairs – much like you'd find at an airport. Every seat was empty, except for one in the far corner, which was filled by the figure of a beautiful woman.

She was probably in her early 20's (certainly no older than me) and although she was seated, I could wager she was 5'6," or perhaps even 5'7." She featured an oval face and small lips pursed in concentration as she flipped through the latest copy of *The Economist* (not the usual reading fare for a girl of her age). Her long golden hair draped past her shoulder blades, and blanketed the back of her lithe, supple frame.

She was thin, but not too thin – splendidly healthy in her wholesome physique. It was impractical to evaluate her breasts, since they were masked by her large green jacket. Likewise, her legs were concealed by a pair of comfortable blue jeans. Overall, she was the archetype of an angel – a classical beauty who captured the essence of what femininity can and should be.

I must have gazed at her for at least fifteen seconds, until she finally lifted her eyes and glanced in my direction. By instinct, I turned away from her, and stared outside the window. Remarkably, I couldn't overcome my shyness, even for what seemed to be the perfect woman.

I started shifting my eyes around the room – first, at the receptionist in the background, then at the strangers shuffling through the entrance, and finally back at the object of my affection: this Renaissance sculpture come to life. She stared at me for a second time, but once again, I hurriedly gazed at the floor below. Basically, I'm hard-wired to avoid eye contact with a woman – even if it means staying a loner for the rest of my life.

However, I think she knew I was vying for her attention. I mean, it was pretty freaking obvious. I guess the key question was, "who would make the first move?" If she was waiting for me to do it, she'd be waiting a long time – because, as we all know, I'm like a frightened turtle around girls. But if *she* was going to do it, she'd be entering uncharted territory - because no girl has ever made the first move with me. Not one.

Needless to say, I couldn't realistically expect this woman to break the pattern of history. While I might have recently developed the capacity to excite myself, I hadn't reached that threshold with the opposite sex. In their critical eyes, I'm still a slightly-hunched, pudgy-faced, sad-eyed doofus. I know it's a shame, but it's true. Chagrined by the memory of my romantic failures, I pretended to play with my cell phone – still hoping, of course, that something strange could bring us together.

It did. It was my shoes.

"I think your shoes are untied," she said, pointing at my Nikes. Because of her easy smile, I could see that her words were inspired by friendliness, and not by sarcasm.

"I know," I said, bashfully. "I'd like to tie them, but I have a bad back at the moment. I'm still recuperating from back surgery."

"Oh, I'm sorry to hear to that," she said, sympathetically. "If you want, I could tie them for you."

"No, I couldn't ask you to do that. But thank you anyway."

"Don't be silly," she said in a nurturing tone. Before I could argue with her, she approached me, bent down on one knee, and carefully tied the shoelaces on each foot. Then she returned to her seat with an aura of self-satisfaction.

"Thank you," I said, practically mesmerized by her act of kindness. "Really, thank you very much."

She flashed a bright warm smile, revealing a bounty of pearly white teeth. Then she simply replied, "You're welcome."

From there, the conversation withered and died, even though I desperately wanted to resuscitate it. Deep down, I hungered to blurt out: "I think you're beautiful and sweet, and perfect in every way," but that was probably inappropriate. Luckily, after a minute, she found another topic for the two of us.

"What happened to your back?" she asked.

"Well," I hesitated, groping for a lie, "I had a stupid accident. Nothing serious. I'm going to be fine." Thankfully, she didn't pester me for further details. Perhaps she knew she was treading on personal ground.

"What about you?" I asked. "What brings you here?"

"I'm here for a charity called The Better Day Foundation. Basically, I stop by every Friday and spend a few hours with little kids who have cancer – reading to them, playing with them, all that stuff. Then, when we're done, I take a cab and head back to class."

"Oh, that's terrific. I really admire that."

"Thanks," she murmured.

"Do you see one kid at a time, or a whole bunch of them at once?"

"Lately, I've been seeing them one at a time, usually for a few months, until eventually they pass on. Lately, I've been spending time with a five-year-old girl named Michelle. This afternoon, we played a game of Candyland and finger-painted. Do you want to see the painting she made for me?"

"Sure," I said, enthusiastically.

She rewarded me with another beaming smile, and then rummaged through her gray backpack to find the painting. Eventually, she pulled out a sheet of paper and handed it to me.

The painting was sloppy and amateurish, as you'd expect from someone so young, but it also had a certain beauty to it – a beauty born out of uninhibited self-expression. In the center of the picture was a smiling boy and girl, holding hands as they walked through a vegetable garden with rows of corn, tomatoes, and potatoes, among other foods.

"This is a very nice painting," I said, handing it back to her.

"I know," she replied. "She's such a sweet and talented girl. When she leaves, I'm definitely going to miss her." Then she calmly tucked the picture back into her backpack.

I could only sit back and marvel at the kindness, gentleness and understanding that radiated from her spirit. She was an old soul – smart, experienced, and quietly self-confident - but she was also a young soul – eagerly exploring the planet with a rare form of happiness – a playful happiness that burns bright even when the prize of innocence is taken from us. I had never met someone who was so close to perfection – in a physical, intellectual, and emotional sense. I think I loved her.

But it was not to be. Our connection was cut short by the bright lights of a yellow cab waiting patiently at the entrance.

"Ooh, I see my cab," the blue-eyed cutie announced, rocketing out of her seat. "It was nice chatting with you. I hope your back feels better."

"Thanks," I said stoically, pretending that her lack of romantic interest was totally cool with me – even though it wasn't.

She flung her blonde hair over her shoulder, whispered "bye," and then exited through the automatic doors.

I pretended to play with my cell phone again, but I was secretly staring at her through the window, as she walked hurriedly to the cab.

I couldn't believe I had allowed such a spectacular woman leave my life – without even a word of protest. In all of my life, I couldn't have asked for a better opportunity at a solid relationship, and yet, because of my paralyzing fear of rejection, I had just pissed it away. I have to be the biggest loser in history.

I cringed as I watched her hop into the cab and slam the door shut. The dream was officially dead. There was nothing I could do about it now. At any moment, the vehicle would zoom off, and with it, any hope of a brighter future.

But a funny thing happened. The cab didn't zoom off. It stayed there. A few seconds later, the car door flung open again, and my nameless, would-be girlfriend crawled out with a look of confusion. She marched back to the hospital, re-entered the lobby, and halted just a few yards from me.

"Is your name 'Raines?'" she announced.

"That's my last name. Why?"

"The cab driver says he's picking up a guy named 'Raines.' So I guess that's your cab outside."

"Hmm, that's strange," I said. "Where are you headed?"

"Foggy Bottom. Why?"

"Do you want to split the cab? Foggy Bottom's along the way."

"Are you sure?"

"Definitely," I answered. "I just hope we get there before it rains."

"That's OK. I don't mind it when it Raines," she said, with a wink. "But seriously, thanks for the ride."

"No problem," I beamed. We walked out of the hospital, dodged a few raindrops, and sprung into the backseat of the cab.

"What's your name?" the driver asked me.

"Brian Raines," I replied.

"What's the address?" he continued.

"The corner of 22nd and H," my co-passenger answered. After that, we were officially on our way.

"You know, it's not fair," I complained flirtatiously. "You know my name, but I don't know yours."

The young lady smiled. "I'm Heather. Heather Manning."

"It's nice to meet you," I said. "Are you from this area originally?"

"Not exactly. I spent most of my life in California. Then I went to Duke for college. Now I'm a med student at GW. What about you?"

I quickly regurgitated the Cliff Notes version of my life – Philly, Vermont, Washington, blah, blah, blah.

"Do you like living here?" she asked, perhaps detecting a trace of regret in my voice.

"I'm not sure," I replied, masking my loathing for this city. "I like politics, so in that sense, it's the best place to be. But I have no real affection for DC. For me, it's just a big, crowded swamp of strangers with their inflated egos, petty bickering, and endless drama. Sometimes I think I should leave this place, but then I ask myself: 'Where would I go? What would I do?' Obviously, I don't have an answer to that. So I stay. For now."

"Could you go home?" she asked. "Back to Philly?"

When I heard the word "Philly," my mind flashed back to the setting of my childhood –a sterile suburb of McMansions connected to strip malls and office parks. Back there, you could live on the same block as your neighbor for eighteen years, and never speak a word to him (as in my case). Shit, even my own home was a lifeless void. After all, it was usually just me and my alcoholic mom, and she spent most of her time passed out in bed. Needless to say, I hated my hometown, and I had no intention of going back.

"Back to Philly?" I repeated. "No, I don't think so. I don't have family there anymore. In fact," I sighed, "I really don't have a family at all."

Those words seemed to strike a nerve with Heather.

"I know how you feel," she said sympathetically. "I really don't have a family either – at least not one I can count on, that's for sure. I suppose if I have a family, it's the boys and girls at the hospital. I love those kids, and they love me too, I think."

She seemed to be a rootless person, lacking ties to either kin or community. But, still, she was effortlessly comfortable in her own skin, and happily attentive to the needs of others – even to those whose life was literally almost over. This kind of dedication was a mystery to me.

"Do you ever get depressed around those kids?" I asked.

"Depressed?" she repeated. "Why would I get depressed?"

"Well, because of their…condition," I explained, casually hinting at the fact that they're…um… *dying*!

"No, not at all," she said, plainly. "They're normal children in every way. They just want a playmate – someone who will care for them, entertain them, and sate their curiosity. I know some people might find it strange, but I enjoy being around them. It keeps me focused on the most important thing in life – namely, life itself."

I wanted to believe her, but I wasn't entirely convinced. "So seeing them doesn't make you scared of death?" I asked.

"No," she said, almost amused at my immaturity.

"How come?"

"Well, I don't think I can explain that in only thirty seconds," she said as the cab approached her street. Then she curled her lips in a Mona Lisa smile – friendly, almost playful, but also taunting. She was concealing a delicious secret – a secret that would never be shared.

Finally, the cab pulled in front of a white three-story building. Heather leaned forward and asked the driver, "How much is it?"

"Don't worry about it, I'll take care of it," I asserted.

She opened her wallet and begged, "Let me at least pay for half."

I chuckled. "No way, it's a favor."

"Please let me pay," she insisted.

"No, I can't let you do that. You were nice enough to tie my shoelaces. Now, we're even."

She blushed, and looked down at her feet.

"OK, thanks," she said.

Once again, we stared at each other for a few seconds, waiting for the other person to say something (anything!) to keep the conversation alive. I thought of blurting out, "Can I see you again?" But the words couldn't penetrate my sealed lips. Even now, I was too afraid.

"I need to run to class," she stated. "But it was nice talking with you, Brian."

I pretended that her parting words were meaningless to me, and that I was invulnerable to the indifference of a beautiful woman. But deep down, my heart was shattered.

"Yeah, it was nice talking with you too," I replied.

She shifted to the far end of her seat, opened the door, jumped out, and looked back at me for a final time. "Bye," she said.

"Bye," I repeated, but by this point, the door had already shut.

The cab rolled back onto the street and sped forward until it reached a red light. As the engine idled, I cursed my weakness around women. In my rational mind, I knew I had to be confident, assertive, and ready to swing into action. But by instinct and experience, I was a prisoner of my own emotions; a timid victim trapped in a vicious cycle of hope, fear, and defeat.

I took a few moments to isolate those negative emotions, and conduct a quick equation in my head: If I caught up with Heather and asked her out, and she rejected me, I would feel miserable. No question about that. But if I stayed in this God-forsaken cab, I would feel even *more* miserable – haunted by doubts about what could've been, and *should've* been, and hating myself for being such a damn pussy!

The choice was obvious: I needed to fight for Heather's affection - even if that kind of boldness went against every instinct in my body, and every prior experience of my life. As you certainly know by now, I'm a weak man by nature, but through the power of reason, I was suddenly finding the courage to change a lifetime of self-defeating behavior. Now was the time to take control.

"Stop!" I yelled at the driver.

"What? Why?" he replied.

"Just pull over. I'll be back in a minute."

"No, you can't leave the cab," he insisted.

"Why not?"

"You need to pay first."

I tossed him a ten-dollar bill and then repeated, "I'll be back."

As I flew out of the cab, I was pummeled by a torrent of rain that soaked through my clothes. Grunting through the pain of my lower back, I ran towards Heather's building, where she was fiddling with her electronic key. Eventually, the key worked, and she opened the door.

"Wait!" I shouted in pain, limping in exhaustion. She turned around and smiled.

"Hi!" she said.

I waited a moment to catch my breath.

"I never…Do you…Can I see you again?"

"What?" she asked, genuinely confused.

"Can I see you again? For dinner or something?"

"Why?"

"Why?" I repeated. "Well…umm…because we have a lot in common."

"Oh yeah, like what?"

I couldn't believe she was hassling me with all these dumb questions. I felt like shouting, "Hey babe, I like you! Ain't it obvious? If you don't like me, just say so. There's no point in embarrassing me."

Instead, I controlled my emotions, took a deep breath, and simply answered, "We care about other people."

She seemed perplexed - staring back and forth between me and the ground beneath us. But then she broke into a grin, and beamed, "O.K., sure!"

"Great!" I said, with both relief and excitement. It was almost too good to be true!

"What's your email address?" I asked.

"It's heather_manning@hotmail.com."

"O.K., I think I can remember that." We both smiled.

"Well, I don't want to keep you from class," I said, kindly. Now that I had her email, I wanted to flee like a thief in the night. If I hung around too long, there was a strong chance I might say something stupid, and ruin everything.

"Yeah, I'm late as it is," she sighed. "But I'm glad you came back."

"Oh yeah, me too," I said, in what has to be a candidate for understatement of the century.

"Take care," were my parting words. After a quick wave, I spun around to catch my cab (if it was still there).

After a few paces, I heard her shout, "Brian!" I looked back, and sure enough, she was still standing there in the pouring rain, with her soaking wet hair stuck to her porcelain cheeks.

"Are you really going to email me?" she asked.

I was stunned by her question. Did she really think I *wasn't* going to email her? How could she think that? In light of everything I had done – running out of a car in a roaring storm, mustering the courage to risk rejection – how could that thought even enter her mind?

For the first time, I could sniff a trace of vulnerability. Perhaps she was anxious about giving her heart to another person - and possibly losing it. In that case, I wanted to reassure her that my feelings were sincere, and that it was O.K. for her to feel the same way about me.

"I promise," I said, over the sound of thunder in the background.

She nodded, turned up her lips, and replied, "O.K."

I smiled back, and repeated, "O.K."

Finally, Heather said "bye," for practically the fourth time, spun around, and used her electronic key to enter the building. I watched as she disappeared in a sea of people, and then I marched back to the cab.

When I re-entered the cab, I thanked the driver for waiting, and then slouched by the window to see the rain fall down and cleanse the city.

I thought about how my world had changed in less than thirty minutes– from a hopeless, dreary dungeon to a sunlit field of endless possibilities. I was lucky to meet such a smart, compassionate, and beautiful woman – and I was even luckier that (for some strange reason), she seemed to like me too.

But it wasn't luck alone that had made the difference. I had seized the initiative, reclaimed ownership of my life, and showed an unprecedented level of assertiveness – fueled by the power of my own rational mind, and a conscious decision to ignore my so-called instincts.

I felt reinvigorated by the prospect of a second chance – a second chance to survive, and even thrive, in the Real World. This time, I wouldn't be a victim. This time, I would be the best *me* I could *be*.

I was tempted to thank God for my reversal of fate, but I decided to hold off on that for now. I needed to see if I had a real future with Heather, because at this point, being with her was the only future worth having.

Chapter 9

When I returned to work on Monday morning, everyone pretended they were thrilled to see me – showering me with praise, and suffocating me with hugs. In fact, they even bought a cake for me, with the frosting-written message, "Welcome back, Brian!"

The cynic in me believed their enthusiasm was linked to my ability to lighten everyone's workload. But I deliberately quashed those negative thoughts. The fact was, I was glad to see them too – or more accurately, I was glad to be back in my normal routine. Besides, it's always fun being the center of attention.

The following afternoon, Troy and I cemented the return to normalcy by going out for lunch. I told him about Heather, and how I had dramatically ran out of the cab in order to talk with her.

"Great job, man!" he said, enthusiastically. "See what happens when you follow your instincts?"

"I *didn't* follow my instincts," I corrected him. "I *over-came* them."

Still, it was hard to overcome all of my fears and insecurities, as I pondered the precise time to contact Heather. Even though she seemed genuinely eager to see me again, I still needed to proceed with caution. If I used the wrong word at the wrong time, I might come across as desperate, or needy, or just plain weird. It was a daunting process that could drive any person insane.

After literally hours of crafting the perfect email, I ultimately decided there was safety in brevity. I simply wrote…

"Hi, this is Brian, the guy you met at the hospital. See, I'm writing you back, just like I promised! I hope you're having a great week. Take care."

I hit the send button on Wednesday afternoon, and then clicked refresh about every five minutes for the rest of the day, desperately searching for a reply. I kept searching through all of Thursday, and most of Friday, as well. I was beginning to panic. Did I say something stupid? Did she lose interest in me altogether? I couldn't believe I had invested so much emotion on a woman who couldn't be bothered to write me back!

Finally, on Friday afternoon, I found an email from "Heather" at the top of my inbox. I clicked on her name with the same excitement as a five-year old on Christmas morning. I read it quickly: "Hi Brian!! I'm so glad to hear from you. I hope you're having a great week too. Is your back feeling any better? I certainly hope so. Keep in touch, Heather."

After a few minutes, my initial wave of excitement leveled off, and eventually settled into a self-pitying sadness. I didn't want to "keep in touch" with Heather; I wanted to see her, and date her, and love her. But she didn't seem to want that from me.

Then, I consoled myself with an alternative explanation. Perhaps she was being coy for the same reason I was – the fear of seeming overanxious and earning the stamp of rejection. I guess that kind of made sense. From then on, we exchanged emails every two days like clockwork, until finally, I worked up the courage to ask her: "Do you want to meet up sometime?"

This time, I received an almost instantaneous reply: "I thought you'd never ask," she said in her email. "Do you have any interest in going for a walk with me? I usually take a walk through Rock Creek Park every Sunday afternoon. Let me know."

Needless to say, I jumped at the chance, and wrote back to confirm the time and location. After we worked out the details, it was official. We had a date!

When D-Day finally rolled around, I was surprisingly calm. I figured, I'm going to be myself and let the chips fall where they may. I put on a blue sweater and covered it with a black leather jacket. Overall, I looked pretty darned good, if you want to know the truth.

I rode the subway into the city, and after about half an hour, I hopped off at the closest metro station. I followed the sight of large, lifeless trees into the heart of Rock Creek Park, and rested at the opening of a secluded trail – the place where Heather and I had agreed to meet. The entire area was deserted – probably because the mid-winter chill had scared everyone else away. But not us. For us, nature still had a unique beauty, even when the temperature hovered around freezing.

I waited for a few minutes, repeatedly checking my watch, until I finally saw an angel coming over the horizon. She was comfortably covered by a grey coat, a green scarf, and a pair of mittens. Her blond hair whipped in the chilly wind, and her smile brightened as she drew closer to me.

"Hi!" she shouted.

"Hi!" I yelled back. "How are you?"

"Great. How are you?"

"A little chilly," I confessed.

"Don't worry, you'll warm up soon enough."

By this point, she was standing right in front of me. I was so happy to see her, I wanted to wrap my arms around her. But I decided to hold off. If I seemed overaggressive, it would jeopardize the date immediately.

"Did you find the place alright?" she asked.

"Sure did," I replied.

"Good. Now," she said, pointing to the east, "let's go *that* way."

"Yes, ma'am," I said, with a mock salute.

"Are you making fun of me?" she asked flirtatiously.

"No way," I said, and we both shared a laugh.

After a few minutes of talking and walking, I started to warm up – and not just on the outer layers of my skin, but inside my heart, as well. I felt comfortable with Heather on a physical, emotional, and spiritual level. If there was such a thing as a soul, my soul was at peace with this woman.

Eventually, the conversation turned back to the hospital, and I told her about the weeks I spent there recovering from an injured back (although I never bothered to explain *how* I injured it). Then I prodded Heather to talk about her hospital experience.

"Did you see Michelle last week?" I asked.

"I'm surprised you remember her name," she replied.

"Sure, I remember. She's a great artist."

"Thanks. She *was* a great artist."

"Do you mean…?" I asked, afraid to finish the thought.

"Yes," she said whimsically. "She's gone."

"Oh Heather, I'm so sorry. Is there anything I can do to help?"

"It's O.K., Brian," she said softly, but with an unmistakable confidence. "Death is just another part of life. There's nothing to be sorry about."

"Do you really believe that?" I asked, perhaps a little *too* directly.

She smiled at me. "Yes, Brian, I *really* do." Then she asked me the million-dollar question, "What do *you* believe?"

I pondered the question for a good ten seconds or so. Finally, I replied: "I don't know. I've spent my whole life asking myself that, but I've never found an answer. At this point, I'm not sure there *is* an answer."

"I think there's an answer," she said with a healthy dose of self-confidence.

"O.K.," I smiled. "So what is it? In the cab, you said you didn't have time to tell me. Do you have time now?"

"I have time," she said, "but it's more complicated than that. A person's faith is a very private matter and that's especially true in my case. During the course of my life, there have been several experiences that have created and tested my faith. So the question is, do you want to hear about those experiences? I should warn you, they might sound kind of strange, and I don't want to scare you away or anything."

"I promise you, Heather, there's nothing you could say that would scare me away."

"O.K, good. Well then...I guess I should start at the beginning. I was born in Boulder, Colorado - the only child of a pair of twenty-something high school teachers. I should have had a nice, normal childhood in the suburbs – but then fate intervened. Shortly after my third birthday, my father died after accidentally taking a lethal mix of prescriptions drugs. A brief time later, my mother also died from taking drugs, but this time it wasn't an accident. She took her own life, and by doing that, she made me an orphan. I have no memory of my parents, except for a single mid-summer afternoon, when my mom took me to the pond to feed some ducks. I'm not sure why I remember that, but I do.

"In any case, after my mom died, I went to live with my Aunt Carrie, Uncle Richard, and their two daughters in San Diego. Right at the start, they treated me like an unwelcome guest – even though they reaped a fortune once the lawsuit against my dad's doctor was settled. Nearly all of the money was spent on my cousins, Stacy and Isabelle. I received whatever money was left over, which usually wasn't much. In the meantime, the girls teased me, tormented me, and blamed me for everything – and their parents were quite happy to ignore the facts, and punish me accordingly.

"As you can see, my home life left a lot to be desired – but, on the bright side, I had a much better time at school. I was determined to be the best student in class. I was driven by two factors – a genuine hunger for knowledge, and also a thinly-veiled competitive streak. I wanted to show my adopted family that I could make something of myself – even though they never showed me even an ounce of love.

"I think my efforts paid off, at least in some ways. I ended up skipping the third grade, and then later, the sixth grade, as well. When I reached junior high, I was in the same class as Stacy – even though she was two years older than me!

"But Stacy didn't care, and neither did much of the other kids, for that matter. In their minds, it was nice to have good grades, but it was much nicer to have a wafer-thin body, a chiseled boyfriend, and a brand new Mercedes to drive back and forth from the beach.

"Incredibly, they found a way to merge those superficial values with their religion – partying until 3 a.m. on a Saturday night, and then showing up for church on Sunday morning.

"I usually stayed away from church for a very simple reason: I figured, if my cousins could go to church regularly, and not feel even a sliver of doubt about their lifestyle, then the church's teachings were probably useless. I know that might sound harsh, but that's how I felt at the time.

"During this entire period of my life, I never worried much about God, or Heaven, or any other spiritual matters. As far as I was concerned, all of those topics were irrelevant to the demands of my daily life. After all, why should I believe in a Higher Power when I had no evidence for its existence? How could I judge one religion as more valid than another when all of them scorned facts and demanded absolute obedience from their followers? The whole process seemed totally pointless to me.

"Now, in fairness, I also held a low opinion of all those self-loathing philosophy teachers, who insisted on telling their students that reality is an illusion, and therefore, there is no absolute 'truth.' According to them, everyone can believe whatever they want to believe, and no one's beliefs are inherently better than anyone else's.

"Needless to say, that perspective didn't conform with the world as I saw it. I saw – based on my own experience – that reality exists, and it exists independent of my thoughts, feelings, and prayers. If I'm running toward a table, I will trip and fall down on that table – even if I prayed for it to disappear. If *you* ran toward the table, the same thing would happen to *you*. The consequences are always the same. There is a 'reality' out there whether we like it or not.

"If reality exists, then reason – and only reason – is the faculty to discover, interpret, and master it. Reason is the highest domain of the mind – focused purely on facts, unswayed by emotion, and in every moment, seeking a constant expansion of one's knowledge. Reason is a complex and highly demanding tool – primarily because it forces us to be independent in thought, and responsible for our own judgments.

"Quite simply, this was my life philosophy: Reality exists, and reason is the key to using it. But when I used reason, what was the reality that I found? Well, it was a reality of *separation*. Every human being was separate from one another. No human mind could truly connect with another mind, at least in any meaningful sense of the word. The constant quest for a feeling of union was an illusion, at best, and a fantasy, at worst. And yet, strangely, the universe seemed to work best that way – with each individual acting, well, as an *individual*.

"Look at it this way: The person who knows the most about you is *you*. The person who knows the most about your physical and emotional needs is *you*. The person who is most trustworthy to handle those needs, and to take care of those needs, is *you*. In a very real sense, the world works best when people put themselves first and foremost – and follow the path of rational self-interest. Knowing all this, why do people still yearn for the idea that we should shed our ego and melt our individuality into the cesspool of society?

"I could whip out a pencil," she said, doing exactly that, "and see the ethic of rational self-interest in action: the loggers in California, the miners in Sri Lanka, the millworkers in Kansas, the retailers in Virginia – all of them coming together to create and sell this simple pencil - not for *my* benefit, but for their own –to make enough enough money to survive. The ethic of rational self-interest can unleash powerful creative energies – whether they're used to produce a simple pencil or the Sears Tower.

"Of course, the idea of self-interest conflicts with the message that's been drilled into our brains since childhood – that we must sacrifice our needs to the needs of others. This is not a natural concept for most people to understand. By definition, sacrificing for others requires a sacrifice of our own minds – a surrender of our judgment and responsibility – for uncertain rewards. And yet that's precisely what we've been conditioned to do.

"In my life, when I saw the ethic of self-sacrifice in action, I saw Buddhist monks walking around, literally sweeping the ground in front of them, in order to avoid hurting bugs. On the other extreme, I saw Nazis hurtling Jews into ovens – in service to the collective 'Fatherland.' Despite this obvious insanity, even today, we are still scolded to 'live for others,' and we're reprimanded whenever we question that slogan. But from my perspective, everything worked better when people lived for *themselves*.

"Now, some people might ask: What does that actually mean? What does it mean to live for yourself? What are the ideas and actions of a self-interested person?

"In our society, a 'self-interested' person is commonly portrayed as a ruthless, violent brute - a common criminal who would lie, cheat, and sometimes kill to achieve his narrow goals - and those goals, more often than not, are the exploitation of others and destruction of all. We think of mob bosses like Al Capone, or on a broader scale, maniacal dictators like Stalin and Hitler.

"And yet, I have to ask: Why would any person consider vice and violence, exploitation and destruction, to be in their self-interest? As far as I'm concerned, those traits are contemptible, and contempt is not in anyone's self-interest.

"So what *is* in our self-interest? I would say that a self-interested life is a *virtuous* life, and there are three virtues which are critical: honesty, responsibility, and justice. These are the virtues of the rational person, because they create a virtuous circle of helping yourself, helping others, and then helping yourself again.

"Let me start with honesty – which is the commitment to understand and act upon reality in all cases. This is essential because the temptation to hide from reality – whether through lies or deception – harms our judgment, and therefore, our ability to achieve our goals. We must be relentless and fearless in our pursuit of honesty, confident in its practical usefulness and also in its positive impact on others. After all, if other people see you as an honest person, they will respect you, admire you, and be eager to assist you. The bottom line: Honesty is in your self-interest, and should be practiced specifically for that reason.

"The second virtue is responsibility – which is the appreciation that, in reality, each of us chooses our own actions, and therefore, we are ultimately accountable for the consequences of those actions. Sometimes in life, we are eager to cling to any excuse – any technicality – that can enable us to stare at our failings, and shout, 'Don't blame me! I couldn't help it!' But by assuming responsibility, we can actually liberate ourselves from those failures by seeing them for what they truly are – learning experiences that pave the road to success. When we rationally seize control over our lives, and recognize that we (rather than external forces) are the most powerful shapers of our future, our future is limitless.

"The third virtue is justice – which is the recognition that every person has an equal capacity to live honestly and responsibly, and therefore all of humanity should be treated as fundamentally equal. There is no need to instinctively treat people as either slaves or masters – when a show of respect and a sense of fair play will suffice. This is the 'golden rule' in action ('do unto others as others would do unto you').

"These three values – honesty, responsibility, and justice – provide us with a sense of ownership over our lives, and the confidence to surmount any of life's challenges. When we apply those values to our personal relationships, we reinforce those positive characteristics in ourselves, and grow even stronger. When we choose to practice those values at all times, in all circumstances, we possess the final, all-encompassing virtue, which is loyalty to virtue itself. That is known as integrity.

"We should strive for integrity because it benefits us, and not out of some abstract moral principle. Unfortunately, society continues to insist that morality consists of shedding the ego, and working exclusively for the benefit of others. I find it sad that people are forced to choose between self-interest and morality, because that is a false choice they should never have to make. Is it any wonder that at an early age, people see morality as the enemy, and seek to avoid it? After all, what does morality have to offer them, beyond pain and misery? The most important rules of ethics have been the least practiced because they have never been wedded to the logic of self-interest.

"So there you have it: this was the philosophy I developed in high school, and continued to practice through my early years of college. It was the morality of a restless striver: a woman who wanted to become the world's greatest doctor, and would do anything to achieve that goal.

"Overall, I was satisfied with myself and I was optimistic about my future. But deep down, I had to acknowledge a simple fact: I still wasn't happy. I mean *really* happy – the kind of happiness that treats every day as a gift, and every experience as a blessing.

"Instead, I saw life as a constant, lonely struggle with no greater purpose than my own wish to win that struggle. For a long time, that was all the motivation I needed. But not anymore. Now it wasn't enough that my life *mattered to me;* I wanted my life to *matter. Period.*

"I knew the only way to find some greater meaning was through God, and yet, I had already convinced myself that God was an illusion. There was simply no evidence for His existence, and a lot of evidence against it. I suppose I could've rejected reality, and embraced a fake faith - but I knew, right from the start, that I could never do that. In general, I think it's possible to repress a fact you *think* is true, but not one you *know* is true. Once you *know* the truth, there's no escape. The mind itself becomes a prison.

"When my older cousin Isabelle died in a car accident on the day before my 21st birthday, it enlarged the spiritual void in my life. I had never cared much for Isabelle, but over the years, I had grown close to her daughter, Elizabeth – a smart, spunky little girl who reminded me of how I was at her age.

"Seeing Elizabeth at the funeral forced me to re-examine all of my cocky assumptions and cherished illusions. She ran up to me with tears streaming down her face and asked me the haunting question: 'Why? Why did my mom die?' I searched my valedictorian brain, but it had nothing to reduce her pain. I hemmed and hawed until I saw my pathetic image in her crest-fallen eyes – my own sense of security slashed by the cold blades of truth – and I joined her in a flood of tears. Despite my best efforts, I couldn't relieve the grief of a child who had lost her mother, nor could I shake my own fear that the loss of this person, was, in the grand scheme of things, utterly and totally meaningless.

"However, like any common prisoner, I still held some vague hope that I could escape the jail cell of my mind. I still believed that I could find a philosophical loophole, and walk through it into a lifetime of bliss.

"At one point, I met with one of Duke's most famous philosophy professors, and I practically begged him for any insights he could offer. After several hours of conversation, do you know what he told me? 'Try not to think so much.' Yep, this was the grand summation of twenty centuries of human philosophy: 'Try not to think so much.' It was enough to drive any decent person to despair.

"That night, I sat alone in the middle of our empty football stadium, staring at the stars above me, praying for a sign – any kind of sign that could lead me out of the abyss.

"I stared at those stars for hours, until they finally faded into the blue sky of a brand new morning. Despite my sincerest hopes, I hadn't found any answers. I walked wearily back to the parking lot and hopped into my car to drive home. I switched on the car radio and flipped through the channels, until I heard the words 'search for God.'

"As I listened closer, I realized this was some sort of interview – an interview, in fact, with one of the world's most famous atheists who had, near the end of his life, embraced religion, because in his words, he simply 'had to go where the evidence leads.'

"I pulled the car over to the side of the road, and listened intently as both men discussed how science – after centuries of denying and denigrating faith – was moving back toward the idea of God.

"For a very long time, the conventional scientific view was that mankind was a 'curious accident in a backwater.'

But as scientists learned more about the laws of physics, it seemed implausible that we were any accident. In fact, it seemed all but certain that life was "pre-planned" in the universe right from the start.

"I don't want to get too technical here, but the universe contains 15 fundamental constants – including gravity, electromagnetism, the strength of nuclear forces, electron-neutron mass ratios, etc. – and they all have very precise values. If any one of those constants was off by even one part in a million, or in some cases, by one part in a million million, matter couldn't coalesce, and therefore, there wouldn't be any galaxies, stars, planets, and of course, life itself.

"All of those seemingly arbitrary and unrelated constants in physics have one strange thing in common – they are precisely the values you need if you want a universe capable of producing life. In a very real sense, the universe seems to have been 'fine-tuned' from the very first moment to support life. Instead of being a freak accident, we – as human beings – seem to be the overarching goal of the universe.

"Needless to say, some critics insist this is merely a raft of coincidences, but the shear volume of coincidences – involving vast differences in scale, and across multi-billion-year tracts of time – seems to rule that out. The only way to make sense of these so-called coincidences is to see them for what they are –evidence of design – and if the universe was designed, it had to have a designer.

"Recent advances in the life sciences also provide strong evidence for a 'designer.' The earliest, and simplest, form of life – the cell – contains a digital code (known as DNA), and code is always the result of a mental process. Consider this fact: inside the smallest self-replicating organism on the planet - a single *E. Coli* bacterial cell – is 10 trillion bits of information. That's 10 times the number of letters in all the books of the world's largest library! Now that we're aware of the complexities of DNA in even the simplest organisms, it's almost impossible to believe the traditional scientific explanation that life sprang from non-life.

"For over a century, scientists have been unable to create a living cell using non-living ingredients. Should we really believe that a random glob of chemicals could have succeeded where scientists – with all of their knowledge and training – couldn't? We might as well believe that a random combination of atoms could produce a computer.

"There is also no natural law that can explain how random processes can create *irreducibly complex systems* – and by that I mean systems that require every component to work together at the same time, or the system wouldn't work at all.

"For example, even the seemingly simple mousetrap is an *irreducibly complex system* – whereby if you remove any of its three components, you don't have a *less* effective mousetrap. You don't have a mousetrap at all!

"In our own bodies, the supposedly simple cell has a motor called the cilium, which is composed of about 200 protein parts. If you remove just a few of those 200 proteins, the cilium wouldn't function at all. It would be useless.

"The same principle applies to more complicated systems in our own body – such as the human eye and blood clotting. If you remove just a few parts of the eye, you wouldn't be able to see, and in the case of blood clotting, you'd bleed to death.

"When every part of the system has to be fully present in order to function, it's nearly impossible that such a system could have developed gradually through random processes. A more likely explanation is that – much like the primitive mousetrap – they are the products of design.

"When taken together, I found these advances in physics and biology to be astonishing. But even so, they didn't necessarily inspire hope for a personal God who has a loving interest in our own lives.

"That's when I discovered an incredible medical mystery. In recent decades, hospitals have become more adept at bringing people back from the dead (literally). And when these people return, they usually have detailed descriptions about a realm beyond death.

"There have been literally thousands of people who were clinically dead - with no heartbeat or brainwaves for 20 or 30 minutes or more – and yet they experienced the feeling of leaving their bodies and witnessing medical resuscitation procedures from above.

"From there, many of them felt a sudden sense of peace and detachment. Some described moving through a 'tunnel,' being greeted by relatives who had passed away, and encountering a 'Being of Light' that emanated a powerful, unearthly love.

"Normally, it would be easy to dismiss these stories as hallucinations, or outright fabrications, but in fact, there's good reason to believe them. In a lot of cases, the patients observed details they couldn't possibly have seen from their physical vantage point (not to mention the rather important fact that they were supposedly *dead*)!

"They accurately described advanced surgical instruments, retold conversations that had occurred while they were 'dead,' and recounted the activity of family members who were at home many miles away.

"Since there isn't any physiological theory that can explain these 'near-death experiences,' it seems safe to say that science has inadvertently stumbled on evidence for the soul.

"After consuming all of this information, I felt like a whole new world had been opened to me. I had always assumed that reason was the destroyer of faith, but now, it seemed like reason could be a catalyst for faith. The burden of proof had shifted dramatically. Now it was *rational* to believe in God and a greater purpose to life. I felt like a complete person for the first time in my existence.

"I also felt an inexplicable desire to share this feeling of completeness. So I moved back to San Diego for the summer to spend more time with my niece. This was the first time I had done anything with the purpose of sharing myself – but it seemed like a challenge worth exploring – and there was no one who could benefit more from that challenge than Elizabeth.

"That summer, Elizabeth and I were practically sisters – in the same way I had always hoped I could be with Stacy and Isabelle – going to the beach, riding bikes through the neighborhood, playing board games, eating ice cream late at night. When I did something to make her laugh or smile, I could feel the walls in my heart melt away. Every time I made her happy, it raised my own happiness to a higher level. But did I *love* her? Did I even know what love was? I wasn't sure.

"I had spent my entire life running away from the idea of love, mostly because I thought it invalidated my entire philosophy. I had always believed that the mind is the source of all values – and therefore it must never be submerged to the needs of some vague 'other.' I rejected love because, in my view, it was an abdication of the mind - a surrender of your true, independent self for the uncertain affections of another person. In the same vein, I scorned the idea of 'brotherly love.' I could not love all people in all circumstances, because that would neutralize my judgment, and put vice and virtue on an equal playing field.

"But, over time, I grew to learn that love – or perhaps I should say, *true* love - wasn't a negation of my philosophy – but rather, an extension of that philosophy to its highest, and greatest purpose. True love was an expression of my rational values, projected not inward, but outward into the world. It was the urge to instill the best and noblest parts of me into the soul of another human being.

"I embraced this new idea of love because it preserved the wholeness of the individual. After all, there is no 'I love you' without 'I.' 'I' comes first – and it will always come first whenever love is true. I also insisted that love, like any rational value, must be evaluated based on its costs and benefits. In other words, love should be earned; it is not an entitlement for ungrateful people who may perceive it as weakness.

"As I spent more time with Elizabeth, I could see how my love enriched her life – increasing her knowledge, steering her moral compass, and nurturing her happiness. Seeing my values reflected in her – and enabling her success – increased my own happiness, as well. I was also flooded with an unexpected feeling of 'power,' and I mean 'power' in the most positive sense of the word.

"I felt like I had the power to expand myself – not in a physical sense, of course, but in a spiritual sense. If you think about it, I was leaving the physical limits of my body to recreate a part of me inside another person's soul. When people talk about the 'power of love,' this was it.

"I wanted to direct this power to a greater purpose – helping even more people reach their full potential. So when I returned to college, I renewed my determination to become a doctor, and lead the kind of research that would help save lives. I wanted to ensure that every child – such as Elizabeth - had a real opportunity to live out their dreams. I saw this commitment as my unique contribution to the triumph of love.

"Love was a product of my faith in God. And as I practiced it more frequently, I saw more proof of its power. I drew even closer to Him. I saw how love was the language of God – inspiring us to craft the highest vision of ourselves, and to shape the world in that image. If we choose to create with God – and the ultimate creative act is love – then we become, in a sense, God-like, as well.

"I pray to God every day, and while I won't claim to hear a response, it helps keep me grounded in my faith. I rarely go to church – not because I think church is wrong – but because my faith is such a private, personal matter. I feel like no one could ever truly understand it, or share it with me on a spiritual level. I'm not even sure why I shared it with you, except...well...I sensed you had an open mind about these sorts of things. I know it sounds strange, but even though I truly care for other people, I can't really make a total connection with them. I just don't feel like they understand me, and I think, deep down, everyone just wants to be understood, right? What do you think?"

I really didn't know what to think at this point. I was completely mesmerized by Heather's story – so honest, so unique, and so inspirational. Somehow, completely on her own, she had created some of the most insightful ideas about life that I ever knew existed.

I stammered for a response. "Well, I think you're right about that. I mean, I've spent most of my life trying to be understood too. God knows it hasn't been easy."

"Right, it hasn't been. But do you understand my point of view? If you don't, it's OK. I know it's a lot to swallow at once."

"It is," I said, collecting my thoughts. "But it's more than that. What you're saying is something I've never heard before - that reason and faith can co-exist. Until now, I've always believed they were in conflict – and that I had to reject one or the other in order to make sense of the world."

"I know. It's a false choice," she declared. "And it's uncertain whether our culture can survive such a choice. Right now, we have two separate philosophies about life– the first is traditional religion, and the other is nihilism. They seemingly have nothing in common – except the rejection of man's mind. The first insists on blind faith, and promotes the literal reading of Scripture as the only path to morality. The second rejects faith and morality as illusions, and requires obedience to whims and instincts as the only path to pleasure in a random universe. Sadly, this is the intellectual battlefield of our culture today. There is also a battle inside our very souls, as most people swing back and forth between both views, leading to confusion, inadequacy, and despair.

"But where are the defenders of man's mind – the only organ that can process reality? Where are the promoters of reason – the only tool that has raised mankind up from the swamps to the stars?

"Reason is the only safe home for faith in the twenty-first century. The days of blind faith are over. It's simply too vulnerable to the rapid increase in human knowledge, and the existential doubt that knowledge inevitably produces. But if faith is conjoined to reason, it has nothing to fear from a person's intellectual advancement. This partnership is the only way to preserve an honest faith in a rapidly-changing world.

"Reason and faith are allies, and they're most powerful when used in tandem, although I will say that reason must come first, now and always. It is reason – and reason alone – that provides evidence for God, and the immortality of the soul. From those facts come faith – faith that God loves us, and that love is the highest expression of the soul. Looking back, it wasn't easy to see how losing my parents, or any of the setbacks in my life, were inherently 'good for me,' but through faith in the power of love, I can rise above that sorrow, and believe that the world – even now – is designed perfectly and blessed."

Despite the beauty of Heather's words, I needed to press a point that was sticking into my brain. "But where does this evidence for God's existence and the 'immortality of the soul' come from? I mean, I've never heard about any of this stuff until now. If scientists can poke a hole through your theory, then your entire chain of logic collapses."

"But Brian, it *is* the scientists who are conducting this research. They've been harshly criticized by the atheists and the hardcore believers alike. But that kind of resistance should be expected. After all, the power of ideas moves slowly until it reaches a critical mass. As an old philosopher once said, 'All truth passes through three stages. First, it is ridiculed. Second, it is violently opposed. Third, it is accepted as being self-evident.' I'm confident that these ideas will be regarded as self-evident within our lifetime.

"However, this paradigm shift – as remarkable as it is – will be, for most people, nothing more than a curiosity, unless it's accompanied by a personal life philosophy – a new approach to living in light of this revolutionary information. That's why I've constructed this idea of 'spiritual rational-ism,' which includes the concepts of self-interest, integrity, and love – everything that I've explained here today.

"I know it'll be challenging to advance these ideas into society – but I'm certain that, with enough time, we can open enough minds to their wisdom. As I said earlier, you can ignore what you *think* is true; but you can't ignore what you *know* is true.

"I'm especially hopeful about the new generation – young men and women like you and me– whose spiritual needs aren't being met by today's stale choices. They are hungering for a faith that is worthy of the name. They are demanding an alternative that is consistent with reality as they see it, but also elevates them to a lifetime of happiness."

"So what is that alternative?"

"I can sum it up in three words: Reason. Faith. Love."

"And what does that give you?"

"Happiness."

"So your theory is: reason, faith, plus love equals happi-ness?"

"Brian, that's not my theory. It's my life."

As we walked deeper into the park, the mid-afternoon clouds parted way, and the sun brought a rare burst of warmth to our skin. Looking ahead, I saw a faded green bench, and suggested we sit there for a while to enjoy the change of climate. After seating ourselves, we stared ahead in silence, totally absorbed in our thoughts.

I thought about the stunning beauty of Heather as a person – in her body, mind, and soul. She was virtuously flawless, as far as I could see. Every moment with her was an escape from the usual drudgeries of my daily life – all of the stress and fear. I felt like nothing in this world was wrong – at least not irredeemably wrong – as long as she was by my side. I just wished there was a way I could express my feelings for her – without seeming like a blathering fool.

"I understand you," I said, looking at her face, which was still focused on the horizon. She looked down at her clasped hands, and then over at me.

"I thought so," she whispered, bursting into a huge grin. I stared into her eyes for a good two seconds or so, but then I quickly looked away. I didn't want to create an awkward moment, or anything.

"Why did you think so?" I asked, glancing at the ground.

She gathered her thoughts for a few moments, and then stared back at me. She took a deep breath and said, "Because of the way you looked at Michelle's picture in the hospital. When I showed it to you, you were just so genuinely happy to see it. I could tell you had an open mind and a sensitive soul like me. That's a pretty rare combination. I hope you realize that."

"I do," I smiled. I felt like this was her way of telling me she cared about me, but I couldn't be certain. I needed to press further.

"Do you think of me as…a soulmate?"

As soon as those words fled my lips, I wanted to call them back. How could I say something so stupid? Typical of me!

"Sorry!" I blushed. "You don't have to answer that."

She blushed a little bit too, flinging her blond hair behind her right shoulder. Then she answered, "I do. I *do* think of you that way."

After hearing that, I could literally feel my heart flutter. I smiled in relief, and stared at her – but this time, when our eyes met, there was no need to look away. I was safe in her eyes. I was safe in her soul.

"Can I kiss you?" I asked without any fear or modesty, because I knew she would welcome me. Still, it was quite a thrill when she whispered – without any hesitation – "Yes."

I leaned forward, closed my eyes, and pressed my lips against hers. Then I opened my mouth, and she did the same, creating even more taste and excitement. I stroked her cheek, and she grabbed the back of my neck. We kept kissing – harder and deeper – without any need to come up for air. We were totally caught up in this explosion of pent-up emotion. We continued to kiss passionately for at least ten minutes – without even the slightest interruption. It was the most sensual and exhilarating experience of my entire life.

Finally, I got too greedy. I gradually moved my hand toward her chest – which was abundantly covered by several layers of clothes. I couldn't feel anything through all those layers, but even so, Heather pulled away and said: "Perhaps we should stop for today."

"O.K.," I said, feeling extremely chastised. But if I was in danger of hating myself, Heather came to the rescue with a big grin and an even bigger final kiss. Then she rose from the bench, and I followed suit.

After a few minutes, we reached a park exit that was close to the metro station. We boarded the subway together, totally aglow from today's events. When we reached the Foggy Bottom stop, she gave me a peck on the cheek, and said "Bye." I reluctantly replied, "See ya," and continued on into Alexandria.

It was a wild, incredible afternoon in every way. I had learned so much about Heather – the *real* Heather – and how she managed to survive despite such a difficult upbringing. Through the raw power of her mind, she had created a life philosophy that caused her soul to shine – and that had touched my soul, as well. She gave me a renewed sense of purpose, and a revitalized faith in my future.

As I rode on the subway escalator, I said a small prayer, consisting of three simple words: "Thank you, God." For the first time in months, the idea of God meant something to me – and I didn't want to lose that feeling again. Starting today, I would try to combine reason and faith, and use the power of both to bring happiness into my life – once and for all.

Chapter 10

During the next week, Heather and I exchanged emails every day, sharing even the smallest details of our daily lives, but we never made any firm plans for the weekend. I think that was because we were subconsciously afraid that our second meeting would be a psychological letdown. After all, our initial date was so emotionally explosive it was inevitable that the sequel could never live up to expectations. We wanted to savor the memory of that kiss for as long as humanly possible, and leave it untainted by the inevitable challenges of our future.

When I called Heather on Monday night, I explained my theory to her, and she admitted that it was probably true. "I just don't want to get my hopes up," she said. "I don't want to fall for you, and then hear, all of a sudden, that you've found somebody else."

I could see this was a real concern for her, so I continued to insist that I had no plans to leave her. "I think you're amazing," I said, "and I would never, ever hurt you. Besides, you're a great kisser!"

She laughed, and eventually the conversation turned to other topics – including my crappy job. Ever since I came back to America Next, I had found my paper-shuffling routine to be even more agonizing than usual. I knew there had to be a place where I could better apply my talents – whatever those talents might be.

"Are you looking for another job?" Heather asked me.

"No, not really."

"How come? What's holding you back?"

Well, my biggest excuse was sheer laziness. I simply didn't want to go through the hassle of reading the classifieds, writing a flurry of cover letters, and faxing them to people who would never look at them. But there was another reason: Everyone at the company had been so supportive of me during my injury, I felt like I had an obligation to stay.

But Heather argued that my only obligation was to reach my full potential. "Don't be afraid to see what opportunities are out there," she advised me.

So I started scouring the local newspapers, magazines, and websites for any available job opportunities. Not surprisingly, it was an ugly conglomeration of boring entry-level jobs (like the one I already had) and relatively interesting jobs that I simply wasn't qualified for. The whole process brought back painful memories of my post-graduation job hunt, when I felt like I had so little to offer the world. I was prepared to give up and postpone the search indefinitely when I saw an intriguing job ad in the *Washington Post*.

Apparently, the IMF – the same organization that was regularly protested by Troy's girlfriend – was creating a subdivision called the "Individual Empowerment Fund." The purpose of this subdivision was to provide loans to people living in developing countries so they could start their own businesses. The overall goal was to help these folks become economically independent so they could create a better future for themselves and their families. As part of the operation, the "IEF" was seeking a "Communications Manager" – a person who would oversee their media outreach, including crafting press releases and brochures to promote their success stories.

The position of "Communications Manager" appealed to the self-interested, creative side of me, while also allowing me to participate in a cause greater than myself. Still, despite its obvious perks, I feared the position was out-of-reach. After all, I didn't have any experience in communications – unless you count a single college class. Nonetheless, I decided to apply for the job anyway, and simply hope for the best.

Surprisingly, the next day I received a phone call from the organization's Communications Director – a high-pitched motormouth named Ryan DeMint – who asked me to come in for an interview. When I eventually met Ryan, he was hospitable, gregarious, and eager to learn about me as a human being. Specifically, he was curious about my values – what I prized in myself, and in other people. For the first time in my life, I felt like I could answer that question. I spoke about the power of reason, taking responsibility for my actions, and the need to help others in that mission. Sometimes I worried that I was being overly philosophical, but Ryan seemed to share my conclusions.

"I think your values are consistent with what we're trying to accomplish," he remarked. "We want to help people help themselves. In a very real sense, that's the only way to help them in the long-run."

"I agree," I said convincingly.

When we finished the interview, I felt strangely confident that I would get the job, and sure enough, two days later, I received an offer. I told Ryan that I'd have to think about it, but honestly, there was nothing to think about. This new job was exactly what I wanted: a place filled with creative opportunities in a cause I truly believed in.

I thought about calling Heather, and requesting her advice, but I already knew what she would tell me: the only person who could make the right decision was me. So, with that in mind, I decided to go for it.

After Ryan faxed me a signed offer letter, the deal was completed: I would be a Communicator Manager in exactly one month. I was so excited, I decided to call Heather after all, but she wasn't available. I still needed to tell someone – anyone – so I walked over to Troy's cubicle (where he was playing solitaire), and told him the good news.

"Hey, congratulations, man!" he shouted, leaping out of his seat.

"Thanks," I said. "I appreciate it."

"I'm very happy for you, although I'll miss having you around."

"Don't worry," I laughed, "I'll be just a couple of blocks away."

"Nah, I'm not worried," he scoffed, repressing any hint of vulnerability. "The only constant in life is change."

Troy went on to share a big change in his own life. After two years of dating, he was finally moving in with his girl-friend.

"Wow!" I said. "Congratulations!"

"Thanks," he said, somberly. "But can you do me a favor? Can you come to IKEA with me this weekend, so I can pick out some furniture for the new apartment? I promise it won't take long."

"Sure," I grumbled, dreading the prospect of returning to that God-forsaken place. "But wouldn't you rather have Julia go with you?"

"Nah, I need guy-stuff, and you're a guy. She's not...Thankfully."

I laughed, and once again, agreed to go with him. He promised to pick me up on Sunday morning, even though I could've sworn he didn't own a car. Oh well.

When Sunday came, I walked out of my room and found Mark sitting on the couch, reading a thick book called, *Savior, My Savior.*

"Hello," he said.

"Hi," I replied, picking up my keys from the kitchen counter. "Do you need anything from IKEA?"

"Why are you going to IKEA?" he asked.

"I'm helping Troy look for some new furniture."

"Is he moving into a new apartment, or something?"

"Yeah," I said. "He's moving in with his girlfriend."

As soon as I uttered those words, Mark closed his book, stared at the pitch-black TV screen, and then twisted his neck towards me. He seemed genuinely annoyed for the first time in his life. I must've said something offensive, but I had no idea what it could be.

"Why are you helping him?" he sighed.

"What?" I asked, thoroughly confused. But as he continued to stare at me, I realized what was troubling him: in his worldview, I shouldn't help an unmarried couple move in together. They should each have their own "sex-free apartment," at least until their wedding day. But Mark didn't press the point any further. Instead, he shifted to an even weirder subject.

"Do you know when Troy is going to return my jeep?' he asked.

"What do you mean?"

"When you were in the hospital, Troy asked if he could borrow my jeep so he could visit you – but now that you're out of the hospital, I figure he doesn't need it anymore."

"I never knew Troy had your jeep," I protested. "Why did you even give it to him?"

"Because he asked for it," Mark shrugged. "Besides, I could just take the subway."

"So could *he!*" I exclaimed, literally stunned by Mark's logic (or lack thereof). Somehow, Mark felt obligated to lend his jeep to Troy – and when Troy didn't return it, he refused to stand up for himself.

"Well," I sighed. "I'm meeting Troy downstairs in a few minutes. He's supposed to pick me up. Probably in *your jeep*. Do you want to come with me, so we can talk with him about it?"

"Nah," Mark brushed me off.

"Why not?"

"I don't want to see him."

"Um, why not?"

"Because…well…there's something dark about that man."

This begged the question: if Mark thought Troy was a "dark man," why did he give him the jeep in the first place? I thought about asking Mark about that, but it was pointless. For whatever reason, Mark felt perfectly comfortable sacrificing his most valuable possession to a person who represented the complete opposite of his values – and then relying on *me* to get *his* possession back. I suppose that attitude worked in Palestine, Ohio – and inside the cozy confines of Crossroads – but it didn't work in the rest of the world.

I stuffed my keys into my pocket, and said, "I'll let you know what happens."

When I arrived downstairs, I waited inside the lobby for about five minutes until I finally saw Mark's jeep pull alongside the curb – with Troy, sure enough, sitting in the driver's seat.

I entered the vehicle and immediately asked: "Why do you have Mark's jeep?"

"Umm…because he loaned it to me," he replied defensively.

"But that was months ago," I protested. "Don't you think you should give it back?"

"Why? He never asked for it."

"Well, you could've returned it *anyway.*"

"Come on, dude, don't be a douche."

I laughed as another friend stunned me with his stupidity. "How is doing the right thing 'being a douche?' Can you explain that to me?" But my question was conveniently ignored.

As the jeep strode onto the highway and accelerated, I noticed a loud rattling noise coming from the front of the vehicle.

"What's that?" I asked.

"What's what?"

"What's that rattling noise?"

"Beats the hell out of me," Troy casually replied. "I've heard it for a few weeks now. Whatever it is, it's not a problem."

"Well, it *could* be a problem," I corrected him. "Do you know anything about cars?"

"No. I'm from New York, remember?"

"Well," I sighed, "you'll need to get it fixed."

Troy cursed underneath his breath.

"What?" I asked.

"Fine, I'll get it fixed," he said, totally exasperated.

"And then you'll give it back to Mark?"

"Yes," he sighed, desperate to shut me up.

I smiled at my victory, but it irritated Troy, who stayed silent for a few minutes. Finally, he announced: "I told Julia about your new job."

"Oh yeah," I said with a noticeable lack of interest. I wasn't too concerned about his girlfriend's opinion, which was sure to be negative.

"Needless to say, she's not too happy about it."

"Well, I really don't care," I replied matter-of-factly.

"Geez, what's gotten into you lately?" Troy snapped at me. "Lately, you've been – I don't know – different."

"I've stopped caring about what other people think," I replied.

"Oh really?" he said, somewhat surprised. "Well, in that case, I'm happy for you. I've always encouraged you to be an individual and put away all that conformist bullshit."

"It's more complicated than that," I corrected him. "I've met someone. A woman."

"Oh really?" he repeated, even more intrigued. He triumphantly lit a cigarette and opened the window to carry out the fumes.

"Yeah, her name is Heather, and she's a med student at GW. She has such a unique and inspiring philosophy about life. She makes me feel like I can do anything if I just put my mind to it. Right now, I feel happier and more confident than at any time since I was a kid."

"Is she hot?"

"She's beautiful – but that's not why I'm dating her."

"I see," said Troy, fiddling with the car radio. Almost instantly, a young man's voice burned through the speakers and filled the vehicle, rhythmically chanting to an electronic beat.

You and me baby ain't nothin' but mammals
So let's do it like they do on the Discovery Channel
Do it again now
You and me baby ain't nothin' but mammals
So let's do it like they do on the Discovery Channel
Gettin' horny now.

"Did you bone her?" asked Troy, interrupting Bloodhouse Gang's chart-topping single. I cringed when I heard him say *"bone."* I had no desire to *"bone"* Heather in the way I've wanted to bone other women. Instead, I wanted to make love to Heather, and match our emotional intimacy on a physical level.

"I don't think she's ready for that," I answered. "I feel like something's holding her back, although I don't know what it could be."

"She's probably a virgin," said Troy, teeming with excitement.

"That's possible," I replied.

"In that case, let me tell you something I've learned about women: They don't want a guy who waits forever to make a move and then asks permission at every step in the process. They want a take-charge guy – someone who will bend them over and dominate them, no questions asked."

I laughed at Troy's knuckle-dragging perspective. "Do you ever listen to yourself, man? Don't you realize this is the twenty-first century?"

"This has nothing to do with the twenty-first century, or any century. This has to do with biology – the way human beings were designed by nature. Women want to be dominated – but only by a *dominant* man. They want to surrender to his power. But only if he's worthy of that act of surrender. If he *is* worthy, nothing will make her happier than being banged from behind, with her face firmly pressed against the ground."

"And how would you know that?" I asked, still highly skeptical.

"From a combination of personal experience and the latest scientific developments."

"What scientific developments?"

"The newest science is very straightforward – we are, in a very real sense, 'nothing but mammals.' Specifically, we're nothing but highly-evolved monkeys. We think like monkeys and, more often than not, we act like monkeys - just in a more sophisticated way. This is true in virtually every area of life – including sex. When people try to escape that fact – whether by ignoring it, or denying it through religion – all they get is frustration and disappointment. They should just embrace their instincts, instead of running away from them."

"I don't think Heather is prepared to embrace her instincts," I said diplomatically. "I'm pretty sure that's against her religion."

"Oh Christ!" shouted Troy, practically banging on his steering wheel. "Don't tell me you're hanging out with another religious nut!"

"No, she's not like Mark," I reassured him. "She has faith in God, but it's not a blind faith; it's a rational faith."

"What the hell does that mean?"

"It means she's studied the latest science - apparently different from the science you've been studying – and based on that information, she's found solid reasons to believe in God. I've also done some research on the subject, and I have to say, the evidence is very convincing."

I could see Troy's rage building inside him. "Dude, did you go to school?" he spewed. "Did they teach you anything there?"

"I thought schools were corrupt institutions that teach us to serve our corporate overlords," I replied, mocking his statement from our first conversation.

"Don't be an asshole," he warned. "Nobody who's taken a high school science class can honestly believe in God, or any kind of greater meaning to the universe. It's that simple."

"Why is it that simple?"

"Because the science is irrefutable: God doesn't exist, the universe is meaningless, life is a random accident, and morality is an illusion. I know some people have a hard time accepting those facts, but I've never heard anyone use *reason itself* to deny it. I think your girlfriend needs to take a second look at the evidence. So do you, for that matter."

"But what if it's *you* who needs to take a second look at the evidence? Why are you so afraid of the idea that maybe, just maybe, there's something beautiful out there in the world?"

"Because it's all a bunch of bullshit! I know for a fact God doesn't exist. Do you hear me? I know for a fact!"

"Fine. What's the fact? Tell me. I want to hear it."

Troy cast a skeptical glance toward me, and then asked me a haunting question: "Have you ever lost the only thing you ever loved?"

Despite the pain in my past, there was only one truthful answer: "No, I haven't."

"Well, I have," he said, proudly. "Let me tell you something: When I was growing up in New York, I was very lonely – lonelier than you could ever possibly imagine. Nobody wanted to hang out with a shy, scrawny geek like me. I was all by myself. I pestered my mom for a sibling but she said she was too old to have another child. Even so, I received some encouragement from my Aunt Sylvia (who was the only person in our family who went to church). She said that if I prayed to God, my wish could come true.

"So that's what I did. And when I was nine years old, my wish really did come true. Even though she was approaching 40 years old, my mom gave birth to a healthy baby boy. She named him Adam.

"With Adam in my life, I felt whole and happy. Even though he couldn't think or speak – and his biggest talent was shitting his diaper – I loved him so much, because with him, I no longer felt alone in the world. I had a purpose. And my purpose was *him*.

"I was so grateful to God for that purpose – although I never discussed it with my parents. They were a pair of lapsed Catholics who found salvation through practicing corporate law. But whenever Aunt Sylvia came to visit our family, she would quietly take me to mass. Just the two of us. I didn't understand all of the church's rules and regulations. But I didn't need to. The only thing that mattered was that a big guy in the sky was taking care of us. I took comfort in that, and I had no reason to doubt it.

"Later on, when I entered junior high and high school, our teachers gave us plenty of reasons to doubt it. But I just memorized the information they fed us and proudly regurgitated it, without ever bothering to understand its implications. What was the point of such curiosity? I just wanted to pass my exams and become valedictorian.

"Still, I would have to confront those implications soon enough. Shortly after his fifth birthday, Adam started getting inexplicably sick, staying in bed all day, and losing weight. I figured he must have the flu or something, and I begged my parents to take him to the doctor. On the day of his appointment, I had to stay late at school. When I came home around 7:30, the place was completely empty. My parents weren't home (but that was normal, because of their jobs). What *wasn't* normal was that Adam and our housekeeper were also gone. I knew –deep down inside - that something was terribly wrong.

"I made myself a peanut butter and jelly sandwich, but I was too nervous to eat it. Finally, I heard someone unlocking the front door, so I ran in from the kitchen to see who it was. When the door opened, I could see our housekeeper Maria – standing alone, broken, slouched with the weight of the world on her shoulders.

"'What happened?' I asked frantically.

"She stood there, seemingly oblivious to me, until she whispered: 'Your brother is very sick. He isn't coming home. I'm sorry.' Then she spun around to leave, but I wouldn't let her.

"'What do you mean he's sick?'" I asked, grabbing her shoulder.

"'I'm sorry, Troy,' she repeated, gently removing my hand. "Your parents asked me to come here and tell you that. That's all I know. If you want to know more, you'll have to speak with them.' Then, as she entered the elevator, she looked back at me one last time and said, 'Pray.' And with that, she was gone.

"But I still needed more answers, so I searched my father's desk, looking for any possible clues. Eventually, I found his daily planner, along with the name of the doctor and hospital they were visiting.

I left the apartment, hailed a cab, and went to the hospital to find Adam and my parents. When I arrived, I did a little investigating, and found the rest of my family in a small, sterile room – with Adam lying asleep in the bed, and my parents standing around him.

"'What's wrong with him?' I whispered, pointing my finger at my sick little brother.

"'Shhh' said my father, who rose from his seat and grabbed my elbow, before leading me outside the room so we could chat alone.

"'You shouldn't be here,' he said, with an even mix of sadness and anger.

"'Why not?' I responded with pure venom. 'If Adam's sick, why can't you tell me? Why are you afraid to be honest with me? Aren't you even slightly embarrassed that *Maria* had to do *your* dirty work?'

"My dad lifted his hand to strike me – something he had never done before in his whole life. But he held back, for some reason. 'I did this for you,' he pleaded. 'I wanted you to remember him the right way.'

"'What the fuck are you taking about?' I shouted, briefly forgetting that I was talking to my father, and not some total stranger.

"'Adam has leukemia. He has about six months to live; a year at the most. There, I said it. Are you happy now?'

"I had spent hours imagining the worst – and now that I knew the worst, I kneeled on the ground and broke down in a hailstorm of tears.

"'I want to see him,' I whined, through my blubbering mess. 'I want to talk to him.'

"'No,' my father said firmly. 'I can't allow that. Trust me, it's for the best.'

"Somehow, I accepted his judgment – not just for that night, but for many months after that. My mom quit her job to be with Adam, and my dad split his time between Adam and the office. So I essentially lost my entire family that year. Then again, Aunt Sylvia visited me more frequently, and we prayed together even more fervently, but from what we were hearing, it was totally pointless.

"Finally, one day, my father called me from the hospital, and said I could see Adam for five minutes, but I needed to be 'strong for him.'

"When I arrived at the hospital, my dad repeated his instructions, and then opened the door to Adam's room. Once I walked through, I saw my bald kid brother, or at least what was left of him.

"'Hi, buddy,' I whispered, trying desperately to 'remain strong.'

"'Troy?' he murmured.

"'Yes,' I said, pulling up a chair.

"'I missed you.'

"'I missed you too, buddy.'

"'Troy, why is this happening to me?'

"In my private thoughts, I had asked that same exact question for almost a year, and I was still waiting for an answer. There was none. I could only reply somberly, 'I don't know.'

"'Where am I going?' he asked, hoping I could at least resolve that mystery. But I had nothing to offer except a tired cliché.

"'You're going to a better place,' I reassured him, even though I didn't believe it. I knew I was lying, but for Christ's sakes, what else could I say in that situation? I just wanted to ease the poor boy's pain.

"Finally, my dad re-entered the room, meaning it was time for me to leave – probably forever. I leaned over Adam's bed and kissed him on the forehead. Then I put my hands on both his cheeks, looked into his soft brown eyes, with our noses almost touching, and whispered: 'I love you.'

"'I love you too,' he said, and those were the last words he ever said to me. Adam died three weeks later in the middle of the night.

With those words, Troy's story had come to an end.

"I'm so sorry," I said. In all this time, I had never suspected that my friend had suffered so much. And yet, somehow, it all made sense.

"If you're so sorry, you won't bring up that God bullshit anymore – because no God would allow something like that to happen to His children."

"But if there *was* a God – I mean, if you *knew* there was a God – wouldn't you feel reassured that this was all part of His plan?"

"I don't think you understand," said Troy, defensively. "I don't *want* there to be a God. After what happened to Adam, it's easier for me to believe He doesn't exist. But if He *did* exist, I'd spit in His face. I'd piss on Him, shit on Him, whatever. Fuck Him, man! Fuck *Him!*"

I leaned back in my seat, growing increasingly scared by the words coming out of Troy's mouth. With every passing second, he seemed to be losing more control over his emotions.

"None of it matters, man. When are you going to understand that? We're born. We live for a while. We die. We're eaten by maggots. And then we become maggot shit. That's all. And you know what? That's fine with me. I'm totally cool with that. It might have taken me a while – about three years of psychotherapy - but eventually I made peace with it. Instead of resisting the truth, I embraced it. So should you."

"And what's the truth?" I asked.

"The ultimate truth? We're all maggot shit."

"Oh come on! Is that what you *really* think?"

"Yeah, man. Look, *I* don't matter. *You* don't matter. Adam doesn't matter. None of it matters. And when you come to realize that, my friend, you're free. You're liberated. You can do whatever you want."

"And does that make you happy?" I asked.

"There's no reason to be happy, man. We just have to make the best of the situation – and that means understanding the truth, embracing it, and indulging in the few pleasures life has to offer."

"So you think we should live like animals?" I asked, a little irritated.

"I think the best solution is to follow our instincts," he declared, "and if that means being an animal, so be it. If you look at animals, they might not seem happy, per se, but they definitely don't seem *un*happy, either. I'm pretty sure most people would settle for that. We could probably learn a lot from those four-legged creatures."

"So we – as human beings – *can't* be happy? Is that what you're trying to tell me?"

"If a person can ignore the truth for their entire life, then yes, they can probably be happy. I suppose your pal Mark fits into that category. But for the rest of us, we have to choose – usually in the inner layers of our subconscious – between happiness and truth. You can't have both, buddy."

"But what if you can?" I asked. "Why is that so impossible to believe?"

"Because of what happened to Adam. And what happens to all of us at one point or another. We're all victims of evil, and that evil is senseless and stupid. I mean, you were beaten up by a bunch of thugs with a baseball bat. While you laid there bleeding, they smiled at you. Think about it: they found pleasure in your pain. They enjoyed your suffering. So the question is: How do you account for the 'joy of evil?' How can you consider the world to be 'fair' when evil is *happier* than good? If you're going to challenge my ideas, you better have a damn good explanation for that."

I didn't have an explanation (at least not yet), but I thought Heather might have one. After all, she had a lot of experience dealing with suffering.

"I still think there's a way to change your perspective," I explained. "I mean, Heather helps children with cancer – kids like Adam – and sometimes they die, and…"

"What the hell does she know?" shouted Troy. "None of those kids were her *brother*. I lost my *brother*. That's a big difference!"

For the first time, I could see tears in Troy's eyes, and since I felt responsible for those tears, I put my hand on his shoulder (which is something I never do) and said, "Sorry, man. I didn't mean to..."

In a flash, he slapped my hand away, and angrily said, "Don't touch me, fag!"

I was stunned by Troy's response, and a little annoyed too. After all, I was just trying to help the poor bastard, and he insulted me for it. But I kept my mouth shut. I just stared straight ahead, and waited for an apology.

Finally, as we pulled into the IKEA parking lot, the apology came.

"I'm sorry I called you a fag," he said, without even bothering to look at me. I continued to stare ahead, completely oblivious to him.

"You're a good friend," he continued, this time glancing at me. "You understand me. You may not agree with me all the time. But you understand me, and I appreciate that." Then he stuck out his hand, hoping I would shake it. I looked at him skeptically, but I shook his hand anyway.

"It's alright," I said. "Come on, let's go see the IKEA people."

"If you say so," he said with a wink.

As we jumped out of the car and marched toward the store, I thought about the impact that tragedies can have on human beings. For both Mark and Troy, the death of a loved one had been the seminal event of their lives, but they learned different lessons from that event. In Mark's case, the passing of his father had strengthened his faith, and reinforced his positive outlook on life. But for Troy, when his brother died, his faith died too, trapping him in a one-man prison of hate and nihilism. I was tempted to see these divergent paths as proof of the power of each person to choose his own values, and live accordingly.

But was it really? Did Mark and Troy really *choose* their reactions to adversity, or was the choice already made for them? From the time he was born, Mark was immersed in a small-town, caring community that supported him in a time of confusion and despair. But Troy never had that kind of support system. At an early age, he was estranged from any form of organized religion, which was frowned upon by his workaholic parents. Even worse, he eventually became estranged from those same parents, who worshipped their dead son, but neglected the one who was still living. Even though Troy grew up in a city of eight million people (much larger than Palestine, Ohio), he was utterly, completely alone.

So I could see how my friends ended up on different paths, after all. But it was much harder to see why they stayed there, especially in Troy's case. I was offering Troy a chance to see the world in a new and better way – to escape the prison he had built for himself. But he didn't care. He was strangely comfortable inside those prison walls. In fact, the only time he seemed *un*comfortable was when someone opened the door, turned on the light, and offered him a chance to walk out. While Troy claimed to be an "intellectual arsonist," the truth was the opposite: he was a moral and mental imbecile. But would he ever realize the errors of his way? Would he ever choose to change his perspective? I honestly didn't know.

I suppose the key test is whether Troy fixes Mark's jeep, and returns it to its rightful owner. If he doesn't, I suppose the key test for Mark is whether he'll try to reclaim it for himself. Shit, if you think about it, this whole situation is crazy – and a perfect illustration of the failure of their philosophies. I almost feel stupid for ever taking them seriously. But I guess it's all part of the learning process.

In the meantime, I'm moving forward with my life. I'm starting a new and better job, and more importantly, I have an incredible woman standing by my side: Heather Manning.

Chapter 11

Heather was the most complicated (and interesting) person I had ever met. She was the most rational (and the most spiritual) human being I ever knew. She was the epitome of happiness (and a survivor of great unhappiness). She was an engine of ambition (and a loving playmate of children). And as it turned out, she loved animals too.

For our second date, Heather said we should visit the Washington Zoo, which had a huge collection of lions, tigers, monkeys, elephants, and of course, the world-famous giant panda.

When we arrived at the panda cage, Heather crouched down and pressed her nose against the glass, hoping the cuddly creature would come closer to her. But the panda was too busy chomping on her bamboo sticks to pay attention to anyone else. So Heather kissed the glass and left a foggy imprint of her lips that immediately began to fade. For some reason, that sparked the animal's attention, and she came waddling toward us, pressing her black paw against the kiss mark. In our excitement, Heather and I started kissing the glass in several places, and the bear duly followed us, pressing her paw against each bit of moisture we left for her. The other people in the zoo were staring at us, and probably thinking we were crazy. But we didn't care. We were rediscovering our inner child – exploring the world with an open mind and an open heart – and we were enjoying every minute of it.

When the zoo closed, I put my lips to even better use – by pressing them against Heather's lips, and giving her some tongue, to boot. But I reluctantly stopped there – still chastised by the lecture I received during our last make-out session. Even so, I loved the taste of her mouth, the touch of her skin, and the scent of her body. When she was in my arms, I was in Heaven on Earth. If only I could bring myself to say those fateful words, "I love you." But I wasn't ready for that moment of vulnerability.

On our third date, we took a more intellectual route, by spending the day at the National Archives – which is the home of America's founding documents, including the Declaration of Independence.

When we stood in front of the Declaration, we silently read it to ourselves, until Heather found a part that demanded to be read out loud:

> "We hold these truths to be self-evident that all men are created equal, that they are endowed by their Creator with certain unalienable rights, that among these are Life, Liberty, and the pursuit of Happiness."

"Isn't that beautiful?" she asked me.

"Yeah, I think so."

"Did you notice the word 'Creator?'"

"Of course."

"Do you think other people notice it?"

"What do you mean?"

"I mean, do you think other people notice that our unalienable rights come from a Creator, and not from a 200-year old piece of paper?"

"I'm not sure," I said. "Why does it matter?"

"Our Founders believed that a free country is a country *under God*. Without God, there can be no freedom."

"Why is that?" I asked, always skeptical about bold assertions.

"Because if human beings are made in the image of God, then we have an 'unalienable right' to be free. But if we're 'nothing but mammals,' then our rights can be taken away, with little argument. After all, we're just unruly animals that need to be disciplined.

"But we're not just animals," I declared. "We have free will, intelligence, and morality."

"Oh, I agree," she said with a twinkle. "But not everyone agrees with us, and I wish they'd see the logical consequence of their arguments." Apparently, she had known a few Troys in her lifetime, and she understood the dangers of their philosophy.

On our fourth date, we faced off in a round of mini-golf, one of my special fortes. Early on, Heather could see I wasn't trying too hard, and deliberately letting her win. But that just annoyed her.

"Don't hold anything back!" she warned, playfully threatening me with the golf club. Then she put the club down, put her hands around my waist, and lifted her head up to kiss me. I was dazzled by her unscripted show of passion.

When she went back to hit the golf ball, she bent forward slightly and a necklace popped out from underneath her white shirt. I marched up to her, pointed at her necklace, and asked: "What are you wearing?" It looked like a standard gold cross, but with a huge oval protruding from the top of the cross. It was quite beautiful.

"It's called an ankh," she said, without hesitation. "It's an early Christian symbol that symbolizes the union of Heaven and Earth."

"Why do you wear it?" I asked curiously.

"Because even though I'm a Christian, I don't think most Christians would accept me, as such. So I've adopted the symbol of an older, and I would say, more rational form of Christianity."

"Did the early Christians believe in reason?" I asked, a little surprised.

"Oh yes," said definitively. "I'll have to explain that to you sometime."

"Please do," I said, holding the ankh for a closer inspection. "Actually, it looks like a normal cross, but with a giant head sticking out of it. Considering your philosophy, that seems appropriate for you."

Heather laughed. "I never noticed that before, but you're absolutely right. I hope that doesn't freak you out."

"Not at all," I said confidently. "In fact, I think it's great." She smiled at my compliment, and rose on her tippy toes to give me another smooch.

When our date was over, we discussed plans for the next weekend. I suggested a camping trip in the Shenandoah State Park, about an hour west of Washington. Even though Heather liked the idea, she didn't own any camping gear. Actually, I didn't have any camping gear either, but I knew Mark kept some in the storage room.

When I asked Mark about it, he seemed thrilled about giving it to me. As a general rule, he was always happy to sacrifice his possessions.

"Who are you going camping with?" he asked.

I knew Mark wouldn't be pleased about Heather and me sleeping together in his tent. So I discreetly replied, "I'm going with a friend." Surprisingly, Mark didn't push the issue. We went to the storage room, picked up his rolled-up tent, two sleeping bags, and a miniature grill, and brought them back to the apartment.

"Hey, maybe we can go camping sometime," said Mark, dropping the grill on the floor.

"Yeah, I like that idea," I said, wiping my sweaty brow. I was being sincere, but with Heather in my life, I didn't have a lot of free time anymore. In a real sense, I was growing beyond Mark – even though I would always be grateful that he invited me to share his "sex-free" apartment.

Speaking of which, I faced a genuine dilemma as I packed for our camping trip. Ever since that first (and only) time I had sex in college, I owned a bag of condoms (that had never been opened). I was tempted to finally open the box and bring a condom with me on the trip. I mean, let's face facts: Heather and I would be sleeping next to each other in a tight and cozy tent. We've known each for a few months. We've made out a few times. And I was definitely in love with her. From that perspective, I stood a pretty good shot, right?

But then again, she was strangely ambivalent about getting close to me (at least in a physical sense). I mean, shit, we hadn't even been to second base. I hated her prudishness, but I needed to respect it. I couldn't force her to do something against her will. I just don't operate that way.

But still...but still...I didn't want to be caught unprepared. Even if the odds were 100-to-1, I still needed to put those rubbers in my backpack. I checked the expiration date on the box, and luckily for me, they were still good for another year. That was great news, because I didn't want to go to CVS, buy a brand-new box of condoms, and have the cashier think to herself: "Sinner! Sinner! This man is a sinner!"

But why was I a sinner? Personally, I never thought of sex in terms of sin and salvation. I thought of it as a natural, and appropriate, expression of love between a man and a woman. I just wondered how Heather felt about the whole thing.

When Heather came by on Saturday morning, she arrived in a rented, red jeep, since neither of us owned a car of our own. We filled the jeep with our junk, put our butts in the seats, and then sped towards the campsite. For the most part, we rode with the windows down, breathing in the fresh, early April air, and absorbing the green scenery that lined the small-town roads far from Washington, DC.

When we arrived at the campsite, we paid our daily fare to the teenage boy who was guarding the place, and then drove to the lot he assigned for us. The lot itself was a mostly-grassy plain, shielded by a circle of high-rising, blooming trees, and overlooking a valley with a stream running through it.

Heather and I pulled the folded-up tent from the back-seat of the jeep, and then dumped it in the middle of the grassy plain.

"Do you know how to put this thing together?" she asked.

"I put one together a few years ago," I replied, "but now I forget how to do it. What about you?"

"I *saw* a guy put one together," she said with a straight face. Then we laughed at our own incompetence. Luckily for us, there was a packet of instructions buried inside the deflated tent. Heather read the instructions and I duly acted upon them – kind of like an assembly line. Growing up in the suburbs, I was never very good with manual labor, so I made a few mistakes along the way. But eventually I was able to sort it out, and create a fully usable, upright tent.

"Great job!" shouted Heather, slapping my hand for a high-five. Then we went back to the jeep, pulled out the sleeping bags, and dragged them into the tent.

"Which one do you want?" she asked, sitting on the floor.

"I guess I'll take the black one," I said, hovering above her.

"O.K., in that case, I'll take the white one," she said, leaving a small space between the sleeping bags – just in case I had any naughty ideas.

After we finished setting up, I laid down in my sleeping bag, and announced, "I think I need a nap."

"No way, goofball!" Heather protested, playfully kicking me with her feet. "Get up. We're going for a hike!"

"We are?" I yawned.

"Oh yes," she insisted. "Now get up."

A few minutes later, we started following a narrow dirt trail that weaved its way through the peaks and valleys of the tranquil park. We climbed over giant rocks and fallen trees, and even dodged a mid-afternoon drizzle. As we ran through the rain, I grabbed Heather's hand and guided her to a dry shelter a hundred yards ahead. Once I had her hand in mine, I never let it go for the rest of the day.

A few hours later, we finally emerged at the end of the trail, slightly wet, and *very* hungry.

"Let's jump in for a quick shower and then I'll make dinner for us, OK?" said Heather, taking charge of the situation. I flashed a mischievous grin, but before I could crack a joke, she continued: "I mean, let's take showers *separately.*"

"I know," I said impishly. If there was any shred of hope for sex, it was blown away by that comment. Those aging Trojans would have to wait for another occasion – maybe forever. But honestly, it didn't matter to me. We were having a great time, and I wasn't going to jeopardize that.

When I finished my shower, I changed into a clean outfit and then marched back to our tent where Heather was already cooking a pot of macaroni and cheese.

"Mmm, my favorite," I said, thinking back to my childhood days when my mom would cook mac and cheese for me twice a week! And you wonder why I was fat! But I wasn't fat anymore. Now I could treat myself to a yummy meal every once in a while – without cursing at myself in the mirror for the rest of the night.

I sat down at our picnic table, and Heather poured me a pot of mac and cheese, and then sat across from me to share in the supper.

"This is great!" I said, scarfing it down with reckless abandon.

"Thanks," Heather replied. "I'm glad you like it."

A few forkfuls later, I thought back to the last conversation I had with Troy, and one of his questions that required Heather's attention.

"Did I ever mention my friend Troy?" I asked.

"Yeah, a few times. Why?"

"Well, I was talking to him about some of your beliefs, and he brought up an interesting point: If being good means being happy, why do some people find happiness in evil? I mean, when I was beaten up by those thugs last year, they seemed to be having a grand ole' time. How do you account for that? Isn't that a major hole in your philosophy?"

"Wait, what are you talking about?" Heather asked. "What beating? When did this happen?"

In my haste, I had accidently spilled one of my deepest secrets (although it should never have been a secret in the first place). I went on to explain the incident, and then I apologized for misleading her. She accepted my apology with a full and open heart. So then I returned to my original question: "How do you account for 'the joy of evil?'"

"There is no joy in evil," she corrected me. "But there *is* joy in power. Do you remember, during our first date, when I talked about power?"

"A little bit," I confessed.

"Let me start off by saying that we, as human beings, want our lives to have a greater purpose. We need to matter. And therefore, we're constantly looking for ways to say, 'Look at me! I matter!' But we can't matter when we're all by ourselves. We need other people to validate our existence. We need other people to say, 'Yes, you matter!' And therefore, we're always trying to find a way to plant a part of ourselves in other people. Our ideas. Our values. Our talents. The point is, it's not good enough to be in-charge of our own lives. We need to express ourselves as individuals, and have a lasting impact on the lives of others. That is the power instinct.

"In healthy, rational people, that instinct has a positive purpose – whether it's falling in love, or raising a child, or saving a life. We find pleasure by expressing ourselves through the act of helping others. These creative acts give us a chance to say, 'This is who I am! I matter!' and those acts are done in a way that elevates other people, instead of tearing them down.

"But when it comes to irrational, unhealthy people – the people who have forfeited their minds – the power instinct serves a negative purpose. These people hate the world. They live in a state of fear. But they still desperately want to matter. In fact, they want to feel *superior* to other people. They think to themselves, 'I'm not the same as everybody else; I'm *better*!' So they're always hunting for someone to look down on, and stomp on. They assert their power by abusing people – whether it's verbal abuse or physical abuse. Sometimes they even kill people. Through violence, they feel strong. They feel relieved. The anxiety of their daily lives has disappeared – if only for a brief moment. That's why they smile. But pretty soon, the fear comes back, and with that fear comes the need to commit more evil. The cycle continues, until they finally choose to escape it.

"So, you see, Brian, there is no 'joy of evil.' The people who hurt you are sad, miserable cowards. Even what they see as power is powerless. Evil itself is powerless. Evil is nothing."

"Evil is nothing?" I asked, incredulously.

"In the grand scheme of things it is," Heather replied. "I won't claim – like some Buddhist monk – that reality is an illusion. I'm sure it hurt like hell when that baseball bat hit your body. That pain was real. That pain was something. But evil itself is nothing."

"What do you mean?" I pressed her.

"The good is the mind. Evil is the anti-mind. The good is the creator. Evil is the destroyer of that which the good has already created. Evil is a parasite that can only feed on the good. It can accomplish nothing on its own. It is intrinsically inferior. It is virtually powerless. Evil can only triumph when good people do nothing."

"How do we get rid of evil?" I asked.

"We should encourage people to think rationally for themselves. When people use reason and a rational code of ethics, they will feel empowered to live in a world that makes sense. They will feel competent and morally entitled to live on this Earth. And they'll be happy. But when people surrender their minds, they feel helpless and powerless, and they mask their powerlessness through the drug of superiority. Oh, Brian, think of the tragedy we could avoid in this world, were it not for this wicked lust to feel superior! Instead, we are left to feel the rage of those who hate to be human, ready to commit any act that screams to the world: 'I *am* powerful!'"

"But they don't know what real power is," I said.

"Exactly," said Heather, scooping up the last forkful of macaroni on her plate. "Love is the real power. Love is the only thing that matters. And that's why I love you, Brian."

"What?" I asked, in shock.

"I love you," she repeated. I had been waiting forever to hear those three magical words, and now, finally, she had spoken them to me. I felt like every emotion I had experienced but ignored over the past few months - every hope I had cherished but doubted, every dream I had adored but dismissed - was real, so very real, after all.

"I love you too," I replied. "I've loved you since the first day I met you." I stood up, emotionally naked before her. Then she stood up, emotionally naked before me. Then we hugged each other for several minutes, like reunited souls who had spent a lifetime trying to find each other. Before, we had dared to hope for love. Now, we knew the truth: Our love was real.

After we watched the sun go down, there wasn't much to do, except hop inside the tent and go to bed. As we changed into our sleeping outfits, we instinctively turned away from each other to avoid any peeks from our partner. I guess some habits are hard to break.

When I was finished, I asked: "Is it alright if I turn around now?"

"Yes," she replied meekly. When I saw her, she was already buried underneath her sleeping bag, and turned on her side. I opened my own sleeping bag, and wrestled inside to get comfortable.

"Good night," said Heather, lifting her head to give me a kiss.

"Good night," I replied, smooching her lips.

"I really do love you," she said, tossing her hair back.

"And I love you too," I responded. Then I reached up for another kiss. And then another. And then another.

"One second," she whispered with a smile. Then she opened both of our sleeping bags and pushed them together, so it was almost like we were laying in a single bed. We took advantage of our newfound flexibility by moving closer together, and wrapping our legs around each other. As we kissed passionately, I stroked her long blond hair, and she caressed my cheek. Then all of our hands started moving south.

First she placed her palm on my hairy chest, and rubbed my pecks provocatively. Next, feeling emboldened, I lifted her t-shirt and touched her left breast. I expected her to jerk away, but she welcomed my aggression, and even moved closer toward me. So I squeezed her plump tit with lustful fury, and then massaged her erect nipple. Needless to say, I was having an erection of my own – as my crotch throbbed in anticipation of unknowable bliss. Impatiently, I moved my hands even further south – from her tits to her lower back, to her firm, round ass.

But I wanted even more. I wanted to touch her most cherished possession, and then go inside it – to a place where

I presume no man had even been. I wanted to be the first –
and only – man to know her fully in mind and body. And she
seemed to offer no resistance. In fact, she spread her legs
ever-so-slightly, as if to invite me to advance further. I had no
choice but to take her cue, and follow my convictions. So I
pushed my fingers further down, and latched onto her sweet
spot.

"What are you doing!" she shrieked, slapping my hand
away, and recoiling back into her sleeping bag.

"What?" I asked meekly, stunned by her response.

"Don't touch me there," she lectured me, pulling her
knees against her chest, like a frightened child.

"I'm sorry," I said, afraid I had ruined everything forever. "I just wanted to express my love for you – not just in
words, but in action."

"Is that what you call it? Love?" she asked disdainfully.

"Yes. I love you, Heather. When I touch you, it's out of
love. There's no hidden agenda there. I just want to share a
wonderful experience with you."

She looked at me skeptically, but not angrily. I could
sense that she needed to be comforted and reassured. So I
aimed to soothe her with my words.

"Look, I know you're a virgin," I began sympathetically.
"But I feel like…"

"I'm not a virgin," she said, interrupting me in a coarse
voice. Now it was my turn to be shocked and appalled.

"What?" I asked.

Then she looked away in embarrassment. We sat there
silently, unsure of what to say to each other. Finally, Heather
started talking about an issue she was familiar with: philosophy.

"What is evil?" she asked stoically.

I thought about it for a few seconds, reminiscing from
our conversation earlier in the day. "Evil is the anti-mind," I
responded. "Evil is the mind gone blank."

"In your lifetime, have you experienced that?"

"Yes," I said reluctantly. "I was beaten up and left to die. I already told you that."

Then she looked back at me, staring at me with sad, vulnerable eyes that cried out for help. Suddenly, I knew what was happening. But I didn't want to say anything. At least not yet.

"I've never told anyone this before," she began, "and I'm only going to tell it *one time*." After a brief pause, she continued, "During my freshman year of college, I had a crush on this guy. His name was Paul. He was in my pre-med class. Nice. Bright. Good-looking. He just seemed different from all the other guys. Like he had emotional depth or something. I don't know. But I liked him.

"Anyway, sometime in the fall, my roommate invited me to come to some frat party, and naturally I declined. But then she told me Paul was going to be there. So I put on a, shall we say, 'revealing outfit,' sprayed on some perfume, and headed off to the party.

"When I got there, I found Paul playing beer pong with some of his friends, and it was easy to see he was already smashed. We spoke for a little bit, but I was no longer interested, and I left as soon as I had the chance.

"When I got home, I took a shower, watched a little TV, and then went to bed." Then she stuttered. "And when I woke up, he was there."

I wrapped my arm around her shoulder, and she buried her head in my chest. Soon, my t-shirt was drenched with her salty tears.

"I never thought that could happen to me," she said, reliving the torment. "I always thought I could fight it off. And I tried to. But he just overpowered me. And I was so scared. I thought he might kill me."

"I know," I said, kissing her hair.

"I just thought to myself, 'God, why have you forsaken me?' I wanted to keep that gift for the man I loved. But it was stolen from me. It was stolen! Oh Brian, I'm so sorry."

"You have nothing to be sorry about," I said, fighting my own urge to cry. I just couldn't believe that anyone would want to hurt my innocent angel like that. I started to imagine the scene in that room – the darkness, the pain, the tears, the feeling of betrayal. I wished I could go back in time and protect her from that experience. But she was also a *product* of that experience – and so many others, as well - both good and bad. I thought to myself: Can we really condemn our past – even one small part of it – without condemning ourselves, as well? I'm not so sure. But Heather seemed to have an answer.

"I accept what happened," she said bravely. "I've come to terms with it. Every person must – at one point or another – confront an awful, inexplicable experience, and choose how to deal with it. I've *chosen* not to be a victim. I refuse to be a victim. It's an act of willpower. My mind – my identity – is mine alone. I will *never* surrender it to the darkness. I will never let it win."

"So why are you crying now?" I blurted out, insensitively.

"Well," she hesitated. "Because when you touched me there, it retriggered all of the emotions from that night. I hadn't been through that in years. It all came back to me in a rush. It overwhelmed me."

"I'm sorry," I said, genuinely ashamed of myself.

"It's OK," she replied. "The truth is, even though I've tried to be rational, I know that night has badly affected me – at least in terms of my sexuality. In the past few years, I've tried to isolate and remove all of my sexual feelings, and I've succeeded, for the most part. In fact, I no longer see the point of those feelings at all."

"You don't see the point in sex?" I asked incredulously.

"Not really," she said thoughtfully. "I just see sex as a way to relieve a physical urge, like eating, or – forgive me – going to the bathroom. It seems anti-mind. And I can only follow my mind."

I saw how Heather – that paragon of reason – had succumbed to the same perspective on sex that Mark and Troy adopted – that it was an animal act – to be avoided or indulged in for that purpose. I, on the other hand, always wanted sex to be something different, and better.

"I can only follow my mind too," I protested. "And my mind has led me to *you*. I love you so much. I want to spend every single moment with you. And I want to be as close to you as possible. I want to be *one* with you. I see sex as the expression of that ideal. I view it as the highest form of love. I just wish you saw it that way too."

"I know," she said somberly. "but I'm just not ready yet. I'm sorry."

"Don't be sorry," I said, hugging her, and wiping away the last of her tears. "I thank God for you. And I thank God for this experience." She smiled at me, and then opened her lips to speak. But I quickly put my finger against her lips, and she obeyed my instruction to stay silent. The time for talking was over. Now it was bedtime. This time, for real.

We slipped back into our sleeping bags, and rolled over onto our sides. I closed my eyes, let out a loud sigh, and drifted into that strange place between sleep and reality. But before I could cross into full sleep mode, I felt a tap on my shoulder, and a whisper in my ear:

"Brian...Brian."

"Whuhh?" I said, rubbing my eyes.

"Look at me," she said. I stared into her calm, purposeful eyes, and smiled.

"Please don't give up on me," she pleaded.

"I will *never* give up on you," I replied forcefully, touching her smooth, round face. "I *promise*." Then I sealed the deal with a kiss. But she refused to stop kissing me back. She stuck her tongue down my throat, and swirled it around with intensity. Then she mounted my body and rubbed her butt provocatively over my groin.

"Brian?" she whispered.

"Yes?"

"Will you make love to me?"

I couldn't believe what I was hearing.

"What? Are you sure?" I asked.

"Positive. Absolutely positive."

I still didn't quite believe her.

"Why don't we wait for another time?"

"No," she begged. "I need to have you now."

I could tell that she meant it. After all, Heather never did anything she didn't want to do, and she pursued every action with focus, passion, and commitment.

"O.K.," I said. "Hold on one second." I rose from my sleeping bag and walked over to the other side of the tent to unzip my backpack. Inside the backpack, I found the condom wrapper I thought I'd never use. I opened the wrapper, and pulled down my shorts, and placed the condom over my erect penis. Once I took off my t-shirt, I stood naked before her, and it didn't bother me at all. I didn't have a perfect body – far from it – but I felt accepted, and loved, and needed.

Heather had used the time to strip off her remaining clothes, and through the darkness, I could see the outlines of her nude body. Unlike me, she *was* physically perfect – at least according to my tastes. But after I had absorbed her feminine parts, I couldn't stop staring at her face – and the hopeful smile that invited me to explore her in a new and profound way.

I tossed the opened condom wrapper onto the ground, walked a few paces, and kneeled down just below the temple of her body.

"I love you," I said.

"I love you too," she replied, and those words never meant more to me than they did right now.

I put my hand on each of her ankles, and spread her legs apart. From there, I kneeled between her legs, and checked to make sure that my condom was still on properly. It was good to go. And so was I.

"Are you ready?" I asked tenderly.

"Yes," she smiled back.

"O.K.," I said. And then, I leaned forward over her body, put my fingers on the base of my penis, and directed it toward her entrance. Admittedly, it took a few seconds to find it.

But when I *did* find it, it was a moment of ecstasy. A bolt of electricity traveled instantly from my shaft to every inch of my body. I moaned in delight, and I could hear Heather sigh, as well.

From there, I pushed the rest of my penis inside of her, and I rested my entire body comfortably over hers. We were now one. One body. One soul.

"Does it hurt?" I asked, staring at her from above.

"No," she said, with shortened breath. "It feels good. Because I know it's *you.*"

We both smiled at each other. Then we kissed passionately, without any inhibition. I waded my fingers through her hair, and she wrapped her arms around my back. Those actions spurred my desire to get even closer to her – closer than I was now, closer than the laws of the universe would allow. In physical terms, my aspiration was translated into thrusting and pumping – sliding myself in and out her, at a faster and harder pace.

The friction from our bodies produced a tremendous amount of pleasure – both physically and mentally. This experience was so much better than my first conquest years ago. Back then, I thought to myself, "I am a man," but in truth, I was still clueless about what "being a man" actually meant. Granted, I knew how to fuck someone, but any animal could do that. Now, finally, at this magical moment, I could say, "I am a *real* man." Because I know what that word truly means. It means "I am love." I know to give love, receive love, and make love.

"Oh God," Heather sighed. She closed her eyes, bit her lower lip, and thrust her head back against the pillow. Then she unleashed a sharp, piercing yelp which forced her to cover her mouth with both her hands. I couldn't be sure, but I think she came. This was fine with me, because I couldn't hold my stuff in any longer.

"I'm going to come," I whispered.

"O.K.," she replied, happily.

Then I released myself. It was the most explosive and blissful feeling I had ever experienced. After the life force flowed out of me, my body went limp. I lied on top of Heather completely motionless, unable to move at all.

Finally, I mustered the energy to roll over next to her, and we lied there side-by-side, staring at the top of the tent.

"How do you feel?" I asked.

"Good," she said peacefully. "You?"

"Pretty good." Just then, I remembered I had a used condom dangling on me, and I needed to get rid of it.

"Gimme a second," I said, as I leaped from the sleeping bag. I walked over to the other side of the tent and put the condom in a plastic bag we were using for trash. Then I lied down in the sleeping bag again. Heather nestled her head on my chest, and wrapped one of her legs between mine.

"I love you," she said, twisting a strand of my chest hair.

"I love you too," I replied. And then we kissed for a final, memorable moment. Not long after, I fell into a deep, deep sleep, and I expected to stay there until morning. But, once again, I was awakened by a tap on the shoulder, and the chant of, "Brian...Brian."

"Whuhh?" I replied.

"Are you awake?"

"I am now," I said playfully.

"Get dressed and come with me," she said, planting a kiss on my cheek.

"What for?" I asked.

"You'll see."

I was too drained to argue, so I dutifully put on my clothes and shoes, and followed her outside the tent. From there, we walked hand-in-hand through the thick, dark forest.

"Where are we going?" I asked.

"You'll see," she repeated mysteriously.

We continued to wade through the area for at least two miles. Finally, we approached a long, flowing stream, and stood beside it. In the distance, we could see the sun coming up – slowly lighting the sky in a breathtaking mosaic of bright colors.

Heather reached into her pocket, and pulled out a gold necklace with a cross.

"He wore this," she said solemnly, referring to the man who had violated her. "When I was struggling, I managed to pull it off. And then he left it behind."

"I'm sorry," I said sympathetically. I stared at the token of that cruel night she was assaulted, and my heart flooded with rage.

"I've kept it in a box for over four years," she continued. "Every now and then, I'll open the box, and look at it, and study it. I'm not sure why I torture myself like that. I guess I do it to remind myself: 'Don't let a man come too close to you, or you'll get hurt.'" Then she looked up at me. "I was afraid to believe in love – the kind of love where you allow a single person to share your deepest feelings, and penetrate every form of your existence...But I'm not afraid anymore."

Then she rifled her arm over the back of her head, and threw the gold chain into the middle of the stream, where the rushing waters would carry it to some unknown destination.

"Thank you," said Heather, holding onto my shoulder. "Thank you for allowing me to believe in love – our kind of love."

I wrapped my arms around her, squeezed her tightly, and stared at the beauty of the sunrise. I started to cry – but it was a cry of joy, not of sorrow. I was just so happy that it jolted my very being. It seemed like every moment in my past – every heartache, every setback, every time I felt alone and frustrated in a random, meaningless universe – had molded me into the man I was today – and that was a man who had earned the love of this perfect woman.

I felt like my entire life had been leading up to this moment, and this experience was my personal reward for pre-serving my mind, and maintaining my integrity. During the course of my life, I had believed in everything at one point or another, but I had never surrendered the integrity of my mind, or the hope for a wonderful truth. Even in my darkest hour, I had extended an olive branch to God, and now that branch had taken me to unimaginable heights. I was home. In Heather's arms, I was home. Our love was the Word made flesh.

"Thank God for bringing us together," I said through muffled tears.

"Yes," she said. "Thank God."

Chapter 12

On Monday morning, I woke up with a nervous feeling, but it was a good nervous feeling, because I was about to start my new job. After I rubbed my eyes, scrubbed and dressed myself, I stared at my image in the bathroom mirror. I looked like a different man from the one who had been in this same situation nine months ago. The changes I had made on a spiritual level could be seen on a physical level. My back was straighter, my stomach was smaller, and my eyes fixed confidently upon my reflection, instead of darting to other parts of the room. I was no longer being dragged, kicking and screaming, into the "Real World." I was now a card-carrying member of it.

When I arrived at the company's headquarters, I spoke briefly with my new boss, Ryan, and then he threw me into a whirlwind of work. Apparently, the United Nations was planning to release a report that would be critical of the IEF, and other groups that provide loans to needy individuals. Not surprisingly, the IEF team was afraid of any bad press, and wanted to start circulating our message. That's where the Communications Department came in. Over the next four days, we planned a full-scale media blitz, including a press conference, a half-dozen TV interviews, and a 20-page report to counter the UN's claims.

Every day, I arrived at the office at the crack of dawn, and left around the stroke of midnight. The entire experience was exhausting, but also strangely exhilarating. I felt like

Ryan and I were hunkered in a foxhole, defending one of the few truly effective aid programs in the world – a program that was improving the lives of thousands of people. And yet that program was being assaulted by a corrupt institution with an ideological axe to grind. The fact that IEF promoted individual responsibility and private sector development was enough to target it for destruction. But we weren't going to let that happen. Not by a long shot.

During the process, I enjoyed working with Ryan, but more importantly, I enjoyed using my mind. From start to finish, it was *my* ideas that were being considered and adopted – whether it was selecting talking points for IEF's President, or pitching news stories to different editors. Finally, I was using my creative energies as part of my career, and that gave me a tremendous feeling of satisfaction.

When the U.N. report was finally released on Friday, we were prepared for the media shitstorm, and we managed to survive it. In fact, we even turned the tables on the U.N. by persuading a couple of journalists to write articles attacking the organization. Overall, it was a great success. Ryan congratulated and thanked me – which never happened at my old job.

The whole experience was a baptism by fire. But I liked it. In fact, I loved it. When I hopped onto the subway later that night, I looked forward to relaxing, basking in the glow of victory, and calling Heather to make plans for the weekend. But I never got that chance.

When I finally arrived at the apartment – a little after 9 o'clock – I saw Mark sitting solemnly at the dining room table, slowly tapping a pencil against his thigh. I could tell something was wrong. But I had no idea what it could be.

"Hey," I said, nervously, but he barely moved. I plopped my briefcase down on the ground, and walked into the kitchen to fetch a can of soda.

"Do you want one?" I asked, showing him the can, but my roommate remained motionless.

"Is everything OK?" I asked, taking a swig of the drink, and banging the can on the counter.

"Why did you move in here?" he asked with a hint of pain.

"What?"

"Why did you want to live here?"

"Umm," I said, thinking back to the first day we met. "Because I liked you, and I liked the apartment," I stated, confused by the weird question. "Where are you going with this, man? What's wrong?"

"Why did you like me?" he continued.

I laughed apprehensively. "Because I thought you were a nice guy, and we had a lot in common."

"I felt the same way," he said, sadly. "But apparently I was wrong."

"Wrong? Why do you say that? What are you talking about?"

"I thought we both wanted to live a good life – and by that, I mean a moral life; a life with God."

"Umm, yeah," I said, still feeling very unsure of the situation. "I think that's right."

"I thought you were willing to listen to me, and learn from me, and share in my experiences."

"What is this about, Mark?" I asked, starting to get annoyed. As far as I was concerned, I *was* a "moral" person, and I resented the insinuation that I was some sort of degenerate. I couldn't think of anything I had done that would give him reason to shame me. But then he whipped something out from his pocket – some sort of small wrapper. I walked over to Mark, and leaned forward to get a closer look. It was...No...Was it???...Could it be???... Incredibly, it was the discarded condom wrapper from my camping trip! Somehow, in the heat of the moment, I had recklessly thrown the wrapper into the darkness of the tent, completely unaware of where it would turn up. A smarter man would've found it and thrown it away, instead of recklessly leaving it in the property of his super-religious roommate. But I wasn't that smart. I had carelessly forgotten about the damn thing. And now it was lying in Mark's hands. Along with my pride.

"I finally got around to putting my camping equipment away, and I found *this* in the tent." He looked at me sullenly. "I'm sure you know what this is."

I thought about denying it ("What? Me? I don't even know what that thing is!"), but it was pointless. I was totally busted and humiliated, although I *did* want to clarify one point.

"It wasn't with a guy," I said, since I feared Mark was under that impression. "It was with my girlfriend, Heather. I love her. She means the world to me." I thought about apologizing, but in my opinion, I didn't do anything wrong. I mean, obviously, I was humbled by the situation, but in my philosophy, sex was a celebration, not a sin. I couldn't violate my own ethics to please my roommate. "I really don't have anything else to say," I concluded.

"Well, I have a lot to say," Mark said confidently, rising from his chair. For the first time, I sensed negative energy from his soul.

"Do you know what you did?" he asked. "You betrayed me."

"Now wait a second," I replied, defensively. "I did *not* betray you."

"Sure you did," he said, dismissively. "You betrayed my trust. You promised to give faith a chance, but you never kept that promise. Instead, you went out and succumbed to the temptations of the flesh."

"So a spiritual person can't have sex? Is that what you're telling me?"

"Sex is something you're supposed to save until marriage – and even then, it's reserved for only one purpose: having children. The Bible is very clear about all this stuff. It has very specific rules that have been obeyed for thousands of years. If you bothered to read the book, you would know that."

"I don't think there should be arbitrary rules on the expression of love between two people," I replied defiantly.

"Sorry, Brian, you don't have the right to decide what is, and what *isn't,* arbitrary."

"Actually, I do. I believe that every person should make their own moral decisions, based on the judgment of their own mind."

"Oh really?" said Mark, with a sneer. "I think that's very naïve. If everyone did that, the world would be in chaos."

"The world already *is* in chaos. But that chaos has nothing to do with the free mind of the individual. Rather, it has everything to do with the blind faith of the herd – certain of their own righteousness, and oblivious to the reality around them.

"There's a basic problem with your theory," said Mark, refusing to give an inch. "By nature, we're all sinners. Every person is born with original sin. If we tell people, 'basically, do whatever you want,' there will be an explosion of sin: sex, theft, murder, war. Face it, Brian: There's a dark side to mankind, and that's why we need the Bible: to restrain us from temptation, and keep us disciplined."

"Dude, you're twisting my words," I said, barely containing my frustration. "I never said people should 'do whatever they want.' I am *not* an advocate of hedonism. Rather, I am a proponent of reason – the study of reality, rather than revelation, to find and live by the truth."

"Brian, you're so naïve: There are different kinds of truth. There are scientific truths – like, say, the distance from the sun to the Earth. For stuff like that, reason is fine. But then there are religious truths – like, say, the nature of God, and how to obey God's will. In that area, reason is useless. Most Christians believe that reason and faith should be separate. Most scientists support that separation, as well. Both groups are satisfied with this arrangement. So why can't you just accept it?"

"The early Christians didn't accept it," I corrected him. "They believed that reason and faith should be joined together." As proof, I opened up my wallet, and started reading from a piece of paper that Heather gave me.

"Listen to the words of the second-century Christian theologian, Quintus Tertullian:

'Reason is a thing of God, inasmuch as there is nothing which God the Maker of all has not provided, disposed, ordained by reason – nothing which He has not willed, should be handled and understood by reason.'

"In the same spirit, Clement of Alexandria warned in the third century:

'Do not think that we say that these things are only to be received by faith, but also that they are to be asserted by reason. For indeed it is not safe to commit these things to bare faith alone, since assuredly truth cannot be without reason.'

"Now, listen to Saint Augustine - the most respected theologian of them all. In the fifth century, he wrote that while it was necessary...

'For faith to precede reason in certain matters of great moment that cannot yet be grasped, surely the very small portion of reason that persuades us of this must precede faith.'

"Let me repeat that: According to Saint Augustine, reason 'must precede faith.' Surely you wouldn't call the great Augustine 'naïve,' would you?"

Mark was unfazed. "All of those men would've condemned you as a sinner. They knew the power of sex – and they understood how controlling your sexual urges is essential to your relationship with God. This has been a major part of the church's teachings for a very long time, and believe me, we don't take it lightly."

"I don't take sex lightly, either," I insisted. "Sex is the life force. All of us are here because of it. None of us could exist without it. Literally. That's pretty damn powerful. And positive too. If you think human life is positive. And I do.

"I'm not sure why the church has chosen to pick a fight with sex. Right now, there are so many young people who are discovering their sexual feelings, but at the same time, they are hungering for a connection to God. Don't you see how absurd it is to force people to choose between the needs of their body and the needs of their soul – when in reality, the needs of both are the same? By condemning sex, you have turned away probably millions of potential believers who refuse to hate themselves for engaging in acts of love?

"And why *should* they hate themselves?" I continued. "Sex wasn't meant to be an act of guilt and shame. It was meant to be an act of celebration and joy. Of course, every person must treat sex in a responsible way. Drinking alcohol must be done in a responsible way. Sticking a plug into a socket must be done responsibly. That's not the issue here. The issue here is that you have condemned as a sin – and 'sin' is pretty strong language – all sex acts outside of marriage, and even most sex acts *inside* marriage. Doesn't that strike you as unfair?"

"No, not really," said Mark, shaking his head. "Sex is a part of our animal nature that needs to be controlled, wherever possible."

"It's funny," I said wistfully. "I know you'd never believe it, but you and Troy have at least one thing in common. Both of you consider sex to be an animal act – although, while you condemn it for that reason, Troy revels in it. As for me, I take a different perspective. I think sex can be, and should be, a *human* act, and I mean that as a compliment, not an insult."

"I see you've given this a lot of thought," said Mark, dismissively. "I never realized sex was so important to you."

"Sex is important to me because it *is* important, objectively. It *is* the act of Life itself, and yet it is so tragically misunderstood. I believe that if we could look at sex rationally, we could remove a lot of barriers to spiritual acceptance."

Seemingly exhausted, Mark sat down on the couch, and stared into the void. "I just wish you had spent less time thinking about sex, and more time opening your heart to others. If you had been less selfish, I know things would've worked out better for the two of us."

"I am not selfish – at least not in the way you understand the term," I said, hovering over him. "I believe in the integrity of the individual, and I have very good reasons for that belief. If you accept that existence exists, and that reason is the faculty to master existence, then you inevitably realize that each person must have control over his mind, and that he can never surrender his judgment to others. Every person has the right to live for his own sake. His own dreams. His own goals. His own future. He is not obligated to care for other people – unless he chooses to do so. And his choice should be dictated by the following consideration: Does helping other people help *myself*? Does it advance the principles and values that I cherish? If the answer is 'no,' he should remain uninvolved. Here's the bottom line: morality should be about the *celebration* of oneself; not the disownership of oneself. If you think that's 'selfish,' then so be it."

"I *do* think that's selfish," said Mark, recharging his energy. "And I think it's sad and pathetic, as well. A happy life is a life of service – both to God, and to His Children."

I sighed deeply. "Even now, after all this time, I'm still not clear what a 'life of service' truly means. I still haven't received a clear definition from you, or anyone else for that matter. Does it mean I should constantly ask people what I can do for them, and then *do it* (like some 'eager pleaser')?" What are the boundaries of such an ethical system? Is there anything I can do for *myself*? Is there anything I'm *not* required to do for other people? How do I know other people aren't just talking advantage of me?"

"Listen to me, Brian. Instead of asking those questions, have you ever thought about why you need to ask those questions in the first place? As I've said before, it's because your heart is closed to God. If you would open your heart to the Lord, He would answer every question you ever had – not through words, but though feelings – positive feelings – and the most positive feeling of all is the one to serve."

Like everything else Mark said, his arguments were vague and meaningless. From his perspective, my problem always came down to a lack of *feeling,* a lack of *commitment,* a lack of *love* – or at least his understanding of the word "love." There could never be any answers to my questions. As he put it himself, the only answer was to banish the need for answers. And I could never do that.

Mark rose from the couch, stood next to me, and put both his hands on my shoulders. "Brian, you went to church with me. You went to Palestine with me. You saw happiness there. Real, true happiness. You met people who want nothing more in life than to share their happiness with you. Why do you push them away? Why do you fight them so much? Why do you refuse to be happy?"

I could only laugh at his comment. "I *am* happy," I insisted. "And I will stay happy – because my happiness is based on reality. In fairness, I think you're happy, as well. At least for now. And why shouldn't you be? You've always been surrounded by people who love you – whether it's your family in Ohio, or your congregation in Virginia. I wish you could see that. I wish you could see that it's been love (not faith) that has supported you throughout your life. I am a witness to the power of love. It's a logical consequence of my philosophy – to share the best parts of myself with others, and to accept their best parts, as well. But only when it is rational to do so. Inevitably, there are times when it is rational to deny the demands of others – especially when their values conflict with your own. That's a lesson you need to learn."

"Oh really?" asked Mark. "How is that?"

"Well, for starters, why did you lend your car to Troy? I could never understand why you trusted someone who was so disrespectful to your religion. And then, when he abused your trust, you stayed silent and did nothing. Absolutely nothing."

"And what was I supposed to do?" asked Mark, looking confused and vulnerable for the first time.

"You were supposed to stand up for yourself, and say 'no.' But you couldn't do that, could you? Because that would mean seeing yourself as an individual with certain rights – instead of a sacrificial animal with obligations to others. Don't you see the dangers of such a worldview? Can't you see that the only people who benefit from that arrangement are folks like Troy? In a very real sense, you're enabling your enemies. In the long-run, your faith cannot survive unless it's conjoined to a confident assertiveness…an assertiveness provided by individualism…an individualism provided by reason."

Mark started pacing around the room, letting the logic of my words absorb into his brain.

"So you think I'm a loser?" he asked. "Is that what you're saying? I'm a loser?"

I looked into his eyes, and even though I wanted to say something supportive, the fact was, I *did* see Mark as a loser – a kind humanitarian, to be sure, but ultimately, a loser. And with that, a nine-month role reversal was complete. When I first met Mark, I thought he was the winner, and I was the loser. But now I believed the opposite, and I couldn't hide that judgment any longer. I could only stare at him with a trace of pity.

"Fine," said Mark, spinning on his heels and storming into his room. I followed close behind, and watched as he sat on his bed, and put on his shoes.

"I think you're a good person," I clarified. "I just think you need to improve in some areas. That's all."

"Oh. So now I'm the one who needs to improve?" said Mark, dismissively. "I'm the one who needs to learn from *you*? Don't even bother, dude."

"Can we please talk about this like rational men?" I pleaded. But it was too late for intellectual discussion. Grabbing his keys and his wallet, Mark bolted out of the bedroom.

"Where are you going?" I asked.

"None of your business," he replied stoically.

"Don't you think you're being a little overdramatic?"

"No, I don't," he said, opening the front door. Then he muttered, mostly to himself, "I can't believe this is happening to me again."

"Wait," I said. "What are you talking about?" But by then it was too late. Mark was gone.

I felt terrible about the whole situation. I never intended for Mark to find out about my– shall we say – intimate encounters. I respected him too much to throw that in his face. But once it *was* in his face – intentional or not - I felt obligated to heal the breach in our friendship. I sat on the couch patiently, waiting for him to return. I figured he needed to cool off somewhere, and when he came back, we could make amends.   By talking in a rational way, I knew we could put this episode behind us.   But as the hours passed by, with Mark still far away, I grew restless, nervous, and finally, sleepy.   I curled up on the couch, laid back, and fell asleep. But before I could get too comfortable, I was awakened by an obnoxious ringing sound.   After stammering from my slumber, I realized it was the telephone – so I walked wearily into the kitchen and picked up the receiver.

"Hello?" I said, groggily.

"This is Officer Lynch at the 39th Precinct," said a gruff, mysterious voice.   "Who am I speaking with?"

"Umm.   This is Brian."

"Brian who?"

"Umm, Brian Raines," I replied nervously.

"And what is your relationship with Mark Williams?"

"Umm.   I'm his roommate."

"Could you please describe Mr. Williams physically?"

"Umm.   Well.   He's about six feet tall.   He has…" And then it hit me.   Mark was hurt.   "Oh God," I pleaded, "Is he OK?"

"I'm afraid there's been a car accident.   A young man didn't make it.   It could be Mr. Williams.   We just don't know. We found a…"

I kept listening to the officer's words, but I couldn't mentally process them, because my mind was blank, paralyzed by fear.   No words.   No thoughts. Just the vague, haunting sensation: "Is this real?   Is this really happening?"   But when I stared at the row of cereal boxes in front of me – and they stayed there, instead of disappearing like at the end of a dream – I knew the answer was "yes." This *was* really happening.   And with that, my stomach clenched.   My throat closed.   And my heart shattered into a million pieces.

"Could you please come here and identify the body?" the officer continued.

Instead of answering his question, I formed an image of Mark in my head – the way he looked on the first day I met him. Smiling. Kind. Handsome. A hopeful young soul who always had the sun on his back. And now he was gone. I mean. Gone! Completely gone! Just like that! Of course, I couldn't be sure of it. After all, the officer said, "we don't *know*" if he's dead. Then again, I think the cop was trying to let me down gently. "Standard police procedure," or something.

"Hello?" said the voice on the phone.

"Sorry," I said, instinctively. "I can come there. Whenever."

"OK. We'll send a car to pick you up in ten minutes. Please be ready by then. Good bye."

Then the line went dead. But I kept the phone in my hand pressed against my ear – straining to remain frozen in the moment, fearful of what the future held for me. I couldn't bear to think of the consequences of what just happened. I needed to suppress my mind and keep it submerged in a fog of nothingness. I needed to distract myself from the reality of the situation.

So I did what any normal person would do: I sat on the couch, flipped on the TV, and surfed the channels – one after another. But I couldn't find anything entertaining enough to keep the demons in my head at bay. Finally, I stumbled on an episode of *Jackass* – a reality show where overgrown boys perform reckless stunts and laugh at each other's pain. There was one scene where a nude midget skateboarded into a streetlamp, fell onto the ground, and then recoiled in agony. And my only reaction was: Yes! Yes! This is exactly what I need!

But the distraction didn't last too long. A few minutes later, a couple of cops knocked on my door, checked my ID, and then brought me down to the police car. As I rode alone in the backseat, the mood was somber and silent, except for the sound of the dispatcher every now and then. I stared outside the window and searched endlessly for a single star, but there was nothing to be found in this cloudy, drizzly evening. The universe was a mirror of my emotions – a sea of blackness, hiding anxiously from the light of truth.

When we finally arrived at the station, I followed the two officers up a flight of steps, passed the main entrance, and entered a small, cluttered room where they left me by myself. Luckily, there was a *People* magazine and a *Sports Illustrated* to keep me distracted.

Later, a balding, middle-aged geezer wearing a pair of red suspenders and a loosened brown tie slowly walked in.

"I'm Lieutenant Shelton," he said softly, sticking out his paw.

"I'm Brian Raines," I replied, shaking it, gingerly.

"Let me begin by thanking you for coming down here," he said, pulling up a stool. "I know this can't be easy for you."

I just nodded.

"Were you close to Mark Williams?"

"Yes," I replied, feeling that pain again inside my chest.

"Well, from what we can gather, Mark's jeep was on the corner of 9th and G Street when – for some reason – it jerked full-speed into the wrong lane, and into oncoming traffic. About a second later, his jeep was struck by a truck speeding in excess of 50 mph. He died instantly.

"How did he die?"

"We still have to determine that, but it seems likely that his neck snapped upon collision. It was all very quick."

But how quick, I thought to myself? Did Mark know what was happening? Did he know he was dying? Did he suffer? How long did he suffer? I tried to recreate the scene in my head – cars swerving and smashing, glass shattering, body parts flailing. I could see the events from Mark's perspective, but I couldn't imagine how he *felt* as they happened.

I've heard that no one dies in their dreams (and I think it's true), but it's also true that no one dies in their own thoughts – because it requires a level of experience that no living person – by definition – could ever possess. The bottom line: I couldn't understand dying. I mean *really* understand it. And that scared me a little bit.

"Did Mark have any reason to commit suicide?" the lieutenant asked me.

"Oh no," I replied instantly. "Mark was a very religious person. He would never do that."

"I see," said Lieutenant Shelton, stroking his suspenders. "Can you think of any other reason this might have happened?"

I was ready to respond with a quick "no," but the strangeness of the question forced me to give it some more thought. Could there be another reason?

Well...umm...yeah! For months, Troy had driven that car into the ground, letting numerous problems fester and worsen. I begged him to get the car fixed. But despite numerous promises, he never actually did it. Could his negligence have actually *caused* Mark's death? Did Mark's altruism fall victim to Troy's narcissism? I had no proof to support that, and perhaps none would ever emerge. But if it was true, it reflected poorly on both of them. In a very real sense, the car accident proved the failure of both their philosophies.

"I think the car had some mechanical issues," I finally replied.

"Such as...?"

"I'm not sure. I know there was a rattling sound coming from the front, but it didn't sound very serious."

"I see," said the lieutenant, scribbling a few words in his notebook. Then he sighed, leaned forward, and stared at me.

"Are you ready for this?" he asked.

"I think so," I answered automatically. But how could any man be ready for what was to come?

"Come with me," said the lieutenant. We walked out of the room, into the hallway, and down a few flights of stairs. When we reached the basement, we entered a large gray room with acres of filing cabinets, and, in the center, a single bed with a white sheet on top, covering the contours of a human body. This had to be the morgue.

"Hello, Lieutenant," said a voice from behind us. We turned around and discovered a short, bespectacled man wearing a white lab coat.

"Hello, Doctor. Could you take us to the body that was discovered at tonight's car crash?"

"Yes," he repeated, matter-of-factly. We marched over to that single bed in the center of the room. When we arrived there, the doctor stood above the head, while the lieutenant and I hovered by the side.

"Ready?" asked Lieutenant Shelton, gripping my elbow.

"Yes," I nodded, while secretly hoping for a miracle: that the body underneath those sheets belonged to someone else.

"Are you sure?" he continued.

"Yes," I sighed.

I expected the cop to keep asking me pointless questions - anything to postpone the inevitable – but then, all of a sudden, the doctor lifted the sheet over the corpse's head. Oh God! It was Mark! Yes, it was definitely Mark. But he looked different – eyes closed, lips sealed, the rosy glow of his cheeks replaced by a cold, beige hue. The frenetic energy of his body replaced by an irreversible stillness. He was dead. I had never seen a dead person before. I had never been exposed to the finality of death. As a kid, Mark had experienced the death of a loved one. So had Troy. So had Heather. I alone had never seen its stunning power. I know it sounds crazy, but I expected Mark to look like he was sleeping. But no. What I saw was quite different. I saw a corpse. A hunk of flesh. A monster. Mark – as I knew him – was truly gone.

And that made me cry. And cry. And cry some more. I thought about that picture of Mark and Mary Beth sitting on that old park bench, smiling, holding hands, desperately in love. Now that love – sustained by the shared memories of the past, and fueled by the shared hopes for the future – was no more. But even the loss of that love – as painful as it was – wasn't the greatest treasure that was stolen. Each person, in the inner recesses of their heart, carries a hidden stash of dreams and memories. They belong to that single person. They can never be seen or heard or understood by anyone else. But once the heart stops beating, do those dreams fade away? Do those memories turn to black? Does anything of us remain?

Still, as crazy as it sounds, I could imagine Mark looking down at me from Heaven, smiling and laughing at me precisely because I *was* crying. After all, it was Mark who believed that God "has us exactly where we need to be," and that life is eternal for those who love Him.

"Brian, why are you torturing yourself like this?" he would probably ask me, with a pat on the shoulder. "Even now – after everything you've seen - you can't come to terms with God's love."

But I wanted to come to terms with it – and I believed that I could –through reason. I had always tried to "go where the evidence leads" and now, in the springtime of my life, it led to *Him*. I knew God was real. I also knew God loved us. Because the facts said there *was* life after death, and only a Loving God would grant that life to His children.

But when I glanced at Mark's corpse – and reflected on the pain he had suffered, and the suffering of his loved ones still to come - it was hard to accept those intellectual conclusions. Those rational, optimistic thoughts were assaulted by the sight of pure death. I had to fight on a mental level to contain the dreadful thought that, in the end, we're all "maggot shit" – just like Troy warned. I needed all of my strength to overcome the pure sadness of that conclusion, and shout, "No! This is not the *real* reality! This is not the truth! The truth is good! GOD DAMN IT, THE TRUTH IS GOOD!"

"Is it him?" the lieutenant asked me, although my trail of tears surely provided the answer.

"Yes," I said, after catching my breath. "That's Mark."

"We'll have to notify the next of kin," said the lieutenant, mostly to himself. "Do you have their name, and contact info?"

"Yes," I said, regaining my composure. "But can I be alone for a minute – just to, you know, pay my respects?"

"Sure," said the lieutenant, and then he walked away and stood outside the door, leaving me alone with Mark's body.

"Can you hear me, God?" I whispered over Mark's corpse. "Why did you take Mark away so quickly? He was young and energetic. A decent man. A good man. Why? *Why?* Are you listening to me? Why won't you answer me? Why are you always silent? Why are you such a fucking riddle? What do you want from us? What do you want *from me*?"

I pushed my head back, and took a deep breath.

"Look, just take good care of Mark. I have nothing else to say right now." Then I reached out and touched my old friend's face – even though it wasn't his face anymore.

"Till next time," I whispered. Then I looked up at the lieutenant, nodded stoically, and declared: "I'm ready."

"OK," he said, and then we walked back up the stairs.

As we marched forward, I thought about the last time I had been in such a challenging situation – recovering from that awful beating, laying in that hospital bed with Mark and Troy sitting next to me. Back then, I concluded, "my life is meaningless. Everything is meaningless." But now I wasn't ready to make that same assertion. I knew I could make sense of the situation – but only if I was strong enough to keep reason on her throne, and resist the sad emotions that swirled beneath it – ready to topple her at any moment. Given enough time, I was sure I could find a meaningful answer.

But four words from that cold, December night were just as valid as ever: "God, please help me."

Despite everything I had learned, I needed His help once again to answer the most profound question I could ever ask:

"Why did Mark have to die?"

PART THREE

PART THREE

Chapter 13

Early the next morning, the cops dropped me off at my apartment, and I immediately crawled onto the couch for a nap. But a few hours later, my sleep was once again disturbed by the ring of a telephone.

"Hello?" I whispered.

"Hi," said a voice that sounded like Heather.

"Oh hi," I repeated. "How are you?"

"I'm pretty good – now that I'm talking to you," she said enthusiastically. "How come you didn't call me last night?"

"Well…umm…something happened."

"Oh no. What?"

"There was…a car wreck," I sighed. "Mark is…well…he's no longer here. He's…gone. He's…dead."

"Oh my God," said Heather. "I'm so sorry to hear that. Are you OK? How do you feel?"

"Well, I'm not so sure," I replied thoughtfully. "When I first heard the news, I felt shock – just total shock. Then, after I went to the morgue and saw Mark's body, I felt a wave of negative emotions – anger, frustration, despair. Of course, I expected to have that reaction. Throughout my life, I've always reacted to adversity by lashing out at the world - and especially at God. I guess I figured, in the inner recesses of my brain, that by lashing out, I could shed any responsibility for my actions. I could sit and wallow in my emotional filth without even the slightest twinge of guilt. But, in the last few hours, I've felt different. Now that I've had a chance to absorb Mark's death, I feel...well... numb. I'm not sure why. I guess the full impact hasn't hit me yet. Or perhaps this is the start of a new understanding. I just don't know."

"Can I come over?" asked Heather.

"Please do. I miss you."

"I miss you too," she replied, and within half-an-hour, she was at my doorstep. When I opened the door, we embraced in a record-long hug – as if it had been years since our last meeting.

For the next two days, Heather kept me company as I worked out my feelings. We didn't do anything in particular. But that was on purpose. While I needed to do my own thinking, I also wanted to be close to Heather, because she made feel sane and supported. I also wanted to be close to the phone, in case anyone called. I figured someone would contact me about the funeral arrangements. Sure enough, on Sunday night, I received a call from John – the pastor from Mark's church – and he gave me all the details.

"I know Mark would've wanted you there," John said. "He always thought very highly of you." I almost laughed when I heard those words, considering how our relationship actually ended.

Then he asked: "Can you speak at the funeral?"

"What do you mean?"

"Can you give a eulogy about Mark?"

"Umm, I guess so. If you want me to." Like most people, I had a natural fear of public speaking, but I also wanted to overcome that fear – especially if it could provide some hope to others.

"I would really like you to do it," he replied solemnly.

Later, after I hung up the phone, I asked Heather if she wanted to come to the funeral with me.

"Of course," she replied. "I'll be there."

I smiled and thanked her. "You're the best."

Then, later in the day, I felt the need to talk with someone else: Troy. I hadn't spoken to him since I left my old job, but I needed to reach out to him. When I called and told him that Mark was dead, he seemed pensive and withdrawn – which was quite unusual for him.

"So…are you going to the funeral?" he asked me.

"Yeah," I said. "Of course."

"I want to come too."

"What? It's all the way in Ohio."

"I don't care. I want to come."

"Umm, OK." I had no idea why he wanted to be there, but I wasn't going to fight him on it.

On Monday, I packed a suitcase, went to work, and put in a full day, as usual. After the day was over, Heather picked me up in a rental car, and we loaded up the trunk. Then we drove a few miles to Troy's apartment, so we could fetch him (and as it turned out, Julia, as well).

"Why are you coming?" I asked Julia innocently. "After all, you didn't know Mark."

"I'm not coming for Mark," she answered abruptly. "I'm coming for *Troy*. He needs me there."

For the next eight hours, Heather drove us all the way to Ohio. I used that time to draft some remarks for the eulogy. I wanted to speak candidly about Mark, and his impact on my life. I also wanted to comfort his family, who loved him so much. But how could I comfort them? What could I possibly say to heal the pain of Mark's death? Even now, I had no answers. I had a bunch of thoughts and theories. But not a single answer.

As I scribbled some words on a yellow notepad, Troy remained shockingly mum. In fact, he barely said a single word for the entire trip. Next to him, Julia was equally quiet. She spent the whole ride jamming to her CD player, except for the two times she yelled, "I need to pee."

Finally, at close to two o'clock in the morning, we arrived at the local Day's Inn. We plucked down about sixty bucks apiece for two separate rooms. Once inside the room,

I unpacked my suitcase, took a quick shower, and then I was ready to go to bed.

"How do you feel?" Heather asked me, as I changed into my bed clothes.

"Well, I'd say…tired," I replied with a grin.

"There's something I want to give you," she said, mysteriously, as she reached into her suitcase.

"Oh yeah? What?"

"Close your eyes," she answered, and I duly obeyed her. A few seconds later, she said "open them," and when I did, she was standing in front of me, holding a gold ankh necklace in both her hands. Then she reached around my head and placed the ankh around my neck. "Now we both have one," she proudly declared.

I stared at the ankh she gave me, and then at the other ankh which draped above her chest. I've never been a huge fan of religious symbols, but for me, this object represented a powerful, beautiful union between me and Heather (and between the two of us and God).

"Thank you," I said, reaching my arms around her. "I love you so much."

"I love you too," she said, and then we kissed.

After that, we curled underneath the bed covers, turned off the lights, and held each other in the darkness. Despite my desperate fatigue, I felt aroused by the warmth of her body. I ran my fingers through her hair, down her arm, and past her shoulder blades. I felt the need to whisper to her: "I am so grateful for you." But by this time, Heather had already fallen fast asleep. In the silence, I let that sentence echo through my brain: "I am so grateful for you." And then I had a breakthrough. In fact, it was a genuine epiphany. I dashed across the room, opened my notebook, and wrote: "I am so grateful for you." And with those words, I finally had the answer I was looking for – an answer I would explain in more detail tomorrow.

When morning came, Heather and I went through our normal routine, and then we waited patiently for Troy and Julia to join us outside. Once they finally arrived, we drove to the nearby church – a small, old building whose humble features fit the temperament of the town.

When we walked inside, we found a large, grieving mass of over 100 people – most of them huddled near the casket, chatting amongst themselves, and sharing each others' pain. Once again, I was jolted back into a depressing reality: This is a funeral. This is a place of death. Be prepared!

I grabbed Heather by the hand and led us down the aisle - slowly approaching the open casket. Standing in front of it, I stared at Mark's face – still cold, empty, and downright scary. I could feel the dark emotions brewing beneath the surface. But then I whispered to him: "I am grateful for you." And then I focused on the cross above us, and quietly repeated: "I am grateful for *You.*"

I stepped back so Heather could view the body. She just smiled softly, like she was beholding a newborn baby. I guess she had come to terms with death a long time ago, and she wasn't going to fake grief just for the sake of conformity. A short time later, Julia took a peek at the corpse, and examined it with all the morbid curiosity of a fourth grader in science class. I practically expected her to poke at Mark's face, and yell, "Cool!" But eventually she just walked away.

Lastly, Troy strode up to the stage – grim, solemn, dutiful. I could only imagine what was going through his mind: Did he think he killed Mark? Did he feel guilty about it? I would never know for sure.

As we marched away from the casket, I spotted Mrs. Williams holding court with a couple of middle-aged women. She wasn't crying, but you could tell that she had been bawling recently.

"Mrs. Williams?" I asked softly.

"Yes?" she said, a little surprised.

"I'm Brian – Mark's roommate. We met at Thanksgiving."

"Oh yes," she said with a smile. "John said you were coming. I'm so glad you're here." Then she took my hand, and asked, "How are you?"

"I'm…I guess I'm OK – under the circumstances. How…how are you? Is there anything I can do for you?"

"Pray," she said seriously. "I need your prayers to keep me strong. I know the Lord suffered for us, and suffering brings us closer to Him, but this is all…it's just…I miss my boy. I miss him so much."

As the tears rolled down her cheeks, she grabbed me by the waist, and hugged me tightly. I could hear a muffled cry behind my shoulder blade– and I cried too, caught in the emotional power of the moment. But I refused to hide my tears. I was proud of them, because they reflected the honesty of our loss.

"I will pray for you," I whispered. "I promise you that."

"Thank you, Brian," she said, backing away from me, and returning to the care of the other ladies. "God bless you."

"God bless you too," I said, amazed by this woman's remarkable courage, even in the darkest of hours. From there, I walked past a few pews, until I noticed a short, red-headed girl huddled by herself. It was Mary Beth.

"Mary Beth?" I asked quietly. "Mary Beth?" When she didn't answer, I sat down next to her, and said: "I'm so sorry for your loss. I know this has got to be -"

"Get away from me," she grunted.

"Excuse me?"

"Get away!!!" she screamed with so much force that it startled everyone inside the church. Then she continued: "Can't you see how I feel? Can't you see that I'm dead inside? My life is over!"

As I pulled away, I thought to myself: "What about Mark? His life is *truly* over. Doesn't that matter at all?" But then I realized I wasn't dealing with a rational person.

At that moment, John rushed over and rescued me from the insanity. "Come here, Brian," he said, wrapping his paw around my shoulder. When he had me alone, he continued: "This has been a hard experience for Mary Beth. I would suggest leaving her alone for now."

"Sure," I said, a little shaken from the experience. "I think I've learned my lesson."

John smiled and said, "Now, just so you know the game-plan, I'm going to speak first. Then Luke will speak. Then you. Got it?"

"Yes, sir," I replied forcefully.

As John rallied everyone to take their seats, I sat down with Heather, Troy, and Julia in one of the final pews.

"Let us begin with a prayer," said John, his voice boom-ing from behind the lectern. Everyone rose to their feet, and joined him as he repeated words from the Bible line-by-line.

After we returned to our seats, John began his eulogy. If you're interested in what he said, here are some of the high-lights:

"Mark was a fine young man – one of the most honest, decent, and righteous individuals I've ever known. He was a committed Christian – a model, indeed an inspiration, to the other members of our church. He loved God, he loved life, and he never doubted his faith.

"At this challenging time, it is surely tempting to ques-tion God's goodness, and even His very existence. But we shouldn't give in to that temptation. If we feel estranged from our Heavenly Father, we should ask ourselves: 'What would Mark think of that?' And if we choose to abandon our Lord, we must ask ourselves another question: 'Did Mark die in vain?'

"No, Mark cannot – and will not – die in vain. Because the promises of our Savior are true. And if we stay true to

Him, we will be rewarded for our faith in Heaven. That's where Mark is now: Sitting on the lap of our Lord, bathed in his warm love for eternity.

"However, even though we know Mark is in a better place, we still suffer from his absence. But please know something else: the Lord God feels our suffering, and He wants to heal our sorrow. That's because He loves us in a way that no words can ever describe. And we must love Him now more than ever. Let's use this occasion to come together and embrace our Father with renewed passion, dedication, and commitment. If we can do that successfully, Mark's legacy will live on forever."

When John wrapped up his speech, Luke calmly approached the lectern, and whipped out a crumpled piece of paper. Reading from the script, he shared a few stories about Mark – including an amusing tale about his younger brother's Little League days. Apparently, Mark stood at the plate, swung at a pitch, and smacked the ball right off the pitcher's knee. But instead of running to first base, Mark rushed the mound to see if his opponent was OK. Inevitably, Mark was called out by the umpire, and his team lost the game by a single run. This strange lesson in sportsmanship elicited some much-needed laughter from the audience. But then, as Luke neared the end of his speech, his demeanor became solemn:

"I remember when Dad died a few years ago, and I had to break the news to Mark. We cried a lot together that night, and for days and weeks afterward. It's never easy for a child to lose a parent, especially when it's so sudden and unexpected. But even in our darkest moments – when the well of anger and grief was ready to explode inside each of us – we could console ourselves by knowing that our father had lived a rich and fulfilling life.

"I'll never be able to say that about Mark. He was cut short in the prime of his life. And we – as the survivors – are forced to see the wreckage: Hopes dashed. Dreams demolished. Prayers unanswered. Love unfulfilled. Each of us owns a heart that can never be whole again. Our faith – so strong in better times – has been shaken to the core.

"And yet I agree with everything John said here today. In our time of sorrow, we cannot abandon our Lord – even though it feels like He's abandoned us. We cannot fall victim to a restless mind – always questioning and doubting the love of our Savior. When we're flooded with doubt, we must strive to remove it like a cancer on the soul. We can and must do that, because even now, we are surrounded by a loving community of family and friends. Despite our suffering, we must come together, support each other, and love one another. Through shared faith and sacrifice, we will one day, not far from now, experience the true joy and beauty of Heaven."

After Luke finished spreading the gospel, John took his place on the podium, and introduced me as Mark's roommate: someone who – in his words – was a "close friend, confidante, and fellow seeker."

As the pastor's words filled the church, I could feel Heather's hand on my left knee. I looked up at her, and we smiled at each other. No words were shared. No words were needed.

Eventually, I left my seat and approached the stage. When I finally arrived, I looked out at the scores of people sitting in their pews. The sea of strangers made me surprisingly nervous. But then I focused on the familiar faces in the back row – Heather, Troy, and Julia. Then I stared at the most familiar face at all: Mark. We were all here together for the first and last time. The sense of community calmed me. So I took a deep breath and started speaking:

"I am humbled to be here. In a simpler time, I never could have imagined standing on this stage, and having to give a eulogy about Mark. There are two reasons for that: The first is that Mark loved life with a full and open heart, and the very idea that his own life could ever end seemed absurd. The second reason is more personal: I am not a man of scripture. By most standards, I am not qualified to speak about spiritual matters. Before today, I had been inside a church only a single time – and that was with Mark almost a year ago.

"Nevertheless, the quest for faith was always the prime focus of our relationship: the spark that initially drew us together, and eventually – I must admit – drove us apart. But through it all, we shared a profound longing to see the unseen, and be a part of something larger than ourselves. Those feelings came easily to Mark, but regrettably, I struggled with them. For a long time, I failed to understand why there was such a huge discrepancy between our experiences. But then I had the opportunity to come here to Palestine last Thanksgiving. I met Mark's mom, his brothers, his girlfriend, and so many of you out here today. I could feel the love you had for each other – and also the love you had for a stranger like me. I could see how your love shaped and molded Mark's character. The beauty of his soul is a testament to each and every one of you, and you should take pride in that. Always. The caring community you gave to Mark is rare in today's America. But it is still the best of America.

"When I was here with Mark, I felt a powerful urge to build a similar life for myself– and I wanted to use the foundation of God, love, and family. But my enthusiasm was cut short by an awful event: I was severely beaten, and left for dead on the streets of Washington. The experience left me bitter and angry with God. I felt like God had violated my trust in Him. But Mark didn't see it that way. As I lay in the hospital bed, he told me: 'Something good will come out of this. You'll see. Don't give up. Don't ever give up.'

"I didn't want to believe Mark back then, but he was absolutely right. A few weeks later, in that very same hospital, I met a kind, intelligent, truly amazing woman, and we fell in love. In loving her – and accepting her love for me – I found the happiness I had been searching for my entire life. She is here with us today. Heather, I love you."

As I gestured in Heather's direction, a herd of heads twisted awkwardly to stare at the final row. Despite the unwanted attention, Heather looked straight ahead at me and smiled. She knew what was coming next.

"From Heather, I learned a life philosophy that is very relevant for this occasion. The premise of her philosophy is simple: Number one, reality is real. And number two, reason is the only way to master reality. On the surface, those don't seem like controversial facts, but the consistent application of those facts can lead to some powerful ideas: the primacy of the individual, the morality of enlightened self-interest, the usefulness of the Golden Rule, and the beauty of unrestricted love.

"In my case, unrestricted love came with a cost – and that cost was my friendship with Mark. I'm sorry to say that on the day Mark passed away, he was angry at me – furious at me, actually – because I had dared to love Heather in a way he thought was sinful – but for me, was nothing short of magical.

"Nonetheless, our argument over relationships with women was only the symptom of a larger argument about our relationship with God Himself.

"As I mentioned a few moments ago, I believe in the power of reason – and it is through reason that I believe in God. There is strong – and I would argue, overwhelming - evidence that the universe was designed, and if it was designed, there was a Designer: namely, God. Like most people, I find this fact to be inspiring.

"But every now and then, we are confronted by acts of God – like the death of a close friend – where reason alone can provide no explanation. No amount of raw intelligence can decipher its meaning. During these troubling times, reason itself must be transcended and substituted with faith. Needless to say, this doesn't mean that reason is pointless. Not at all. Reason must always come before faith, and even God Himself must be evaluated by the facts as we understand them. But ultimately, at the end of the process, we must put our faith in God – because we know, through reason, that God is worthy of that faith.

"This philosophy was unsettling to Mark because, for him, reason was an obstacle to faith – or at least, an obstacle to his own brand of faith. Instead of trusting his mind, he followed his feelings – feelings of love and devotion, not just for God, but for all people. Those feelings came naturally to him, and he was convinced they could be stirred inside anyone (even inside a skeptic like me) if only we wanted them badly enough.

"But the problem is...feelings change. I know that from experience. One minute, you're on top of the world; the next minute you're bleeding in a gutter. One minute, you're at peace with all creation; the next minute you're mourning the death of a close friend. The roller coaster of emotions can become overwhelming. Given enough time, they can persuade most people to adopt a safe and dreary agnosticism. Even worse, when the valleys of life are at their steepest and longest, those feelings can harden into atheism.

"The atheists usually claim to be defenders of the mind – constantly clamoring for 'proof' of God's existence, and happily claiming that none exists. But their willful blindness to the evidence that's been accumulating for years exposes an obvious fact: they're *not* defenders of the mind. They're simply another band of ideologues driven by their own feelings - in this case, the feelings of separation. They enjoy their separation from humanity. From a biological perspective, they love being the 'animal' that is blessed with no responsibility for his moral choices. From a mental perspective, they love being the 'machine' – a cold-hearted contraption that loves the feeling of its own superiority – the superiority of knowing that, unlike the rest of us, it doesn't need the comfort of a Higher Power. But is that true? We can never know what's inside the mind of another person. Perhaps, late at night, when it's quiet and dark, and they're all alone, the truth seeps through and whispers to them: 'God is real.'"

As I uttered those words, "God is real," I stared directly at Troy: the very definition of the "animal machine." I honestly thought he would sneer at me, or even walk out in protest. But he just frowned bashfully, masking the shame of being picked apart so decisively.

"The bottom line is, feelings are a part of life – but they're ultimately unreliable. And a life philosophy that is based on feelings is equally unreliable. What *is* reliable? Reason. Intelligence. Judgment. The power of the mind. The *individual* mind. These are the roots of a superior kind of faith – a faith that, in time, blossoms into a sturdy oak that can survive any storm. Despite the heaviest rains and the strongest winds, it stays there unmoved, confident, secure in itself, and secure in its place in the universe.

"This faith has been greatly tested by Mark's death. The feeling of loss – and all of the feelings that come with it (anger, despair, guilt) – are natural, and understandable. But those feelings must be reigned in by the mind – which knows the truth, despite the scenes of coffins and car wrecks. And the truth is that God loves us. Each and every one of us. And because He loves us, death itself is an illusion. Life for all of us is eternal. It goes on forever. And that means Mark is in Heaven right now – smiling at us, waiting for us. And one day we will be with him again.

"If we stay focused on those facts – and brand them into our brains – our feelings of sadness will gradually melt away, and a new feeling will spring forth and reenergize us: a feeling of *gratefulness*. We should be grateful to God because He has given us the gift of Life – the Life we have now, and the Life we have to come. We love life. Every day, when we wake up and get out of bed, we affirm the value of life. Every breath we take is our personal vote of confidence in God's plan. After all, very few of us choose to end our lives. And why should we? We are all artists, and the world is our canvass. Each day, we take our paintbrush to the world, and redesign it with the colors of our own image. The colors can change – bold, primary colors or bland shades of darkness – but the choice is ours. The choice is always ours. There are endless possibilities for acts of self-creation. We are what we choose to be. We love the canvass. We love life. We protect it, we fight for it, and when it ends, (or at least seems to end) we mourn it.

"We should also be *grateful* for it. We should be grateful because it's an appropriate response to reality. God has been good to us – and we should honor that goodness. We should say to God, 'I am grateful to You. I am grateful for my life. I am grateful for Mark's life. I am grateful for the time we spent together.' This shifts our attention from what we've lost to what we've gained: the wonderful memories that we'll treasure forever. And it keeps us focused on the future: *new* opportunities for *new* memories, so long as we're unafraid to love and be loved, once again. Gratitude for yesterday's blessings heal the sorrows of today. Gratitude for today's blessings spur the hopes of tomorrow. Gratitude is truly the cure for a wounded soul."

I scanned the audience and looked for Mary Beth - armed with the faint hope that my words might sooth her, and give her strength. But when my eyes finally found her, her head was buried in her hands, and her body was convulsing with a fresh outbreak of tears. I could only ask myself, "Why? Why was she reacting so badly to my speech?" I needed to know the answer – but that answer would have to wait.

"I'd like to conclude where I began – with humility. I've said a lot today, but I won't claim to have all the answers. In fact, as I said earlier, we shouldn't expect to have all the answers in this lifetime – and that's precisely where faith comes in. Mark had the power of faith. He lived it. He practiced it. And he wanted to share it with me. But as it turned out, I needed to find it in my own way, on my own terms - and after some early stumbles, that's exactly what I did.

"I found a new faith – a faith where the mind is prized, not surrendered; where love is celebrated, not repressed; where creativity comes before conformity; and gratitude comes before all.

"The world has changed a lot over the past few generations, and religion should change with it. So therefore, as we pass through these trying times, I urge all of you, not to *return* to faith, but to *discover* it. Thank you."

I stepped away from the podium, walked down the aisle, and returned to my seat. The church was silent. Dead silent. I instinctively feared the worst. I was worried that I had offended people with my thinly-veiled criticisms of Mark, and my unconventional views about faith. But my goal was not to offend people; it was to enlighten them. I wanted to offer them a new way of seeing the world – a better way that could empower them to withstand the rocky currents of life. But perhaps I had overreached. Perhaps my gentle words of wisdom had been misinterpreted as arrogant words of ignorance. Perhaps my religious views had been mistaken for blasphemy. Perhaps I had failed. Nevertheless, I had spoken the truth – or at least the truth as I saw it. The truth was my mission – and no matter what happened in the future, one woman would always stand with me in that mission.

"I'm very proud of you," Heather whispered in my ear.

"Thanks," I said with a smile. Then I grabbed her hand and kissed it. "I love you very much."

"I love you too."

John closed the funeral with a prayer, and then provided directions to Uncle Jim's home for the postmortem. "Don't eat anything on the way there," he warned. "We'll have drinks and sandwiches at the house."

I gathered Julia, Troy, and Heather together, left the church, and returned to the car. After a few minutes on the road, Troy broke the silence by casually stating, "Nice speech."

"Thanks," I replied cautiously, unsure of whether he was being sincere or sarcastic.

"I mean, I don't agree with everything you said," he clarified, "but I respect the fact that you said it."

"I agree," said Julia, with surprising enthusiasm. She then peppered me with a series of questions – "Why is reason superior to emotion?" "Why is rational self-interest the best foundation for morality?" "What is the 'overwhelming' evidence for God's existence?" During the eulogy, I didn't have time to address all of those issues in detail – but now, with a 45-minute car ride ahead of us, I carefully answered them. In most cases, I simply remembered my first date with Heather and repeated her main points, although I usually provided a unique twist of my own. Julia patiently listened to me, and quietly absorbed the information I gave her. Apparently, my speech had genuinely opened her mind. Meanwhile, Troy remained strangely silent – unaware, or unconcerned, that he was losing his greatest disciple: his own girlfriend.

When we arrived at Uncle Jim's house, I was surprised by its immense size; it was practically a mansion, surrounded by endless acres of green fields. We walked through an unlocked door, and found dozens of people mulling around – most of them munching on sandwiches and slurping on sodas. Some of the men were watching a baseball game on TV. In the distance, I thought I heard a woman laughing. For most of the folks there, I suppose the time for mourning had come to an end. I looked at Heather, who knew exactly what I was thinking, and also the best way to comprehend it.

"Life goes on," she explained to me. "Life goes on."

"Let's eat," said Troy. So we followed him into the kitchen and studied the selection of meat – ham, turkey, salami, roast beef, etc. There was also a huge supply of chicken salad. While I filled my plate with a small sampling of each food, I felt a tap on my shoulder. When I looked behind me, I found John staring at me ominously.

"Can I talk to you privately?" he said.

"Umm, sure," I replied. I expected to receive a modern version of the Spanish Inquisition: "How could you say those things at a funeral? Don't you have any respect for Mark's family?" But when we stepped outside the kitchen, John struck a different tone. "Would you mind speaking at my church – you know, the one in Alexandria?"

"What? Are you serious?"

"Yes. I'd really like you to do it."

"But why?"

"Because there are many paths to God, and I think people could learn from yours."

"But isn't my path dangerous?"

"If it leads to faith and love, how could it be dangerous?"

"Because my faith empowers people. It says to every person, 'You are the owner of your life. Everything you need to build a happy and successful life is right here: inside your own mind.' The power to think – and by that, I mean the power to think *rationally* - is the power to grow, and to be everything you wish to be, including your highest manifestation: pure love. But even in our most loving state, we must never surrender our minds – not to society, not to the church, not even to God. God doesn't need blind animals. He needs human beings. And I mean that in the best, most noble sense of the term."

"Fine. So say that," said John, totally unfazed by my statement. "After all, I need human beings too." Then he smiled.

"Alright," I said. "I'll do it." Then we shook hands. I have to admit, I had misjudged John. He was a good guy. A *great* guy, actually.

A short time later, Mrs. Williams approached me. She was equally impressed by my eulogy. "I think you're absolutely right about gratitude," she said. "I *am* grateful to God for all of my blessings – including the chance to hear you speak today. You're a wonderful young man."

"Thank you," I said. Then we hugged.

As we held each other, a smarm of relatives encircled us. Everyone wanted to chat with me, learn some more about me, and thank me.

"I appreciate everything you said," said a 60-something man with a deep scar on his left cheek. "It was fantastic."

"I hope you'll visit us again," said a plump woman who was using a cane to support herself.

"I will," I said. "I promise."

As the hours passed by, Troy grew increasingly anxious.

"Don't you think we should leave now?" he asked, as the sun started to set. "We have a long drive ahead of us."

"Yeah, you're probably right," I surmised. "But first, I need to speak with Mary Beth." I hadn't seen her in Uncle Jim's house, so I asked John where I could find her.

"She's in one of the bedrooms," he told me. "But she doesn't want to be disturbed by anyone. She was very clear about that. I would suggest calling her in a few days."

"OK," I said reluctantly. Then I looked over at Troy. "I guess we can leave now. Are you ready?"

"Not quite yet," he warned. "First, I need to take a leak."

"Yeah," I murmured, "I guess I should do that too."

We both headed toward the restroom. But when I turned the knob, it was already locked. "Gimme a minute," shouted the voice from behind the wall.

As we waited patiently for the bathroom door to open, we heard the sound of another door opening behind us. When we turned around, we found Mary Beth standing on the outskirts of her bedroom – her hair frazzled, her clothes wrinkled, and her make-up smeared beyond all recognition. She stared at us with narrow eyes and tight lips, as if she was thinking to herself: "I've been waiting for you assholes to show up. Now y'all are gonna get a piece of my mind."

She stepped forward and jabbed her finger into my chest: "Well, Brian, I hope you're pleased with yourself," she said, barely containing her fury. "Since the day you came into Mark's life, you laughed at his faith, criticized his church, and preached endlessly about 'following the facts.' But then, when the facts are clear, you're afraid to face them. The fact is, God *doesn't* love us. Isn't that obvious? I mean, Mark is dead. You hear me? He's *dead!!* I'll never see him again. I'll never hear the sound of his voice; I'll never feel the touch of his hand; I'll never taste the warmth of his lips. But, according to you, I should be *thankful* for that! I should be *grateful* for that! Do you really expect me to believe any of that crap? Normally, I would expect that sort of bullshit from one of my relatives, but not from someone like you. After all, you were the one who always wanted to be held to a higher standard. But I guess you've become a sell-out just like the rest of them."

"Now, hold on a second," I said defensively.

"No, I won't hold on. Do you have any idea how I feel? Let me tell you something: I am a broken woman. When Mark died, I died too. But do you care? No! In fact, you honestly think your life – not mine – is the tragic one. Why?

What's so tragic about *your* life? So your parents got divorced? Big deal! So your back hurts? Boo-hoo! So it took you a while to bang a girl? Well, you shouldn't have banged her in the first place! Let's face it, there's nothing tragic about your life. But *my* life? *My* life is the *real* tragedy! I've lost the only thing that ever mattered to me. The love of my life is gone forever. But what do you say? 'Be grateful.' No, I'm *not* grateful. I'll never be grateful. I'll never be able to overcome this loss. Listen to me, Brian: Once you've seen the abyss, it never leaves you. But you know what else? One day, you'll see it too. We all have it coming to us." Then she looked at Troy and repeated, "We all have it coming to us."

"If you're so focused on facts," I said, "here's the *real* fact: Mark *is* in a better place. If you believe that (and you *should* believe it, because it's true), you'll have the strength to carry on."

"No," said Mary Beth, shaking her head, "that's not good enough. Even if I believe that, the question remains: Why now? Why did God take Mark away *now*? I mean, he was only 23 years old. We were supposed to get married, move back to Ohio, and start a family. Couldn't God have waited a little while longer to take Mark? Like 60 years from now? What's the big hurry? I suppose if Mark was a *bad* person, I could understand what happened. But Mark was a *good* person – a *great* person. He followed all of God's commandments. Doesn't that count for anything? Shouldn't good people be treated better in this hellhole called Earth? If not, what's the point of being a good person at all?"

I put my hand on her shoulder and said, "I honestly believe there is a moral code built into the very fabric of the universe. In this code, good is more powerful than evil, and evil can never truly win. But I also believe in free will – and because we possess free will, bad things can, and will happen to us – even to the *best* of us. During those bad times – like now – we must focus our minds, and absorb the big picture – which is that God loves us, we must love each other, and 'there is a purpose to all things under Heaven.'"

"Sorry Brian, I still don't buy it. I mean, He's God, after all! He can do *anything!* Why should I excuse his failures? Why should I be thanking Him, when in reality, he should be begging for my forgiveness?"

"So forgive Him!" I blurted out.

"What?"

"If you think God has failed you, forgive Him."

"I can't do that."

"Why not?"

"Because He's *God!*" she shouted, with a trace of laughter. "God doesn't *need* my forgiveness. He doesn't need *anyone's* forgiveness. He does what He can, and we suffer what we must."

"If God needs our love, maybe he also needs our forgiveness. I think we all need forgiveness. Even God."

For the first time, Mary Beth seemed receptive to my words. She pursed her lips, unfolded her arms, and then stared at Troy to gauge his reaction. But the thought of forgiveness could not penetrate his brain.

"What if He doesn't deserve forgiveness?" Troy interjected. "Back in the hospital, you agreed that forgiving evil only leads to *more* evil."

"I suppose that's true for human beings, but not necessarily for God. We can change people's behavior, but God Himself is immune to our rewards and punishments. We know God loves us, so we can safely forgive Him. Later on, when we feel comfortable with Him again, we can then experience the ultimate truth – which is gratitude.

"So I ask you again, Mary Beth: Can you forgive God?"

She looked down at her shoes, and then up at the crucifix hanging on the wall. Finally, she cautiously answered, "I guess I can try."

"Good," I said. "Now, is it O.K if I hug you?"

"Oh Christ!" shouted Troy, clearly irritated by my victory. Then he stormed into the empty bathroom and slammed the door shut. But his rudeness couldn't contain Mary Beth's emotions. She embraced me tightly, and stayed in my arms seemingly forever. When Troy re-opened the door, he looked straight at me sighed, "Knock it off, dude. Go take a piss so we can get outta here."

I lifted Mary Beth's head from my chest and said, "I guess I have to go now. Call me when you're back in D.C., O.K?"

"O.K.," she said, wiping away a tear. "Thanks. Thanks a lot." Then she walked downstairs to see the rest of her family.

After using the restroom, I gathered my crew together, and we exchanged some final words with Mark's family. Then we hit the road.

The ride home was quiet, as usual, and I was able to spend some extra time thinking about this whole experience. Needless to say, I was emotionally drained from it all, but I was also mentally invigorated. I had brought some hope to the hopeless – even to a lost soul like Mary Beth. I had stopped tears of pain, and inspired tears of compassion. I had – as Heather once explained – "expanded myself" into other people's souls. I had closed the natural separation between me and everyone else – not by denying myself, but by exalting in myself. I would never forget the happiness that came with it.

In fairness, I never found an answer to that haunting question, "Why did Mark die?" and Mary Beth quickly called me out on that. But together we were still able to find peace – by putting our faith in God, and even, as strange as it sounds, *forgiving* Him. In Mary Beth's case, the road to recovery would be long and difficult, but I knew she would succeed. I was certain of that. She had a whole network of friends and family to support her, and I was willing to do my part, as well.

In some ways, I was less optimistic about Troy's prospects. As always, he was closed to God, but now, for the first time, he also lacked self-confidence and a sense of purpose. At some point, he would need to make peace with God, or the consequences would be deadly.

As for me, I was alright. I had lost a great friend, whose memory I would always cherish, but I had also gained rock-hard proof that I could overcome any challenge. In many ways, I had taken the ultimate test – the test of staring death in the face and refusing to crumble– and I had passed it.

In her own way, Heather had passed a test, as well. By supporting me during this crazy time, I knew I could count on her for anything. She was my rock. Our love – never in doubt - was now complete.

Knowing that, there was only one thing left to do.

Chapter 14

When I returned to Washington, I was determined to bring my life back to normal as quickly as possible – and that meant, first and foremost, finding a new roommate. This was a complete role reversal from a year ago. Back then, I was the new kid in town, desperately searching for a place to live, and genuinely unsure that anyone would actually want to live with me. But now I was the experienced veteran – carefully screening applicants with all the emotional detachment of a computer. Every night, after work, I met with a different candidate and showed him around the apartment – but all of them were lacking in some capacity. The whole process made me miss Mark more than ever.

Every now and then, I called Mary Beth, hoping I could provide her with some support and encouragement. But whenever I called her apartment, her roommates insisted she was still in Ohio. I started to fear Mary Beth would be stuck in Ohio for the rest of her life.

Sure enough, about a week after the funeral, I received a phone call from Luke, which confirmed that fear.

"She's going to stay here and build a new life for herself," Luke explained to me. But in order to build that new life, she needed all of the stuff she left behind in D.C. So Luke, along with his brother, Matt, were planning a trip to Washington to pick up that stuff. Since they would already be in town, they wanted to take Mark's belongings too.

"Is that alright?" asked Luke.

"Sure," I said. "I'll help you guys out."

Later on, when I spoke to Troy on the phone, I casually mentioned my upcoming project with Mark's brothers. Surprisingly, Troy jumped at the chance to help us.

"Are you sure?" I asked. "I mean, you're not under any obligation."

"Actually, I think I am," he said mysteriously, before changing the subject.

When everyone arrived on Saturday morning, we exchanged a few pleasantries, chatted awkwardly about the NBA playoffs, and then cautiously entered Mark's room.

I hadn't been inside his room since the day he confronted me about Heather and then stormed out of the building to meet his awful fate. I wanted to avoid reliving that painful memory, but I couldn't avoid it any longer. As the four of us surveyed the room, the moment of truth had finally arrived – and it was a shocking truth, indeed – more shocking that I ever could have expected.

"So this is Mark's room?" asked Luke, slightly confused.

"Yeah," I answered.

"Did he switch rooms, or something?"

"Yeah. When Mark's old roommate, Bret, moved back to Ohio, Mark took over Bret's room, and I took over Mark's room."

"Bret moved back to Ohio?" Luke asked skeptically. "Well, I suppose that's one way of putting it."

"What do you mean?"

"You mean Mark never told you?"

"I guess not."

"Well…Bret committed suicide."

"What? Why?"

"Nobody knows. Bret was a strange kid. Back in college, he was an alcoholic or something. But then he met Mark, and everything changed. Because of Mark, Bret found the courage to quit booze, join a church, and eventually, he became a deeply religious person. I think Mark saw Bret as his protégé, or something. But they were also very good friends – so good, in fact, they moved to DC together. But a few weeks after moving here, Mark came home one day and found Bret lying in his bed – dead of a drug overdose.

"What?" I repeated. "That's crazy. Why didn't Mark tell me about any of this?"

"Geez, man. I don't know."

I sat on Mark's bed, rubbed my eyes, and took a deep breath.

"So that's what I was – another protégé?" I asked myself rhetorically. "Someone to make up for the failures of the past?" If that was true, Mark's final words (*"I can't believe this is happening to me again"*) made sense. Once again, Mark had lost his roommate's soul. Once again, he saw himself as a failure to his faith. But was he?

I stood up from Mark's bed, and walked toward one of the posters hanging on his wall: *"The Mustard Seed."* For the first time in almost a year, I carefully read its message...

"The kingdom of heaven is like a mustard seed, which a man took, and sowed in his field. Though it is the smallest of all your seeds, yet when it grows, it is the largest of garden plants and becomes a tree, so that the birds of the air come and perch in its branches." (Matthew 13:31-32)

When I first met Mark, he planted a mustard seed inside my soul - convincing me that faith in God was worth finding, and worth living. But as time passed, that mustard seed of faith blossomed into a tree that Mark would never recognize – a powerful, yet colorful oak tree that stood out in a forest of conformity. Still, it was Mark who had planted that seed – and he deserved credit for that. Even more, his death had brought my faith in God to a new and higher level. By enabling me to accept God's power, even in its most tragic form, Mark's death had transformed my faith from an idea into an experience; an entire way of life. Almost a year ago, Mark said he wanted to make a "sacrifice for the betterment of mankind," and in a very real sense, his death *was* that sacrifice. Like Christ, he used his death as a tool for inspiration. In death, as in his life, Mark was the mustard seed.

"I always liked that poster," said Luke.

"Yeah," I replied. "Is it O.K. if I keep it?"

"Keep it? Why?"

"I think Mark would want me to have it."

"Umm, ok. Go for it."

So I removed the poster from Mark's wall and hung it up in my room. "Alright," I said. "Now we can get started."

For the next six hours, we gathered all of Mark's stuff (his desk, bed, computer, clothes, and books), brought them downstairs, and loaded them into the U-haul. Inevitably, we also found a few *Playboys,* but we threw them into the trash. When it was over, Mark's room was completely barren – a white, empty void where a young man once lived and dreamed.

"I guess that's it," said Luke, wiping his sweaty brow.

"Yeah," I sighed. "I guess so."

"Thanks for your help," he said, sticking out his hand. I shook it and replied, "Do you need any help with Mary Beth's stuff?"

"Nah," he said. "Matt and I have it covered. Plus, we'll have both of Mary Beth's roommates to help us. So don't worry about it."

"O.K.," I said reluctantly. Then, Luke approached Troy, and thanked him, as well.

"You're a good man," he told Troy.

"I hope so," Troy replied. "I really do hope so."

"Good luck to you," I yelled to Luke and Matt, as they approached the front door.

"Good luck to all of us," Luke replied. Then the door slammed shut. They were gone.

"Damn, I could use a beer," said Troy. "Do you have any?"

"Look in the fridge," I suggested.

"Ah, jackpot!" he shouted, pulling out a can, and taking a long swig. "I feel like getting trashed tonight. What about you?"

"Not really. Why do you want to get trashed?"

"I'm just tired of all this shit, man."

"What shit?"

"Mark's shit. I mean, that kid was a total asshole – and yet, here I am, cleaning up all of his shit. I never asked to deal with it, dude. Even now, I want to say, 'fuck it,' but…but I can't…I can't walk away."

"Because of the guilt?"

"Guilt?" he asked. "What guilt?"

I was ready to say out loud what I had been thinking for weeks – that Troy's reckless narcissism had caused Mark's death. But as I opened my mouth, Troy realized his mistake. So he leaped from his seat and pleaded: "Don't say it." Of course, by saying it, Troy had basically confessed, "I did it."

Still, even if he *did* do it, I felt sorry for him – sorry for the guilt he carried in his heart – a guilt so painful and over-whelming, and yet its source could never be revealed – not by him, not by me, not by anyone.

"Fine," I said. "I'm not here to judge you, man. But you need to release that guilt. There's no virtue in spending the rest of your life hating yourself."

"But the guilt is *good* for me," said Troy, with surprising conviction. "I mean, I'm here, right? I spent the whole day helping Mark's family – sacrificing my time and energy to make amends. Now, of course, I didn't *want* to do it. In fact, I *hated* doing it. But I did it, anyway. Why? Because of the guilt. The guilt made me do the right thing– and for that reason, I can't suppress it, or condemn it. I have to let it work its way through my system – until I've earned the right to live for myself once again."

"Good Lord, you've changed a lot. When we first met, you laughed at people who 'drowned in their own guilt,' 'hated themselves,' and 'sabotaged their lives in service to others.' Now you're falling into the same trap. Is that what you really want for yourself? Come on, man. For your own sake, forgive yourself."

"No way, dude. If I forgive myself, I'll lose the motivation to be a good person. I'll feel like I can be the same prick I've always been. I can't do that – at least not yet."

"Listen, Troy: The key to being a good person is quite simple: keep an open mind, believe in yourself, love yourself, and share that love with other people. But you can't apply those principles unless you release the guilt and forgive yourself. Guilt is not the answer. Guilt will block your mind, lower your self-confidence, and make everything you do for others a painful sacrifice.

"But I *should* be in pain," Troy answered. "I *should* be unhappy. I made a terrible, horrible mistake. I have no right to be happy unless that mistake has been atoned for – somehow." Then he sighed and concluded, "I'm sorry, my friend, but that is justice."

"I support justice," I countered, "but you can't create justice by stripping away your self-confidence and judgment. If you do that, you'll never know when your debt has been paid – at least not from a *rational* perspective. Instead, your debt will go on forever, because after all, 'you're a bad person, and you deserve to be punished,' or at least that's what you've led yourself to believe. Don't go down that road. Face reality: Nobody is perfect. Everybody makes mistakes. Forgive yourself. Start over, and say: 'From now on, I will commit to a rational, honest life – and everything that comes with it. I will do the best that I can. No more. No less.' Can you do that?"

Troy refused to answer.

"Look man," I continued, "don't make this any harder than it has to be. When it comes to life, you can either love it, or hate it. And I choose to love it. What do you choose?"

"I chooooose..." he said overdramatically, slurring his words, and raising his beer can high in the air, "I chooooose not to chooooose." Then he rose from the couch, and concluded, "Thinking's a bitch. I'll see ya later, man." Then he opened the door, and left.

On Friday night, Heather came to my place and stayed for the weekend. Since I no longer had a roommate, we could do whatever we wanted – including sleeping in the same bed and making love. Our lovemaking was incredibly powerful and pleasurable – although it didn't feature the clothes-ripping, toe-curling lust that I had fantasized about as a teenager. Rather, if I could use two words to describe our sexual experiences, I would say: "playful" and "spiritual."

After the slight awkwardness of our first encounter, the idea of making sex a "playful experience" came naturally to us. By nature, we were explorers – and now, we were taking that sense of exploration to a new frontier – our own bodies – learning what felt good, what didn't feel good – with no sense of shame or fear. In a strange way, there was something almost innocent about us – because we weren't tainted by a million so-called "adult" emotions – whether it was lust or greed, submission or domination, or keeping up with the neighbors – but rather, we were motivated by the joy of pleasure for its own sake.

But that pleasure – as intense as it was – wasn't strictly physical. It was also spiritual. I could only have sex – at least such truly enjoyable sex – with one woman – Heather - because she was the only woman who encompassed all of my values – my entire concept of what life can be, and should be.

Because we connected so perfectly on a mental level, I felt comfortable enough to connect with her on a physical level – and once I was inside her, the last remnants of my "false self" – all of the masks and armor and shackles I had put on myself through years of so-called "growing up" – completely melted away, unable to survive the heat of such a powerful energy – an energy so powerful, it could lead to the creation of life itself. When we climaxed, our connection - from mind to body to soul - was complete.

On Monday morning, when I woke up, I hurriedly prepared for another workweek – showering, primping, and getting dressed – but Heather, who had the summer off – stayed comfortably underneath the sheets.

"Is it OK if I stay?" she asked me.

"Sure. Stay as long as you want. Just call me when you get home."

"No, sweetie. I mean, can I stay here and live with you?"

"Oh," I said, "you want to live here? With me?"

"Yeah," she said, bashfully – perhaps afraid I might reject her. "What do you think?"

I thought about it for a moment. "Well, I need a new roommate anyway...so...it might as well be someone I love...Of course...Let's do it!"

"Oh baby!" she said, leaping out of the bed, and running over to embrace me. "This is going to be so much fun!"

We started kissing and caressing, and within a few minutes, we were naked once again. Needless to say, I was late to work that day.

The next weekend, Heather and I went to her dorm room, collected all of her stuff, and brought it back to my apartment. Now, it was *our* apartment. By living together, we were entering a new phase in our relationship – a phase that had killed other couples, but seemed to suit us just fine. Every morning, I got up early for work and let Heather sleep for a few more hours. Since Heather didn't take classes in the summer, she had the freedom to come and go as she pleased – although she usually spent a few days each week at the children's hospital. No matter what, she would be home in time to cook me dinner, and from there, we would curl up on the couch and watch TV. Nearly always, we would end the day with sex. I loved having her around – and I think she liked having me around too.

During the middle of July, Heather suggested that her six-year old niece, Elizabeth – the one she loved so much – come and stay with us for a few weeks. I wasn't thrilled with the idea (to be honest, I've never been good with kids), but I accepted, anyway.

Elizabeth was a pretty young girl – a miniature Heather, in some ways – but she was also painfully shy. I tried to engage her in conversation, but she seemed uncomfortable around me – which, of course, made me even *more* uncomfortable. By the end of the first week, I was discreetly trying to avoid her. I'm not proud of that, but it's true.

A few days later, I came home from the office, and found Elizabeth and Heather lying on the floor, surrounded by dozens of scattered papers – all of them splashed with a variety of bright colors.

"What are you doing?" I asked.

Heather looked up and smiled. "We're finger painting."

I kneeled beside Elizabeth, and stared at their pictures – half-finished portraits of dogs, kids, and smiling suns.

"Are you having fun?" I asked her. She stopped drawing, but didn't answer the question.

A few seconds later, Heather poked her niece's elbow, and repeated: "Elizabeth, are you having fun?"

"Yeah," she said quietly. Then she bit her lip. "Do you want to play with us?"

I hesitated for a moment. "I…uh…sure…OK. Let me just change my clothes."

When I came back, I sat down between the girls and grabbed my own sheet of paper. From there, I started dunking my fingers in small pools of red, green and yellow paint, and then I began drawing a picture of a young couple walking in a garden – the same portrait that Heather had shown me on the first day we met. But there was one thing missing.

"Where's meeeee?" Elizabeth pleaded.

"Don't worry," I said with a chuckle. "I'm getting to that."

I fulfilled Elizabeth's wish by sketching a small girl, holding a pink flower in her hand.

"Do you like it?" I asked.

"I think you need some practice," she replied in a dead-pan voice.

"Alright," I laughed. "Teach me."

For the next few hours, Elizabeth taught me the intricacies of finger painting – but despite her helpful instructions, I couldn't live up to her exacting standards. Still, with every silly picture I drew, she grew closer to me. By revealing my inner child – and exposing my playful side – I earned her trust and affection.

Later on, her new feelings were clearly proven when Heather and I took Elizabeth to the Arlington County Fair – an annual kid's paradise filled with Ferris wheels, pig races, cotton candy, and numerous games. Despite the torturous heat, Elizabeth insisted that I come with her on all the rides. She wouldn't let me out of her sight. She also called me "Uncle Brian," which made my heart melt every time I heard it.

I could honestly say that going to the County Fair with Heather and Elizabeth was one of the happiest days of my life – and yet, throughout the day, there was virtually nothing to stimulate me on an intellectual level. From start to finish, there was absolutely zilch to nourish my rational mind. This was strange to me. After all, I had grown accustomed to thinking that *thinking itself* was the key to happiness - certainly not petting llamas or eating ice cream cones.

However, even going back to my first dates with Heather, we found some of our greatest pleasure not just in books and museums, but also in nature, in the bedroom, and now, at a county fair. At first, I was confused by this situation, and justified it through an analogy: "If the body needs sleep every night, the mind also needs a break from the intellectual challenges of daily life." By creating this analogy, I had moral permission to enjoy "trivial" experiences like the County Fair, along with other stuff, like baseball games and *Seinfeld* re-runs. Basically, anything that rested the mind was OK. But things that *impaired* the mind – like, say, getting totally drunk – were still off-limits.

Still, as I went on the Ferris wheel, and held Elizabeth's hand, and shared her joy as we went 'round and 'round in a circle, I realized the situation was more complicated than that. These childlike – seemingly "mindless" - pleasures weren't an escape from the demands of a rational life. Rather, they were a natural expression of that rational life. After all, a child, like any rational person, puts her own happiness first. A child instinctively resists the straightjacket of adult life, with all of its rules and regulations. Unfortunately, as kids grow older, most of them fall victim to its overwhelming power. Then, as adults, they'll look back at their own past, and yearn to have, once again, a child's outlook on the world. But what does that even mean? What does it mean to "be like a child again?"

Both Mark and Troy had their own theories, and they were quite different from each other. Nearly a year ago, Mark told me that a child's unique quality is her "open heart" that accepts everyone "without judgment." But Troy, on the other hand, believed that kids have "virtually no understanding of love." Rather, they are "huge egoists who are barely concerned with the needs of others."

Despite their differences, Mark and Troy shared a common view that we, as adults, should strive to recapture the essence of a child, and see the world through their eyes. For a long time, I resisted the idea – mainly because the phrase, "be like a child again," sounded like a tired cliché. But now, I had a better understanding of its wisdom.

For Elizabeth – like most children - the world was a wonder; a place with endless opportunities for creative expression and happiness. In her world, life was an adventure, an endless journey of discovery - and therein lay her wisdom. Needless to say, this didn't mean every moment would be beautiful and wonderful. Every now and then, a child's eyes would be filled with tears. Sometimes a lot of tears. But those tears would never lead to cynicism and despair. A child – like any rational person with a loving spirit – was immune to those emotions.

Over the last few months, I had quietly absorbed that lesson– and now that I understood it, I could never forget it.

A few days later, with first grade rapidly approaching, we sent Elizabeth back home to live with her father. She didn't want to leave, but we promised to come see her at Christmas.

"Do you pinky promise?" she asked me, extending her little finger.

"I pinky promise," I said, wrapping our fingers together.

Elizabeth wasn't the only person who was heading back to school. On the last day of August, Heather began her second year at GW University. Needless to say, her life suddenly became very busy again – and we started to see each other less and less. When Heather wasn't in class, or at the hospital, she was at the library studying. In the meantime, I was becoming more preoccupied with my job – slaving away to generate interest in our programs. Still, we usually found time to have dinner together every night. Sometimes we moaned about our crazy-ass schedules, and expressed the hope that we could be with each other all the time. Even so, despite our misgiving, our careers were blossoming, and we were definitely happy about that. So long as we kept a healthy balance between loving work and working at love, we were going to be OK.

But I wanted to be *better* than OK. I wanted to take our relationship to a new and higher level – marriage. I know, you're probably thinking: "Brian, are you nuts? You're only 23 years old! Plus, you've only known this girl for about 6 months! Don't rush into any stupid decisions! I thought you were a rational guy."

Well, I *am* being rational. I see marriage as a rational choice to secure my happiness. When I am with Heather, I am not only a *happier* man, I am a *better* man – because she inspires me to think clearer and love stronger than I ever could by myself. Even so, I've reached a point when it's no longer enough to *be* with her. I need to *commit to her.* If I'm serious about living with integrity, I have a responsibility to make that commitment. I need to get down on one knee, and make a promise to share my life with her – and to love her now and always.

If you think about it, the permanence of love is what makes it truly powerful. It's one thing to say "I love you now, and maybe I'll love you a little while longer." But it's entirely different to say "I love you now, and I will love you forever." With a ring, I could say that.

While at work, I did some Internet research on wedding rings, and I realized, holy crap, those things cost a lot of money! I couldn't believe people pissed away so much cash on a piece of jewelry. Don't get me wrong: I'm definitely in favor of symbols of love. But some of those prices were flat-out ridiculous. Luckily for me, Heather showed little interest in material possessions – and even less interest in impressing her girlfriends. So I felt comfortable choosing a rather –shall we say – "affordable" product. After I picked out the ring, I went to the local jewelry store, studied it carefully, and bought it.

I should mention, however, that a funny thing happened when I got home: Instead of rushing to see Heather and instantly propose, I was paralyzed by a series of nagging doubts. First and foremost, there was the practical consideration: "When and where should I ask the question?" I wracked my brain for the perfect time and location – but every scenario had its drawbacks. Not private enough. Not romantic enough. Too tacky. Too strange. But there was an even greater, overarching consideration: "Did Heather even *want* to get married?" Surprisingly, it wasn't clear to me. Despite our sincere love for each other, we had never addressed the topic of marriage. Deep down, I feared that maybe she didn't see herself as the "marrying type." After all, she was a strong, independent woman. Perhaps she viewed marriage as a surrender of her freedom. Even worse, perhaps she liked the idea of marriage – just not with *me*. Although I knew that she loved me, perhaps she didn't love me enough to be with me forever. I spent days torturing myself with these haunting questions. But eventually, I decided to quit dragging my feet and take action.

On Sunday night, just after 11 o'clock, Heather and I were in bed, comfortably underneath the covers, reading separate books, as the TV hummed in the background.

"I'm getting sleepy," said Heather. "What about you?"

"Yeah," I said. "I'm ready for bed too. Let me just go to the bathroom."

When I entered the bathroom, I opened an empty Tylenol bottle where I had been hiding the engagement ring. I buried the ring in my hand and then walked outside. When I stood in front of her, I asked: "Honey, could you get out of the bed?"

"Why?" she asked, closing her book. "What for?"

"Please."

She rolled her eyes (but not in a mean way), and sat upright on the side of the bed, her bare feet dangling above the floor.

"O.K., I'm out of the bed," she announced, flipping her hair behind her white, low-cut nightgown. "What now?"

"I have something important to tell you," I said, my voice shaking a little bit. Before Heather could respond, I dropped to one knee, presented the ring, and asked: "Heather, will you marry me?"

I waited for an answer, but none came. Instead, Heather just stared at the ring – completely devoid of all expression. Finally, she asked, "Why do you want to marry me?"

"Because I love you," I answered, still in a crouched position.

"But honey, love fades," she warned me. "One day, you might not love me anymore. If that happens, I don't want you to feel obligated to stay with me. Because then you'll resent me, and hate me. Then I'll hate you. We both deserve better than that."

"What?" I practically shouted, completely unable to imagine falling out of love with her. "Are you serious?"

"I'm sorry, Brian," she said, sympathetically, rolling back onto the bed. "I can't say 'yes.' At least not now."

"But honey," I said, crawling by the side of the bed, "When I say, 'I love you,' that means forever. Always. Don't you love me too?"

"Of course I love you," she said, rubbing her finger against my cheek. "That's why I'm saying 'no.' I want you to be happy – which means I want you to be *free.*"

"I want to be free – but I want to be free *with you,*" I said, standing up, and getting slightly annoyed. "We can be free together. And happy together. Why are you resisting me so much?"

"I'm not resisting you," she said, rising from the bed, and pacing around the room. "I'm just...protecting you. I don't want you to feel obligated to be with me. I don't want to be a burden on you."

"Oh my God," I said, grabbing her by the shoulders, and staring into her eyes. "Heather, you are *not* a burden on me.

You're the greatest thing that ever happened to me. You have given *me* to myself. You have given me the confidence to think for myself, and chart my own destiny. I love you, Heather. Please don't abandon me."

Heather looked down at her feet, somewhat embarrassed. "I want you to promise that if you ever stopped loving me – for whatever reason - you'd tell me, and leave me. I want you to promise me that, OK?"

"No," I said, putting my finger on her chin. "I will *not* promise you that. I will fight for our love. *That* is my promise."

Heather's eyes started to well up, and then she started to wail – covering her eyes as she ran back to the bed. I followed her, and sat next to her.

"You passed," she said, wiping away her tears. "You passed the test."

"What? What test?"

"I was testing you. I wanted to make sure you *really, really* wanted to marry me. If you took 'no,' for an answer, I figured you weren't ready. But you fought for our love – just like you promised. Thank you, sweetie."

"Wait," I said, with a shocked smile on my face. "What does this mean? Are you accepting my proposal? Are you saying 'yes?'"

She nodded, and smiled, and wrapped her arms around me. "Yes, Brian!...Yes! Yes! Yes!"

"Oh God," I said, letting out a deep breath. "I can't believe it...So you're going to be my wife?"

She looked at me with such sweet, innocent joy. "Yes, I'm going to be your wife. And *you* will be my husband."

"Wow!" I said, as the reality of the situation slapped me in the face. "This is incredible." Then I noticed that Heather had engulfed herself in another round of tears.

"What's the matter?" I asked.

"It's just that...when I was a little girl growing up...I could never have imagined that this day would ever come.

Oh Brian, I was so lonely. I had nobody. No mom. No dad. No one who loved me. The only person I had was myself. Of course, I hoped that one day, I could find someone who could truly understand me, and love me, and appreciate my struggle. But I never thought it would actually happen. I learned to become an independent spirit – to take pride in that role – but even then, I never felt complete. That's because the world itself seemed incomplete. I couldn't love the world with all my power, because I couldn't experience the best that I thought this world could offer – and *that is you.* I've waited my whole life *for you.* And I want to spend *the rest of my life* with you."

Seeing Heather's tears triggered my own flood of tears. I held her hand tightly, and said, through a broken, craggily voice: "I know how you feel. I spent most of my life alone too – a mystery to myself and others. I wanted to be happy, but I wanted that happiness to be based on truth. Still, I was afraid – so afraid – that when I examined the truth – and I mean, *really* examined it – it would horrify me. But, even then, I had hope – a faint hope – that maybe, just maybe, life was good, love was real, and happiness was my destiny. I never lost that hope. Now I have you – and because of that, I feel vindicated in some sense. I feel like God is patting me on the back, and whispering, 'You did good, son.' I feel like every challenge, every defeat, every time of crisis was worth it – because it led to this moment. I love you, Heather."

"I love you too," she said, with a perfect smile. We looked into each other's eyes, and I brushed her long blond hair. Just then, I remembered that I hadn't completed the occasion. I returned to my knees, and slipped the ring on Heather's finger.

"Heather, will you marry me? I asked.

"Yes," she said with passion and determination. I held her hand, and stared at it – so beautiful now with this special symbol of our love.

"Never let me go," she whispered calmly.

"I'll never let you go," I promised.

She smiled and got down on her knees, facing the bed, right beside me. "Pray with me, Brian," she requested.

We had never prayed together before, but it seemed like an appropriate action in light of everything that had happened – not just tonight, but throughout our lives. I closed my eyes, rested my elbows on the edge of the bed, and put my hands in the praying position. Next to me, Heather was already deep in prayer.

In the sacred, inner recesses of my mind, these words flowed through me:

"Dear God,

I am so grateful for the opportunity You've given me to create my life anew. For many years, I was one of Your most difficult children –constantly questioning, frequently angry, always on the cusp of quitting. Now, I am still Your child – but I am also an adult – an adult who is the owner of his own life – a proud embodiment of creativity and love, instead of a flailing zombie, shackled by the contradictory beliefs, slogans, and clichés he swallowed from others.

I am especially grateful for Heather – this wonderful, truly amazing woman – who will share that life with me. At least I hope she will. I know that nothing in life is guaranteed – except perhaps, the constant drumbeat of change – and, as human beings, our carefully laid-out plans can be swept away in the blink of an eye. Life is a process of learning, growing, and adapting – which can be quite daunting at times. But to help master that process, You have given us a powerful tool: our own mind.

By developing my mind, I have found the self-confidence and sense of purpose to achieve *peace* of mind. In

271

addition, I have discovered an amazing idea - that the Kingdom of Heaven - that tiny mustard seed – the 'smallest of all seeds' – can blossom inside the soul of even a humble creature like me. I cherish that idea, and may it sustain me for the rest of my days. Amen."

I said the word, "Amen," aloud, and a few moments later, Heather repeated it: "Amen." Then, she looked at me and smiled. "What did you pray for?" she asked.

"I didn't pray *for* anything," I said. "I expressed *gratitude* for *everything*."

"Do you really mean that?" she asked.

I gave her question some serious thought. I never wanted to be the kind of person who let his beliefs cloud his judgment. I had already seen how dogma could spoil a man's life, and I wanted no part in that.

"I think so," I said optimistically. Then I held her hand again, and we both stared at the engagement ring, shining like a beacon to our better selves. "But there's only one way to find out. I have to live my life. That's the only real test. Do you care to join me?"

She laughed, and hugged me. "Sure," she said, and then planted a kiss on my lips. "Let's do it."

So, with those words, I come to the end of my story – the story of my first year out of college. In the opening chapter, I promised that it would be a "hell of an adventure," and I hope I've managed to meet that high expectation.

As I told you in the beginning, when I entered the Real World, "I didn't know who I was. And I sure as hell didn't know where I was going." Now, I can confidently say: I know who I am: I am a child of God. And I am a rational adult. And I am going into a career and a marriage where I can express my rational values into action.

I have found that sense of purpose by adopting a life philosophy that Heather calls "spiritual rationalism." If I had to summarize the message of that philosophy into a single word, it would be "think." I mean, *really* think. Think about everything! Especially about yourself! I know some people are afraid to think about their own lives. As human beings, we fear what we don't understand, and all too often, what we understand least is ourselves. But the reality is, when we understand ourselves, we empower ourselves, and the feeling of self-empowerment is the greatest of all feelings. The root of happiness is the conviction (supported by experience) that you are competent and morally entitled to succeed on this Earth. And you are.

After a long period of trial and error, I have finally achieved that conviction. Now, does this mean I'm going to be happy all the time? No. Does it mean I am perfect? Definitely not! I can't and won't expect perfection from myself, or anybody else, for that matter. I will only expect that I will keep an open mind, and that I will defend my right to use that mind. Of course, I might slip up from time to time. Sometimes, I might harbor anger, or sadness, or frustration. But I won't give up. I'll give life my best shot. I will go on.

A friend once told me that God always has us exactly where we need to be. My friend, *you* are exactly where *you* need to be. You didn't read this book by accident. You are a seeker too. So my final message to you is: Love your life, and take control of it. Break free of the shackles you've imposed on yourself, and grow the proud pair of wings that will fly you to your destiny.

Your future begins now.

CPSIA information can be obtained
at www.ICGtesting.com
Printed in the USA
BVOW03s1424050117
472562BV00001B/36/P